DEFYING GRAVITY

SUNY series, The Margins of Literature
Mihai I. Spariosu, editor

DEFYING GRAVITY

*Jean Paulhan's Interventions in
Twentieth-Century
French Intellectual History*

MICHAEL SYROTINSKI

STATE UNIVERSITY OF NEW YORK PRESS

Published by
State University of New York Press, Albany

© 1998 State University of New York

Printed in the United States of America

For information, address the State University of New York Press,
State University Plaza, Albany, NY 12246

Production design by David Ford
Marketing by Fran Keneston

Library of Congress Cataloging-in-Publication Data

Syrotinski, Michael, 1957–
        Defying gravity : Jean Paulhan's interventions in twentieth-
century French intellectual history / Michael Syrotinski.
              p.   cm. — (SUNY series, the margins of literature)
        Includes bibliographical references and index.
        ISBN 0-7914-3639-X (hardcover : alk. paper). — ISBN 0-
7914-3640-3 (pbk. : alk. paper)
        1. Criticism—History—20th century. 2. Paulhan, Jean,
1884–1968—Criticism and interpretation. 3. France—Intellectual
life—20th century. I. Title. II. Series.
PN94.S97   1998
801'.95'09440904—dc21   97-23071
                                                              CIP

10 9 8 7 6 5 4 3 2 1

CONTENTS

Acknowledgments   vii

Introduction. Figures of Duplicity   1
   Paulhan and Contemporary Literary Theory

1. Allegories of Ethnography   25
   i. Malagasy Proverbs
   ii. Sacred Language

2. Underwriting the Personal: Modesty and the *récits*   47
   i. Jean Paulhan and Jacques Maast
   ii. Modesty, Mania and Other Wor(l)ds
   iii. Coda: Progress in Love?

3. Blanchot reading Paulhan   77
   i. Who Said Anything About Terror?
   ii. Poetic Justice

4. Resistance, Collaboration,
   and the Postwar Literary Purge in France   105

5. Domestic Spaces, Aesthetic Traces   127
   i. Cubes, Cubes, and More Cubes
   ii. Painting by Letters

Conclusion   151

Notes   157

Bibliography   193

Index   201

ACKNOWLEDGMENTS

The debts incurred in writing this book are varied and numerous. I owe thanks to the British Academy, the University of Aberdeen and Illinois State University for travel and research grants at different stages of its genesis. Parts of the book were given first as lectures or conference papers at the Universities of California at Berkeley and Los Angeles, the 1993 Modern Language Association conference in Toronto, the Institut Français in London, the Twentieth Century French Studies conference at the University of Iowa, and the Universities of Stirling and Aberdeen in Scotland, and I would like to thank the many people who gave me the opportunity to present my work publicly and those whose comments and criticisms helped to focus and redirect my own thoughts.

Portions of the manuscript were published in earlier versions, and I wish to express my gratitude to the editors concerned for their kind permission in allowing me to reproduce this work in part or in whole. Portions of chapter 4 first appeared as an article in *Studies in Twentieth Century Literature* (16:2, summer 1992). Sections of chapters 1 and 4 appeared previously in my article, "Jean Paulhan's Allegories of Translation," *Translation and Literature* 3 (1994), Edinburgh University Press. A brief discussion of Paulhan's *récits* appears in my introduction to Christine Laennec's and my translation of *Progrès en amour assez lents* and other *récits*, in *Progress in Love on the Slow Side* (University of Nebraska Press, 1994). The second half of chapter 1 was first published in French in *L'Autre et le sacré*, ed. Christopher Thompson (Paris: L'Harmattan, 1995). The text of "Manie" is reproduced with the kind permission of Gallimard, and the Dubuffet portrait of Jean Paulhan on the front cover is reproduced with the permission of the Fondation Jean Dubuffet.

I would like to extend the warmest thanks to the following people, who have been involved with this book in different ways from its early stages as a doctoral dissertation. Firstly, Kevin Newmark, my thesis director, whose relentless rigour and subtle, perceptive mind kept the project on track. Various readers of the manuscript as it progressed towards its current state have helped to make it a much better book than it might have been; Allan Stoekl, Charles Porter, Mary Lydon, Malcolm Bowie and Douglas Clayton. I am particularly indebted in this regard to Denis Hollier and Ann Smock, who have been the most faithful and encouraging supporters of my work on Paulhan. Special thanks also go to Mme Jacqueline Paulhan, secretary of the *Société des Lecteurs de Jean Paulhan* for her interest in my work and her friendship over the years, and to Claire Paulhan, archivist extraordinaire of Paulhan's manuscripts at the *Institut Mémoires de l'Edition Contemporaine* in Paris, who generously gave up her time and office space for me during a memorable research visit to the Archives.

More personal and less easily definable debts of gratitude are owed to Michael Sheringham, whose infectious passion for French literature was the spark that ignited my own as an undergraduate, and whose unwavering support and friendship over the years have kept my interest as fresh and alive as it was when I started out. To a couple of close friends who have meant more to this project than they know: David Alan Black and Torri Thompson. To our son Ricky Calum, who is a constant reminder of the joy of being alive, and who is teaching me much about the pleasure of reading. To our two cats, Tinker and Mischka, who witnessed this project from beginning to end, and whose luminous presence and rare insight inspired many a late night's writing. And finally my greatest (and immeasurable) debt is to my own "Manie," Christine Laennec, my proofreader, co-translator, sounding board, and spiritual sustainer.

FIGURES OF DUPLICITY

Paulhan
and Contemporary
Literary Theory

*"I'm reading Derrida. Yes, he has a nice, subtle
mind: very engaging"*

Letter to Francis Ponge, 14 March 1968[1]

Max Ernst's 1924 painting "Rendez-vous der Freunde" (Rendez-vous with Friends) depicts Jean Paulhan in a posture which will typify his paradoxical role in French intellectual history over the subsequent 40 years. Here is a young Paulhan, already as secretary of the *Nouvelle Revue Française (NRF)*, an increasingly influential presence on the Parisian literary scene, tellingly occupying a central position amongst the French and German avant-garde painters and writers of the time, and yet not truly in any sense himself a Surrealist or Dadaist. Even though he was one of the founders of the Dadaist movement, and was certainly a friend of many of the figures who surround him in the painting, he—along

1

with the *NRF*—was soon to part company with André Breton following a particularly acrimonious exchange of letters. Probably no other figure in the twentieth century was as closely in contact as Paulhan with happenings on the French literary scene, and perhaps no one as impervious as he was to the many intellectual, artistic and ideological forces which helped shape French literary history this century. To say he was at the center of the literary world from the 1920s to the 1960s is really to understate the case; as director of the *NRF,* and subsequently as its editor, he played a key role in defining that center, and—it may be said without exaggeration—in creating a whole generation of writers.

The reputation he earned for himself as the "grey eminence" of French literature is entirely justified. He spotted, advised, promoted, edited, published, befriended (and often became the intellectual guiding light of) many of the major French writers from this period. The list of writers with whom he was associated is as remarkable for its eclecticism as for its length. In his early years at the *NRF* he was already working with established writers such as Breton, Eluard, Reverdy, Aragon, Proust, Valéry, Gide, Martin du Gard and Mauriac. He went on to publish many of the "household" names of French literature; Michel Leiris, Henri Michaux, Antonin Artaud, George Bataille, Maurice Blanchot, Jules Supervielle, Francis Ponge, Valéry Larbaud, Julien Gracq, René Etiemble, Albert Thibaudet, Roger Caillois. He was very close to a score of other half-forgotten, less familiar figures, who were nonetheless prominent writers at the time in France: Marcel Arland, René Daumal, André Suarès, Jean Grenier, Marcel Jouhandeau, Joë Bousquet, Jacques Audiberti, René Crevel, Guillaume de la Tarde, Pierre Drieu la Rochelle, Giuseppe Ungaretti, Barbara and Henry Church, Bernard Groethuysen. Not forgetting, of course, his friendships with painters such as Braque, Picasso, Dubuffet and Fautrier. Lest this seem like merely an expansive use of name-dropping (arguably, any long-serving editor would accumulate a list of similarly indebted authors), it should be noted first of all that the names I have indicated are intended to be representative only, secondly that most of these writers also became close personal friends of Paulhan, and that he sustained a regular correspondence with them over many years (he would get up at six most mornings, and spend a few hours on his correspondence before attending to his editorial duties).

Every one who knew him has an anecdote about Paulhan. His very unacademic attitude towards literature, the lightness of his approach to even the most serious of matters, and the surprising turns and leaps of his thought, naturally steer evocations of him towards the anecdotal. People who talk about Paulhan invariably end up talking about his mystery, his modesty, his disarming playfulness, the subtle balance of contradictory traits, as if one might catch the essence of his elusive character within a fleeting manifestation of its appearance. A few "descriptions" of Paulhan should give an idea of the delicate, prismatic quality of his person as his friends experienced it:

> Yet there is in him a sort of eloquence, but very fine and all flute glissandos, in this bizarre blend of politeness and silence, of reserve and coquetry, of taciturn humor and rare enthusiasm where others are concerned, of fearful goodness and quiet influence. (Roger Judrin, *La Vocation transparente,* p. 110)

> I have always had in my mind the image of a young intellectual . . . his fine, nervous silhouette, his mask as enigmatic as it was affable, his rapid movements, his look that was as clear as it was impenetrable, its intelligence at times hardly bearable, seeming to go right through his interlocutor. (Robert Sebastian, *NRF* May 1969, p. 704)

> A character who was at first exasperating. Permanently, openly, ostentatiously mischievous; not laying any traps, since he gave you a clear warning of the pitfalls. Never saying what he thought, but sometimes saying exactly the opposite, a constant love of paradox. (Roger Caillois, *NRF,* May 1969, p. 734)

> Jean Paulhan's scruples and tactfulness have led some to accuse him . . . of duplicity, dissimulation, and affected mannerism. His generosity remained hidden from them, as did his brand of humor. . . . Whence emerged this parodic character whom he would allow to remain beside him, and whom he would sometimes use. . . . (Jean Follain, *NRF,* May 1969, p. 714)

> When interviewing you, he never failed to make you feel uncomfortable, for his words were not those of a master but

> of someone curious who would try to surprise you, and
> even to fluster you, all the while remaining extremely re-
> served himself. (André Dhôtel, *Jean Paulhan: Qui suis-je?*,
> p. 9)

Given the number of people who knew Paulhan, a composite picture
formed from different testimonies might seem easy enough to put together. However, everyone seems to want to see in Paulhan (the man)
the same enigma we find in his texts. As we shall see, Paulhan's texts
both speak of mystery, and are themselves as frustratingly elusive as
the mystery they attempt to approach. Most of the people who knew
him seem intent on perpetuating the image of Paulhan as someone at
once immediately accessible, open, generous, and secretive, shadowy,
a behind-the-scenes figure, who nonetheless wielded immense power,
as if he were as essentially "unreadable" as his texts.

My intention in this book is not to shed any particularly new light
on Jean Paulhan, the person, except perhaps indirectly, as an effect
of reflection or refraction. While I find Paulhan a fascinating and intriguing figure, I don't feel that I have anything to add to what has already been written on him in this regard, and I would refer interested readers to Roger Judrin's *La Vocation transparente de Jean Paulhan*,
André Dhôtel's *Jean Paulhan: Qui suis-je?*, the May 1969 commem-
orative issue of the *Nouvelle Revue Française*, the many volumes of his
correspondence now available, the excellent annotated edition of his
personal writings, *La Vie est pleine de choses redoutables*, and the series of *Cahiers Jean Paulhan* published by the "Société des Lecteurs de
Jean Paulhan." These biographically oriented writings, together with
a flood of re-editions of Paulhan's texts, have certainly helped to in-
crease his visibility, and to further our understanding of just how pivotal a role he played in French literary history this century. At the
same time, his name has been evoked more and more frequently as a
neglected precursor of contemporary literary theory in France, and
he has even been referred to by one critic, Jeffrey Mehlman, as an un-
acknowledged ancestor to Deconstruction. My interest in Paulhan
falls somewhere between literary history and literary theory, as I think
neither approach to his texts does full justice to their complexity, to
their startling originality, and above all to the challenges they present
to the very foundations of literary study. My own attempt to come
to terms with Paulhan's texts is based on the view that not enough
attention has been paid to him as a *writer,* and that one cannot sim-

ply reduce his texts to their explicit arguments, even though this expository critical labor is both necessary and valuable in introducing one of the most refreshingly jargon-free of literary theoreticians to an anglophone readership. I see a greater attention to the language of the texts, to their poetic as well as their hermeneutic dimension, as a means to understanding more clearly not only their internal dynamics, but also their relationship to the various theoretical, artistic and historical contexts out of which they arose.

This book is thus not a book "on" Paulhan, but more a book "about" Paulhan, insofar as I situate his writing with respect to the different intellectual currents of his times. It is organized as a series of "scenes" of twentieth century French intellectual history, each forming the site of an important critical intervention on the part of Paulhan: the "literary ethnography" which developed out of the French colonial experience; the interplay between autobiography and fiction which has been a prominent feature of much French writing this century; the Sartre-Blanchot debate in the 1940s around the question "What is literature?"; the post-war literary purge and the question of the political or ethical dimension of literature; the relationship between literature and art, particularly in the context of a Cubist aesthetic; and the development of literary theory in France. The sequence of chapters follows roughly the chronological order of Paulhan's writings, but this is more a matter of convenience than anything else. My own resistance to reading Paulhan in terms of a dialectical progression is motivated by a concern to articulate more distinctly the interconnectedness of his different writings, and to respond to the ironic relationship which Paulhan himself adopts towards literary history. I thus want to put on hold the familiar narrative of the evolution of Paulhan's thought, which runs something like this: it was during his time on Madagascar, while learning Malagasy, that Paulhan first became interested in proverbs, clichés, and commonplace expressions, an interest which eventually grew into a more generalized "theory of language," most forcefully expressed in *Les Fleurs de Tarbes,* that informs all of his thinking on everything from politics to aesthetics to sexuality; as his thought turned more and more to mysticism, his lifelong search for the "secret of language" finally ended with the revelation of language's "triplicity" (word, sign, thing) in one of his last works, *Le Don des langues (The Gift of Languages)*, which at last resolved the various models of "duplicity" which had always seemed to lead him up a blind alley. I see this (admittedly oversimplified) "success story" as a false evolution, which does not really address the problems raised by Paulhan's texts, and I prefer to take as more significant his own pronouncements about the failure of his thought to arrive at any kind of synthesis. Consequently, there are many of his texts I will *not* be considering, partly as a matter of strategic choice, partly because I feel that the best chance of correcting the received ideas, or commonplaces, about Paulhan which seem to be gaining ground, is to focus on a few texts, and to read them well.

Having said this, the least I could do in an introduction to a book "about" Paulhan is to provide a brief biography. Jean Paulhan was born in Nîmes in 1884, the son of Suzanne and Frédéric Paulhan. The latter was a well-known philosopher in France at the time, and one can see his influence, if only thematically, on some of Paulhan's early writings (his works were a blend of philosophy and the psychology of the period, and bore titles such as *L'Activité mentale et les éléments de l'esprit* [*Mental Activity and the Elements of the Mind*]). After studying literature and philosophy at the Sorbonne (while a student he was active in anarchist circles), Paulhan became interested in Chinese thought and language, and had planned to spend time in China, but accepted another overseas post that was offered to him in 1908, to become a teacher at the first French *lycée* on Madagascar. He lived there for almost three years, became fluent in Malagasy, and began to write both fiction as well as studies of Malagasy poems (*hain-teny*) and proverbs, the latter being the subject of a proposed thesis (*The Semantics of the Proverb*) under the direction of Lucien Lévy-Bruhl, which he was never to complete. He married Sala Prusak in 1911, and taught Malagasy for a short while at the *Ecole des Langues Orientales,* then enlisted in the French army in 1914, but was wounded in St. Mard in December (an event which forms the basis of Paulhan's *récit, Le Guerrier appliqué* [*The Diligent Soldier*]). He never returned to combat, but became a driving instructor and interpreter for the Malagasy division, as well as a plane-spotter. During this time he was already beginning to establish himself, publishing his essays and *récits,* and making contacts with many of the most prominent intellectuals on the Parisian literary scene. *Le Guerrier appliqué* was particularly well received; it was shortlisted for the *Prix Goncourt,* and earned the admiration of André Breton and Paul Eluard. Paulhan's personal life during these years was fairly turbulent. In 1916 he fell in love with Germaine Pascal, with whom he carried on a secret affair for two years before Sala found evidence of his infidelity while he was critically ill with pneumonia (this again is at the origin of one of his *récits, La Guérison sévère (The Severe Recovery)*. He decided to divorce Sala, who resisted tenaciously (by this time, they had two children, Pierre and Frédéric); the divorce was only made official in 1933, upon which Paulhan finally married Germaine Pascal.

In 1921 Jacques Rivière asked Paulhan to become the secretary of the *Nouvelle Revue Française,* and he became its director in 1925 after Rivière's death. Many consider as the greatest years of the *NRF* those between 1925 and the Second World War, with Paulhan largely responsible for finding, encouraging, and editing the authors it published. During this period Paulhan established his reputation as perhaps the most influential figure in French literature, and yet his self-effacing style led him to marginalize his own writings, which consequently never achieved the kind of popular success enjoyed by his many protégés. These years were also spent painstakingly working away on what was to become his best-known text, *Les Fleurs de Tarbes, ou la terreur dans les lettres (The Flowers of Tarbes, or Terror in Literature),* the final version of which only appeared in 1941.

During the war, Paulhan refused to continue working with the *NRF* once it became clear it was going to fall into the hands of collaborators (it was taken over by Drieu la Rochelle, but only lasted a few months as a collaborationist journal), and he was one of the first and most active writers to become involved in the Resistance. Here again, he played a pivotal role, founding the Resistance journal *Les Lettres Françaises* with Jacques Decour, and using his home to hide the printing press. He was arrested by the Gestapo, and spent a week in prison, before being released. He was a key contact for the *Editions de Minuit,* and helped found the *Comité National des Ecrivains* (National Committee of Writers), the principal organization of Resistance writers during the war, and the group which possessed the moral authority to determine the future of French literature after the Liberation. Paulhan left the group in 1946 when it adopted a policy of "purging" writers who had collaborated during the Occupation, and he took the side of the collaborators, a move which outraged many of his Resistance friends. For several years he obstinately stuck to his position in the face of quite ferocious public criticism.

This again perhaps had the effect of diverting attention from some of his major texts, which were published in the 1940s and 1950s: texts such as *Clef de la poésie (Key to Poetry),* which continued the theoretical reflections of *Les Fleurs de Tarbes;* the short fictional texts entitled *Les Causes célèbres (Famous Cases)*; and the writings on Cubist and Modern Art, such as *Braque le patron (Braque the Boss)* and *La Peinture cubiste (Cubist Painting)*. Paulhan continued as editor of the *Nouvelle Revue Française* (renamed the *Nouvelle Nouvelle Revue Française*) once it reappeared in 1953. He was elected to the *Académie Française* in 1963, continued to write essays and articles, rewrote already published texts, and was engaged in prefacing the five volume edition of his *Oeuvres complètes* when he died in 1968.

The Paulhan who emerges from this biographical sketch is in fact a fairly recognizable, even canonical figure, yet it does not tell us very much about his literary and intellectual achievements, nor the ways in which these relate to the various historical contexts in which they originated. Paulhan was best known as a literary critic and theoretician of language and literature, although part of the difficulty of situating his work within the linguistic and literary theory of this century is that it resists any easy assimilation by genre, or theoretical/ideological affiliation. The singularity of his work comes not from any deliberate effort by Paulhan to position and define himself alongside or against other writers, but rather from the single-mindedness with which he pursued his own "search" for what he often referred to as the "secret of language"; endlessly circling around the same configuration of elements, refusing to be drawn away from this focus by more sophisticated articulations of it; well-informed about each successive literary or theoretical movement (indeed, he was often instrumental in enabling their emergence), he was nonetheless rigorously indifferent to their appeals. This paradoxical position—being both firmly rooted within the literary community of his time, and yet impervious to its influences—accounts for two equally inadequate approaches to his work: attempts to appropriate and "translate" Paulhan's theories in terms of a given historical or theoretical continuum, and perhaps more reverential depictions of Paulhan as a kind of guru figure, who by virtue of his supreme independence was able to transcend all local, circumstantial pressures. In the following chapters I will argue for the need to take into account the "duplicity" of Paulhan's texts, and his paradoxical position within literary or intellectual history is another version of this irreducible doubleness. This produces a simultaneous conjunction and disjunction between Paulhan and his times, across a range of scenes and contexts.

How then could we characterize Paulhan as a literary critic and theorist? We would have to take into account not only his best known interventions, such as *Les Fleurs de Tarbes,* but also his many other modes of interaction with writers, which create a number of different critical contexts. This was largely, of course, a function of his many editorial roles, and he seemed to relish the multiplicity of forms of critical engagement offered to him by his various positions. Thus we have concise, often polemical reviews in the NRF, longer reactions within letters to texts he had read, laconic dismissals or expressions of admiration, or quite elaborate explanations of his response, detailed editorial comments to authors, references to books in the context of arguments within his own theoretical texts, and then longish studies of artists' and writers' works (though never anything as substantial as, say, Sartre's studies of Genet or Flaubert). The latter would often be texts he devoted to writers he knew personally and whom he usually had a hand in publishing (such as Paul Valéry or Joë Bousquet).

These different critical media, however, did not always prevent a certain overlapping of purpose, and Paulhan himself would be uncertain at times whether his criticism had taken the most appropriate form. One of the most painful examples of this, for him, was Valéry's rather cool reaction to the initial publication in the *NRF* (1929), of the essays that would eventually become *Un Rhétoriqueur à l'état sauvage: Valéry, ou la Littérature considérée comme un faux (A Rhetorician in a Raw State: Valéry, or Literature Considered as a Fake).* Perhaps as a result of this experience, he often refrained from writing at all on the writers he felt particularly close to (for example, Marcel Arland, Francis Ponge, or Roger Caillois). We can only assume that he achieved a successful balance most of the time, since while he was engaged in the powerful critique of literary "originality" we find in *Les Fleurs de Tarbes,* with the dizzying condition it leaves the writer in, he was at the same time never less than totally committed to encouraging and publishing new writing. In other words, the last thing he would have wanted was to have descend on "his" writers the "silence of Rimbaud," which for Blanchot is the logical consequence of the writer's predicament in *Les Fleurs de Tarbes.* In any case, we find in his critical writings the same sensitivity and attention to detail he displays as an editor; there are, for example, the same precise and often surprising examples, the same lingering over the quirks of language, and above all the same sense of a transcendent criterion ("literature") by which all works are essentially measured. This by no means implies a kind of reverence for canonical texts or an elitist notion of literary style since what Paulhan understands by "literature" is never a given, but is rather the very question he spent his whole life attempting to answer.

The best way to approach an assessment of Paulhan's contribution to literary theory might be to consider it first of all in the light of his engagement with linguistics, since literature, in his view, is a "fatter" or "expanded" version of language ("du langage grossi"). In this light, Paulhan's interest in linguistic-based analysis, dating back to his studies of Malagasy proverbs in the early part of the century, appears very much ahead of his time, and certainly well ahead of the movement towards using linguistic categories as a tool for literary criticism, although the manner in which Paulhan does this is quite different from Jakobson's or Barthes' structural analyses, for example. Paulhan had clearly read and understood the implications of Saussurean linguistics by the time he was writing *Jacob Cow*, which is based on a similar rejection of language in terms of any "natural" correspondence to the world, a recognition of the arbitrary nature of the sign, and a consequent examination of its functioning as an autonomous system. He goes on to pursue this problematic in a variety of ways; as we will see, it is translated into aesthetic terms in his essays on Cubist painting, and in *Alain, ou la preuve par l'étymologie (Alain, or Proof by Etymology)*, he questions the cratylic assumptions behind what he sees as misplaced trust in the epistemological value of etymology. As Thomas Ferenczi has noted, his study of proverbs could be an application of Saussure's findings to the analysis of phrases as well as individual words. But Paulhan certainly does not develop it into anything like a theory of generative grammar, and we would have to recognize the limitations of its significance for linguistic knowledge generally. As Ferenczi says:

> the difficulties are hardly ever resolved, and are indeed barely even opened up and defined as problems; and even then, these problems are less posed than indicated. The status of the abstract elements which underlie the sentence are not defined, the mechanisms which ensure the *creativity* of language are not studied.[2]

Nonetheless, Ferenczi continues by underlining Paulhan's importance as an example of the "renewal of 'discourse linguistics' now being developed [this was written in 1969] by Benvéniste, and whose repercussions are essential for the analysis of literary language." While it is true that Paulhan's usefulness to linguistics has its limits, these limits are in a sense recognized by Paulhan, and they are self-imposed insofar as the particular enigma he was interested in pursuing was located both within language and outside of it. Paulhan's refusal to stray very far down the path of linguistics could be seen, in fact, as a recognition of its inherent limitations for his own particular intellectual focus. So even though, in *Le Don des langues [The Gift of Languages]*, one of his final works, he was still relying terminologically on de Saussure, Bréal, Max Muller, Bloomfield, Hjelmslev and Bally, and although the particular combination of their ideas corresponded to the structure of Paulhan's argument, none of them taken individually provided the answer to the "secret of language" he was searching for. Linguistics as a rigorously scientific methodology would not allow him to formulate something like "poetic mystery," although its foregrounding of language as the unavoidable medium of thought and expression makes it a necessary point of departure. Paulhan thus incorporates the important insights of linguistics, but clearly, literature is the space within which the "secret of language" is enacted and where he hopes, patiently and painstakingly, as both a writer and a literary theoretician, to track it down.

One thing we can say is that Paulhan as a literary critic was neither a typical literary historian, nor an "academic" theoretician, and in this respect is close to the Barthes of *Critique et vérité (Criticism and Truth);* just as Barthes demystified the mythology of academic discourse, so Paulhan's work was a profound questioning of the function and activity of literary criticism (reading literature becomes a radically *different* practice with Paulhan, as it does with Barthes, even though the paths they follow are far from parallel ones). What were his typical strategies and procedures? His studies were often an extension of his own work on language and literature (for example, *Petite préface à toute critique [Short Preface to All Criticism]*, which starts out as a restatement of his theory of literature, and ends with his critique of Sartre's "avoidance" of the question of language). These readings of other writers' work inevitably contain a moment of reversal, insofar as Paulhan often reads them "against" themselves. This procedure is in evidence as early as his essay on Valéry, which we might look at briefly as an example.

Paulhan's point of departure is Valéry's consistent assertion that writers, such as Stendhal, Hugo, and La Fontaine, whose writing has the appearance of spontaneity and a kind of natural expressiveness, are in fact simply accumulating *commonplaces* of sincerity, and are thus what Valéry terms *faussaires* (fakers, or forgers). Paulhan quotes Valéry talking about Stendhal: "The thing that strikes me, amuses me, and even charms me in the Egotist's desire to be natural, is that it demands, and even necessarily contains a *convention.*"[3] The first twist in Paulhan's essay is to argue that it is quite possible to read Valéry's examples as sincere: ". . . as soon as one is dealing with language or expression . . . this expression . . . can at any moment show one or the other of its two opposite faces," and "Each one of Valéry's reflections could be reversed."[4] In short, Paulhan argues, there is no way of knowing whether the author *intended* his or her work to be "artificial" or "natural." Paulhan then goes on to show that in Valéry's own work he resolutely opts for conscious artistic construction (he is, indeed, the archetypal "rhétoriqueur" for Paulhan), but that Valéry, like anyone else, is prey to the same illusions (believing words to be thoughts, or vice versa). Paulhan's conclusion, which will become the "solution" of *Les Fleurs de Tarbes,* with its "reinvented" terror, is that it is the writer alone, as one aware of the paradoxical conditions of the writer's own practice, who can lay claim to "authenticity."

This same technique can be seen in *Alain, ou la preuve par l'étymologie* (Alain's etymologism is readable as paronomasia, and thus no more epistemologically reliable than mere wordplay); in "Sartre n'est pas en bons termes avec les mots" ["Sartre is not on good terms with words"], which is the last chapter of *Petite préface à toute critique* (Sartre devotes eighty pages of *Situations I* to the "the problem of language," only to say that language is a local detail of the more general question of ontology, so according to Paulhan, he never really even *begins* to talk about language); and in *Enigmes de Perse* [*The Engimas of Perse*] (St.-John Perse, mistrustful of language's capacity to screen us from the world, does everything to write about the world's rich profusion and detail, but ends up producing poetry which is crammed full of the most precious rhetorical flourishes).

These are not to be construed, Paulhan is always careful to point out, as negative criticisms, but they are a consequence of the inevitable aporia within all writing, and as such serve as an illustration of the unavoidable illusions of all literary activity. This strategy is in fact very similar to the one which would become the hallmark of Paul de Man's critical writing from the *Blindness and Insight* period. By reading the explicit assertions within the work of literary critics from Georges

Poulet to Jacques Derrida against the movement of their own critical writing, de Man identified the points where the explicit statements are later undone, producing a "negative insight." De Man summarized this procedure at the beginning of "The Rhetoric of Blindness":

> The insight seems instead to have been gained from a negative movement that animates the critic's thought, an unstated principle that leads his language away from its asserted stand, perverting and dissolving his stated commitment to the point where it becomes emptied of substance, as if the very possibility of assertion had been put into question.[5]

Like Paulhan, de Man pointed to "literature" as the place where this uncertainty, and the rigorous necessity of this uncertainty, is most apparent. De Man later refined his theory, of course, into an uncompromising practice of reading which teases out the rhetorical structures in literary text, relentlessly pursuing the epistemological consequences of the negative insights it reveals, to a degree of sophistication that makes Paulhan's efforts look fairly simplistic. As we will see, however, when Paulhan's critical statements are reassessed in the light of their own literary "performances," this surface simplicity belies a work of unusual subtlety and complexity.

Just before he died, Paul de Man was beginning to work on Paulhan.[6] What is clear is how thoroughly he had read Paulhan's texts, and he saw him as a key figure in the twentieth century's rediscovery and reorientation of the questions that had absorbed eighteenth century French language theorists such as Diderot, Du Marsais, and Condillac. De Man understood Paulhan's playful negotiation of his debt towards rhetoricians such as Du Marsais (Paulhan's *Traité des figures* being an ironic attempt to write a contemporary version of the rhetoric textbooks which were once widely used in French schools), but he also recognized Paulhan's awareness of the epistemological consequences of "pushing Rhetoric as far as it will go." There are without doubt a number of significant points of convergence between Paulhan's and de Man's writings.[7] Although Paulhan's contributions to literary theory as a linguist are overshadowed by the likes of Jakobson, Barthes, and Benveniste, his return to Rhetoric, and particularly the use of rhetorical terminology to analyze literary texts, heralded a resurgence of interest in the rhetorical dimension of literature. Paulhan's mind was too finely attuned to the nuanced dynamics of literary texts to be interested in elaborating a typology of literary figures, and in this regard his thinking echoes that of de Man in "Semiology and Rhetoric," in which the latter describes this tendency to systematize rhetorical figures as the "grammatization of rhetoric." [8] Significantly, Paulhan often refers to himself as a "grammarian" (for example, in his *Lettre aux directeurs de la Résistance* [*Letter to the Directors of the Resistance*]), although he never really explains what he means by this term, or what it might be opposed to. Is it someone who takes correct language seriously? (We know he is never "just" interested in language, and also that he never misses an opportunity for exploiting its playfulness.) Or is it merely a synonym for a rhetorician, in Paulhan's sense of the term? The very uncertainty of its reference seems almost to be an invitation by Paulhan to release the rhetorical energy of the term, and points to an opposite movement, one which de Man, symmetrically, also circumscribes very carefully in "Semiology and Rhetoric" as the "rhetorization of grammar." Just as Paulhan's texts continually dramatize the endless back-and-forth movement between terror and rhetoric, so de Man's essays inevitably pivot around the undecidable moments of tension between the literal and figural dimensions of language. As suspicious as Paulhan was of attempts to bypass language, de Man's insistence on talking not of "reference" but of a rhetoricized "referential function of language," is very much in tandem with Paulhan's descriptions of rhetoric's preempting the terrorist project. Not that in either case "reference," or even more so, the "real world," is denied, but both demonstrate that it can never exist in a state of non-linguistic innocence.

As de Man and Paulhan reflected later on the entirety of their respective critical projects, it was in both cases with a certain wry irony, as they acknowledged the inevitability of failure.[9] Irony, because the failure of their theories to "add up" to a final, climactic summation, or indeed to have made any dialectical progress whatsoever, was built into the theories, being in many ways their most distinctive feature, or even their condition of possibility; for Paulhan this took the form of a "law of failure" ("loi d'échec"), the inaccessibility of something like "poetic mystery" which nonetheless was the theoretical foundation for *Clef de la poésie*; and for de Man it was the continual pressure within his critical texts towards the illusory synthesis of limit-terms like "allegory," "parabasis," and "materiality," which were attempts precisely to articulate the moments at which reading (inevitably) breaks down, the insurmountable points of "resistance to theory." As I will suggest somewhat more speculatively in the essays on Malagasy proverbs, and on Blanchot as a reader of Paulhan, one might compare de Man's "allegory" (as a critical narrative of the deconstruction of narrative) to Paulhan's "récit" (the story of the impossibility of telling a story). Both writers thus end up privileging literature, not as a kind of elitist refuge, or as a safe haven for a "terrorist" rejection of any formal constraints (whether traditional, social, or ideological), but because of its power to continually exceed (in theoretical terms) any systematic efforts to theorize it. For both de Man and Paulhan, "literature" is thus the place both where language's rhetorical energy is most playfully exploited, and where the most serious of questions are allowed to resonate. Both writers, in different ways, measured the epistemological force of literature, saw literature and philosophy as powerfully collaborative, and assessed the destabilizing effect on discourses of knowledge from taking literature seriously.

When Paulhan's name is associated openly with the emergence of literary theory, and particularly of deconstruction, the two names most often cited are those of Derrida and Blanchot. As Jeffrey Mehlman writes, "there has not perhaps been an adequate appreciation of the extent to which this grammarian's obsession with the conundra of language was pregnant with future developments," and he goes on to call Paulhan's *Alain, ou la preuve par l'étymologie* "a local instance of what might be called, before the letter, applied grammatology." [10] This claim is based on three bold points of association between Paulhan and Derrida. First of all, Paulhan's call for a political "amnesty" of literary collaborators after the Second World War is said to prefigure Derrida's amnesic "forgetting" of history in, for example, his reading of Blanchot's *L'arrêt de mort*. Secondly, Mehlman sees an anticipation of Derrida's use of the term "undecidability" in Paulhan's interest in Abel's 1884 work *On the Antithetical Sense of Primal Words,* and his related analysis (in *Alain, ou la preuve par l'étymologie*) of the impossibility of telling whether an etymology is merely a play on words. And thirdly, the admiration of Paulhan by Gerhard Heller, the German literary attaché in Paris during the war, is taken as an early paradigm of a generalized pattern of deference to charismatic French intellectuals by outsiders, of which the American "adulation" of Derrida is the latest example. Thus Mehlman sees Paulhan's work as leading irresistibly to a full-blown

Derridean practice of deconstruction: "With the transcendental signified (or etymon) generated after the fact by a tension between signifiers, the problematic later to emerge as deconstruction was already broached" ("Writing and Deference," p. 8). The rather curious conclusion, motivated by an eagerness to prove the political bankruptcy of deconstruction generally, is that Derrida's rewriting of Paulhan's concerns passes by way of a voiding of the political context which Paulhan bravely confronted, "Deconstruction as a forgetting of the perils engaged by Paulhan" ("Writing and Deference," p. 12).

As Ann Smock pointed out in her reply to Mehlman's article, the argument of the essay is constructed as a "fanciful chain of associations." [11] Indeed, Mehlman in his subsequent rejoinder falls into his own trap by acknowledging his understanding of deconstruction, which he gleefully claims to be mimicking, as simply "*bricolage* and/or the techniques of reinscription." [12] Just as Mehlman's reading of Lévi-Strauss and of Derrida depends on an almost caricatural, decontextualized exposition of their ideas, so the reading of Paulhan can be shown to equally superficial. As I argue in the context of the postwar literary purge, Paulhan's texts cannot simply be reduced to their explicit arguments or themes, but must be read as writing that engages and exemplifies the very problematic it elaborates. An inattentiveness to the narrative dynamic of the texts themselves inhibits an appreciation of their wit and irony, and also prohibits a casually analogical chain of associations leading from "reversibility," for example, as it operates in Paulhan's texts, to "applied grammatology," "undecidability," and "dissemination." Thus, for example, when Mehlman reads Paulhan's *Fleurs de Tarbes* as initiating the future of French criticism, ("what Paulhan calls *clichés,* what has been more generally thematized as *écriture,*" [13] my emphasis), his reading is restricted to the provisional conclusion of Paulhan's text. There are undoubtedly interesting parallels to be drawn between a certain form of citationality in Paulhan's texts which argue for a rehabilitated rhetoric, and Derrida's own invocation of citationality within the context of his discussion of Austin's theory of performative language, in "Signature Event Context." Or between the radical ambiguity or indifference that Paulhan theorizes in, for example, *Clef de la poésie,* and Derrida's use, to very different philosophical ends, of irreducibly ambivalent terms like *hymen* and *pharmakon* in "La Pharmacie de Platon." If we take each term out of the context of its respective narrative, however, and yoke them together in a kind of theoretical identity parade, we stand little chance of understanding how they might truly relate to each other in any historical continuum. It is not coincidental, therefore, that Mehlman's reading of the relationship between Paulhan and Blanchot should rely for its "proof" on an equally misrepresentative decontextualization of passages from Blanchot's "The Ease of Dying" in the coda to his essay.[14] If anything, what Derrida's and Paulhan's texts have in common is precisely a skepticism towards, or an ironization of, intellectual history structured as a continuous sequence of influences, which Mehlman's argument relies upon (including, most pertinently, the claim of a direct thread connecting Paulhan to Derrida).[15]

By abandoning the need to assign Paulhan a determined place in the history of literary theory, we in fact free up his texts for a much more productive dialogue with other writers. Since we know that Paulhan was only beginning to read Derrida in 1968, and since Derrida himself has only mentioned Paulhan in connection with de Man's wartime writing and the postwar literary purge in France, the most we can say is that they were both to some extent, but with markedly different purposes, preoccupied with questions of language, its inherent tensions, and its relationship to other disciplines. Rather than seeing Paulhan as necessarily preceding and prefiguring Derrida, for example, we can put Derrida's writing to use to articulate with greater precision the theoretical stakes in Paulhan's writing (which remain, it must be said, a good deal more implicit than they do with Derrida). As we shall see with Paulhan's *De la Paille et du grain,* for example, the postwar purge can be read at an empirical level as the necessary reduction of the duplicity or doubleness of France to a single essence. At the linguistic level this functions in a similar manner, insofar as most contemporary readings of Paulhan's texts are motivated by a tendency to efface the radical undecidability which is their very theoretical foundation. This act of effacement, whereby the contingent is expelled in order to consolidate the assumed priority of the essential, is itself not accidental, but is, as Derrida has argued in "La Pharmacie de Platon," part of a long and well-established philosophical tradition.[16] Derrida's focus on the radical ambivalence of *pharmakon,* as a disruption of the Platonic privileging of presence, points to a more generalized disruptiveness occasioned by writing. Just as Plato designates writing as a dangerous and nefarious element to be expelled, since it is essentially foreign, so there seems to be no room for Paulhan's duplicity. According to Derrida, however, it is precisely the strange, ambivalent logic of writing that opens up and makes possible the very distinction between language and presence. Paulhan's ambiguity —which is quite different from a simple semantic conflict — is from a theoretical perspective of a similar order as the ambiguity of a term like *pharmakon.*

Similarly, we might consider Derrida's essay "La Loi du genre" (The Law of Genre), an essay devoted to the question of the law in its relation to literary genres, as extremely pertinent to thinking the double-bind of the *récit,* as a general term for Paulhan's writing. Derrida focuses on the unclassifiable yet absolutely necessary mark, or "trait of belonging" ("trait d'appartenance") by which any text indicates the genre to which it belongs. The strange logic of such a *trait* resembles the manner in which poetic mystery operates, and Derrida frames the question in the following terms:

> And what if there were, lodged in the very heart of the law itself, a law of impurity or a principle of contamination? And if the condition of possibility of the law were the *a priori* of a counter-law, an axiom of impossibility which would disrupt its meaning, order and reason?[17]

This "axiom of impossibility" is precisely how Paulhan attempts to define the law of poetic mystery. Derrida's essay is in large part a reading of Blanchot's *La Folie du jour,* a text which is very much a *récit* in the sense that Blanchot himself uses the term to talk about Paulhan's writing. Like *Clef de la poésie* (for example), it is a text whose borders become undefinable, whose beginning and end are impossible to locate. Derrida describes the resulting möbius strip-like pockets and folds of the text as a "double chiasmatic invagination of the edges" ("La Loi du genre," 272), such that "It is impossible to decide whether there was an event, a *récit,* the *récit* of an event, or the event of a *récit.*"

Derrida's very explicit, rigorous and powerful critique of discourses of philosophy, or forms of philosophical thinking, involves, as does Paulhan's more subtle, suggestive critique, a shifting of priorities, taking seriously what had until recently suffered from being relegated to secondary importance (rhetoric, contingency, writing, the signifier, etc.), and tracing the effects of its reinstatement. This can be seen, for example, in *Clef de la poésie,* which sets the discourses of poetry and science in a kind of collaborative opposition.

One might pursue the notion of poetry elaborated by Paulhan in this text by mentioning the affinity between his thought and that of a figure who in many ways opened the way for theorists such as Derrida and de Man, that is, Martin Heidegger. One might, for example, consider Heidegger's readings of Hölderlin and Rilke as poets whose poetry is fundamentally concerned with its own essence, and texts such as "The Origin of the Work of Art," or the later writings where poetry becomes an essential presencing, or a founding naming, of Being. The rift between poetry and language that Paulhan examines in *Clef de la poésie* bears formal resemblances to Heidegger's ontic-ontological distinction, and the revelation of Being, revealed in its hiding, could be read in terms of the phenomenality of poetic mystery's duplicitous (dis)appearance. In this respect, it does not seem accidental that Heidegger's thinking involves a powerful critique of the scientific method (Cf., for example, *Was ist Metaphysik?*, which contains Heidegger's famous "Die Wissenschaft will vom Nichts nichts wissen." [Science wants to know nothing of Nothingness]) and of the foundations of Western metaphysics, this critique also being implicit in Paulhan's writings. Particularly appropriate to this point of convergence between them would be Heidegger's discussion of the mathematical project as the foundation of all scientific inquiry providing the prototype, as it were, of the axiomatic character of all projects. Yet we would be wrong to see Paulhan's project as essentially continuous with a twentieth century philosophical questioning of the nature of being. Rather, as Blanchot puts it in "The Ease of Dying," Paulhan's texts engage "the suspense of being," and as such are somewhere on the borderlines of philosophy, or are between philosophy and something else, "being both a scientific and a nonscientific process, the disjunction as it were between the two, and the mind's hesitation between the latter and the former." [18]

It is, of course, Blanchot who has been most often associated with Paulhan, and we shall see in chapter 3 the importance of the meeting between the two writers around Paulhan's pivotal text, *Les Fleurs de Tarbes*. One can trace the legacy of Paulhan's essay on Blanchot's subsequent thinking. The impact of Blanchot's reading of Paulhan pervades Blanchot's most important theoretical statement of the 1940s, "La Littérature et le droit à la mort" ("Literature and the Right to Death"), which begins with the proposition that "literature begins at the moment when literature becomes a question." [19] The impossibility of writing —one can only be a writer once one has

already written, so one is always either not yet or no longer a writer —
is treated much more extensively in "Literature and the Right to
Death," and it has its exact counterpart in the impossibility of reading, the *Noli me legere* of the opening pages of Blanchot's *L'Espace
littéraire*.[20] This bivalent impossibility is reformulated in "Le mystère dans les lettres" as the priority of poetry (the impossibility of
language) over language, and as the precedence of the impersonali-
ty of reading and writing over a reader and a writer. Toward the beginning of "Literature and the Right to Death," Blanchot notes that
"It has been stated ("On a constaté") with surprise that the question: "What is literature?" only ever received insignificant answers."
We might well identify the impersonal "on" of this sentence as Paulhan, and the anonymity of this inscription would possibly make it
even more important to the essay than the many proper names which
are all key points of reference for Blanchot (Mallarmé, Valéry, Sade,
Hegel, Kierkegaard, Ponge, Lautréamont and Baudelaire).

The final passage of "How is literature possible?" can be read —
if somewhat elliptically —as a prefiguration of another central consideration of "Literature and the Right to Death." The former essay
ends by reflecting on the question of how, if literature is to find anew
its authenticity within its own commonplaces, one starts to read and
to write:

> It is enough to understand that *true* commonplaces are
> words torn apart by lightning, and that the rigors of laws
> found the absolute world of expression, outside of which
> chance is but sleep. (*Faux pas,* p. 101)

The invocation of fundamental laws of expression recalls Blanchot's
allusion to Kant, since Paulhan's essay is clearly a critical examination,
in the strongest sense of the term, of the conditions that make literature possible, and an attempt to articulate, as we will see with *Clef
de la poésie,* something like literature's ethical imperative. That such
laws should be a simultaneous *founding* ("the rigors of laws *found*
the absolute world of expression," my emphasis) and *tearing apart*
("words *torn apart* by lightning," my emphasis), is entirely appropriate for Paulhan's text. Writing or reading that does not respond
to this essential impossibility or non-essence of literature is said to be
inattentive to its own circumstances, or to be "asleep" ("outside of
which chance is but sleep"). But what would, or could, a literature

be that is truly attentive to its own circumstances? As we learn from "Literature and the Right to Death," the way out of this "unsurmountable problem" ("problème indépassable," *La Part du feu*, p. 297) of the impossibility of writing is to make the circumstances of this impossibility the necessary starting point of literature. The corresponding circumstances, and contingent beginning, would hold true for reading, as a way out of the impossibility of reading, and this may well be how we should read Blanchot's "inaugural" double reading of *Les Fleurs de Tarbes*.

De Man, Derrida, Heidegger, Blanchot; these names cannot, in the current repoliticized theoretical arena, fail to evoke the specter of collaboration, and a rather unsavory past. Will Paulhan's name now be irresistibly associated with them (and by contamination, with the ideology of collaboration)? There is a danger in reading collaboration metaphorically as a kind of contamination, which then spreads metonymically to anything that happens to come into contact with it. Who, then, would be immune? Where do we stop once we set in motion the process of guilt by association? What does it mean to be infected by an ideology? If it means to stop thinking critically (or in short, to stop reading), then it would certainly contaminate the proposition itself that Paulhan's writing is thematically linked to the emergence of deconstruction.

Without wishing here to summarize the work already done on these writers' political associations, and its ramifications for their philosophical and theoretical thinking, I would like to focus for a little while on Paulhan's extremely ambivalent status. As I will demonstrate, particularly in my discussion of his texts on the postwar literary purge, it is important not only to read Paulhan's writings thematically, but also to be attentive to their doubleness or duplicity, to the "second" book hidden within the first one, to the literary performance which displaces and rewrites the critical statement. Henri Meschonnic has described this well in talking about Paulhan's language as "anti-theoretical theoretical writing ("écriture théorique anti-théorique")." [. . .] "His interruption of the theoretical is his *writing* of the theoretical. He privileged the performative, not the didactic." [21] If his anti-theoretical theory often appears as reactionary or anti-intellectual, it is precisely because of this inexorable performance of the theoretical at the expense of its explicit elaboration. Even his friends were increasingly unsympathetic to some of his outspoken views towards the end of his life; he was, for example, in favor of Algeria remaining French, argued in the 1960s that Rudolf Hess was being victimized and should be released from prison, was a great admirer of pornographic writing, and was critical of the early semiological writings of Barthes, which he saw as products of Marxist theory.

I'd like to end by looking briefly at this last criticism, since it is a significant and highly suggestive example of the need to look beyond the apparent level of Paulhan's statements. Paulhan's reaction to Barthes's *Mythologies* appeared in the "Chroniques" section of the *NRF* in July, October, and December 1955, under his pseudonym of Jean Guérin. Paulhan took Barthes to task for not adequately taking into account those aspects of society which *escaped* the subordination to "mythology," and suggested that his analyses were in fact merely a sophisticated form of Marxist ideological demystification. Barthes replied by accusing the *NRF* of undertaking a Macarthyist witchhunt, and appeared not to take Paulhan's criticism seriously (or rather, precisely to take it seriously, and not engage its playfulness).[22] To read Paulhan's question "Are you a Marxist?" as a literal question would be to take as genuine (and not ideologically overdetermined) his interest in the relationship of literature to ideology. In fact, as I suggested, we would not be unjustified in seeing a number of parallels between the two writers, especially as Barthes in his later texts such as *Critique et vérité (Criticism and Truth)* became increasingly interested in undoing the myths and ideologies which inhabit literature and literary criticism. Barthes' gradual disillusionment with the possibility of semiology providing an adequate method for cultural criticism was accompanied by a move towards writing, "the pleasure of the text," and as such he might be seen to be moving closer to the position which Paulhan occupied in their polemic in the 1950s. That Paulhan's thinking was already in a sense anticipating Barthes' can be seen in the theoretical essay at the end of *Mythologies,* "Myth Today." Barthes is anxious in this essay to somehow theorize the continuous back-and-forth movement (the "game of hide-and-seek") between the sign as referential meaning, and the sign as form (that is, an instance of a mythological operation), and in fact uses the term "duplicity" to describe this ambivalence.[23] Later on in the essay, when talking about literature itself as a kind of mythical system, Barthes refers to the play between writers in search of a "pre-semiological state of language," and the inexorable effects of myth's powers of recuperation. What better description could we have of the interplay between terror and rhetoric? We have, then, a text—*Mythologies*—that is often taken as the inaugural or defining moment of contemporary French theory, but which has already in a sense been preempted by Paulhan's subtle articulation of the dynamics it attempts to circumscribe. It is precisely this power to disrupt, unsettle, undercut, redefine, and the constantly surprising effects of Paulhan's "naïve" theory that I will be attempting to trace in this study, across a range of different literary, cultural and thematic contexts within twentieth century French intellectual history.

ALLEGORIES OF ETHNOGRAPHY

I would like to have defined the Malagasies in terms of the subtlety of their mind, the openness of their customs, their considerate, polite morality, if I were not afraid that in doing so I was conceding to a European ideal, and perhaps to that part of this ideal which had already been accepted by the Malagasies.[1]

"Les Hain-Teny: Poésie obscure."
Lecture delivered in Monaco, 1930

Malagasy Proverbs

Jean Paulhan spent 33 months, between 1908 and 1910, as a teacher at the first European college on Madagascar, the island in the Indian Ocean that France had colonized in 1896. He was responsible for teaching a variety of subjects, including history, French, Latin, German, and gymnastics, and from the accounts we have of the three years he spent there, he found the teaching very rewarding (his students were

25

a mixture of indigenous children and teachers, and children of French colonial administrators). As time went by, however, Paulhan felt an increasing distance from the arrogant colonialist attitudes of his compatriots. Paulhan commented at one point on the fact, for example, that their ideas about the cultures they were colonizing were drawn chiefly from Pierre Loti's novels, and that they believed, in any case, that "all of the colonies are the same," [2] and later on remarked: "All of these people are living off the Malagasies. What a rotten lot of *bourgeois* they are!" [3]

He spent less and less time with the other colonial officials on Madagascar, and an increasing amount of time with his Malagasy friends, who were mainly Hova.[4] He set about learning Malagasy, and made rapid progress in the language, successfully passing all of the exams (he was the only French person at the time to do so, and even outperformed most of the Malagasies who were taking the exams). As his interest in Malagasy culture deepened, his attention turned to its folklore, and he began noting down legends, stories, proverbs and the traditional oratorical debates known as *hain-teny,* which were rich in proverbs. He collected about 3,000 proverbs, this research being so appreciated on Madagascar that it earned him a place on the Malagasy Academy.

His attitude generally went very much against the grain of French colonialism, in that he argued strongly in favor of encouraging indigenous languages, and failed to see the purpose or usefulness of imposing French language education. His neglect of his "official" duties not surprisingly led to unfavorable reports from his colonial superiors, and he was eventually sent back to France at the end of 1910. He taught Malagasy at the Ecole des Langues Orientales, a temporary replacement post which only lasted a year, but the work he had begun on Malagasy proverbs was to preoccupy him for nearly 30 years, and was at the source of all of his later theoretical texts on language and literature. He translated and wrote an introduction to a selection of 153 *hain-tenys,* which he divided thematically into eight groups, a division he kept until the 1939 edition of the poems was published with an updated introduction. A number of essays, which seem merely to repeat the initial account of his experiences, predate this introduction. They in fact offer diverse perspectives on the question. It is well-known that Paulhan intended his work ultimately to become the subject of a thesis at the Sorbonne, an objective that was never brought to completion.[5]

Paulhan's writings which were inspired by his time on Madagascar might be placed very broadly within the context of French literature born—directly or indirectly—out of the French colonial experience, and the contact with other, colonized, cultures. These texts—both literary as well as ethnological in intention—are representative of what James Clifford has termed "ethnography," by which he understands a "general cultural disposition that cuts through modern anthropology and that this science shares with twentieth century art and writing." [6] Clifford sees manifestations of this in, for example, Victor Segalen's accounts of his travels to Polynesia and China, or in the "discovery" by the Surrealists in the 1920s and 1930s of what was then referred to as "negro art" (a catchall term whose nonspecificity allowed it to assimilate such diverse phenomena as American jazz, African tribal masks and voodoo rituals). Cubist Art, according to some accounts of its origins, owed its inspiration to African and Polynesian sculpture, and although Picasso denied any conscious debt to African art, the angularity of his early experiments with human form clearly borrow stylistic elements from African tribal masks.[7]

It was, however, Surrealist writers who were most directly influenced by or involved with ethnography, to such an extent that Michel Leiris's *L'Afrique fantôme* (1934), the account of the famous Dakar-Djibouti expedition of 1931, on which he was the official secretary of the trip, was considered as important as Marcel Griaule's ethnographic study of the Dogon, the most extensive study ever at that time of a single tribal group. It confirmed the extent to which, even on supposedly "scientific" expeditions such as the Dakar-Djibouti trip, Western writers continued to appropriate less "civilized" cultures as figures of (their own) alterity, as channels for escaping the dullness and rationalism of Western civilization. "Ethnography," apparently the serious counterpart to Surrealism's playful distortions and reappropriations, was in Clifford's view no less caught within the same structural dynamics. As he asks rhetorically: "Is not every ethnographer something of a surrealist, an inventor and reshuffler of realities? [. . .] Ethnography cut with Surrealism emerges as the theory and practise of juxtaposition." [8]

More recently, African philosophers such as V. Y. Mudimbe and Paulin Hountondji have radicalized Clifford's questioning of the assumed "scientific" basis of much early ethnography, and have sought to articulate a specifically African epistemology that no longer relies on the Western models used until now to frame the study of non-Western culture.[9] The articulation of such an epistemology takes as its point of departure the critical re-reading of works produced by ethnographers thought at the time to be "pro-African"; from Frobenius's descriptions of an idealized African society, to Lévy-Bruhl's theories of "primitive" cultures exhibiting a "pre-logical" mentality, and Placide Tempel's attempts to describe the Bantu "soul" in his *Bantu Philosophy,* with its merging of African and Christian spirituality.

To return to Paulhan, the accounts of his experiences do not fit easily into any of the categories sketched out above. He was certainly not on Madagascar for any Christian or other religious evangelistic mission, and his interest in Malagasy culture in fact predates the Cubist and Surrealist "discovery" of African art. Furthermore, Paulhan's position with respect to Lévy-Bruhl, whom he had hoped would be one of the readers of his thesis, is stated clearly in his critique of the latter's cultural hierarchy of logical and pre-logical civilizations. Paulhan argues that Lévy-Bruhl is the victim of what he termed the "illusion of the explorer," that is, the assumption that French is capable of greater abstraction than "primitive," supposedly more "concrete," languages. As Paulhan shows in his essay "La Mentalité primitive" [Primitive Mentality], the attributes of "abstract" and "concrete" are entirely relative, and in fact reversible, as his examples from Malagasy demonstrate.[10] As we have seen, Paulhan was very conscious of the injustices of colonialism, and aware of the various forms of ideological and political hegemony it brought with it. His own attitude to Malagasy culture was one of respect for the people and the language, taking them very much on their own terms, and trying himself to be assimilated, rather than to assimilate.

It would, of course, be naïve to claim that Paulhan was not just as much involved in the establishment and spread of colonial ideology as any of his compatriots on Madagascar, or that his work represents an extremely precocious form of self-critical ethnography. As Marc Augé has correctly pointed out, Paulhan's essays are of fairly limited interest as anthropological studies. This is particularly true of his attempts to perform more conventional anthropology in his *Repas et amour chez les Merinas (Meals and Love among the Merinas).* This short essay is a comparison between the taboos that operate with respect to meals in Merinas society, and the etiquette and morality that surrounds matters of love in Western society, and Augé shows how

Paulhan sets up a false and ethnologically unworkable analogy between the two domains, since he fails, for example, to contextualize the problem of social taboos, and draws erroneous and very general conclusions about Merinas society. Indeed, when Paulhan argues, at the end of one of his accounts of his learning proverbs that "You don't need to go to Madagascar to have the experience of the proverb," [11] thus deriving a *general* linguistic problematic from the *particularity* of his experiences, one might say he fits very well into mainstream ethnography which "recomposes from its own point of view the image of the society it observes." [12] Christopher Miller has characterized this process as one of *projection*, the perilous negotiation between subject and object that may, as he suggests, ultimately inform all ethnographic activity.[13]

What, then, are the value and usefulness of Paulhan's studies, besides being a chapter in the history of Malagasy folklore? What would it mean to take his studies on their own terms, as Paulhan did with Madagascar? If Paulhan could not escape being the traditional "participant observer" of early ethnography, he operates something of a twist on this very notion, since his accounts are narratives in which he gradually *becomes* a part of the life with respect to which he had started out in a position of superiority, and his descriptive account is overtaken by a certain performativity, a narrative destabilization that we will see to be typical of the *récit,* and that needs to be itself accounted for. By reading his texts as *récits,* we might concurrently pose the question of whether they were in fact *intended* to be serious attempts at ethnography, since Paulhan did not come to Malagasy culture with any particular methodological predisposition. In any case, we might at least entertain this hypothesis while we read them. At the very least, it would allow us to see them as only very ironically linked to something like Tempel's "ethnophilosophy," [14] in their effort to reveal the mysteries of the Malagasy "soul" as manifested in the finesse and ingenuity of proverbs.

If Paulhan's inquiry started out, then, as a fairly simple anthologization of the *hain-teny,* an act of literary conservation simplified by the imposition of time-honored thematic categories such as love, abandonment, and pride, its innately constrictive character left him dissatisfied. Most obviously, such a codification failed to take into account both the ways in which a *hain-teny* can lend itself to several differing themes and the fragmented, improvisational nature of their composition.[15] They are, he says, divided into two parts: a "clear part" and an "obscure part," the latter being made up, as he discovers, of proverbs, or of a kind of proverbial language. His first instinct is to see the essential part of the poem's message as being contained in the clear part, with the more obscure ending adding a sort of poetic counterpart or rhetorical embellishment. As his investigation proceeds, and as he pays more attention to the obscure parts, Paulhan shifts the emphasis and suggests that the obscure parts in fact carry the main burden of the poems, and the clearer parts merely "set them up." This change in emphasis comes about as Paulhan focuses more on the *effect* of the poems as opposed to their simple thematic *meaning*. The *hain-tenys* are often pronounced in the context of a debate, or rather of a highly formalized oratorical joust; it is during such contests that Paulhan came to recognize the importance of these proverbial phrases. Indeed, success in these debates is to a large extent determined by the strength and aptness of the proverbs one has at one's disposal ("The value of a hain-teny depends on the quantity of proverbs in it" [16]). In the texts that Paulhan subsequently devotes to proverbs, this shift of focus does not displace the importance of the semantic aspect of the poems, but as a result the interplay between the two becomes the burden of the essays. This same interplay between effect and meaning is carried over into Paulhan's studies of the more quotidian phenomenon that the proverb represents. Probably the most coherent account of Paulhan's own struggle, or joust, with proverbs, that doesn't sidestep the difficulties, failures and dead-ends involved, and the one which allows us to see most clearly the dynamics of Paulhan's "ethnographic narrative" at work, is *L'Expérience du proverbe (The Experience of the Proverb).*[17]

Although Paulhan, in his *Le Repas et l'amour chez les Merinas,*[18] had engaged in more traditional ethnographical writing, the essay on proverbs marks a significant departure in that it presents a narrator who actively involves himself in the phenomenon he sets out to describe. The essay itself is fairly clearly structured as a before/after narrative, in which the narrator's initial frustration in using proverbs is replaced, once he has learnt how to use them, by a symmetrical frustration in not being able to understand *why* his proverbs are successful. It is thus not simply a tale of the acquisition of a particular kind of language, but it examines the enigma of the proverb from two very distinct perspectives: before and after, outside and inside. The terms in which the question of the proverb is first posed recall the essay on *hain-teny.* The proverb is described by the narrator as a kind of "second language," differentiated from ordinary language by its tone, which commands attention and respect. Its authoritative force gives it the status of a kind of law, and it could thus be said to belong to the category of sententious discourse, such as maxims, aphorisms, and sayings.[19] Often a proverb will be used to bolster the authority of another proverb, a process that is also characteristic of the *hain-tenys*. The author initially surmises the possibility of a secret code which it would be possible to crack—he talks of "the strangeness of the words it contained," and of an element that is "foreign to our conversation" (*Expérience*, p.. 102), and this strange element *in* language often serves to interrupt language:

> Sometimes it would disrupt the tone of a discussion that was going on for too long, would hurry it along, get it out; or indeed would cut short some impending quarrel; in the Hova family I was staying with, this was the end of any argument: you needed a proverb, but a proverb was all you needed to end it. (*Expérience*, p. 102)[20]

How does the proverb put an end to discussions? It is not a logical or a dialectical resolution, since there is a very definitive rupture with the discussion leading up to the proverb. Yet neither is it entirely a question of sheer force, despite the manner in which the debates are concluded, since it "stands in for" ("me paraissait tenir lieu") more undignified interruptions of language such as orders or insults: "It stood in for them, if I might say, at less expense, and without there being any need to go outside of language" (*Expérience*, p. 103)[21].

We might examine more closely how this works in some of the examples the narrator provides. In the first example, he is discussing with his friend Rajaona how they should go to market:

> RAJAONA: Let's take a *filanjana* to market. [Footnote in text: "A filanjana is a type of chair carried by porters."]
>
> ME: It's only an hour's walk, let's go on foot. Only old people take filanjanas.
>
> RAJAONA: You have to pay for respect. If you go to market on foot, people will make fun of you.

> *You have to pay for respect* [*Le respect s'achète*] is a
> proverb. I don't notice it, no word warned me it was
> coming. But assuming it's just following on from the
> previous sentence, I reply:
>
> I prefer to do as I please, and people can respect me a lit-
> tle less. Anyway, of course . . . (*Expérience*, p. 103)[22]

The narrator completely misunderstands the function of the proverb, and Rabe and Rajaona, his two interlocutors, continue the discussion as if he had said nothing at all. Although "le respect s'achète" *does* mean something like "You have to pay for respect," in the context of this conversation it is obviously not just this. And it is not simply, as the narrators suggests, that "the meaning was not exactly where I placed it" (*Expérience*, p. 104),[23] since even if we could find an expression that would come close to the Malagasy, the misunderstanding comes from attributing a meaning to it at all. It is not reducible to a cognitive statement, a sentence, about respect ("Such a detailed consideration is foreign to the actual sentence uttered by Rajaona" [*Expérience*, p.104]),[24] but it is a code that has to be learnt and applied mechanically. It is, to anticipate the following example, "le-respect-s'achète."

In the second example Rainipatsa is counseling his son, Ralay, on the need to get married soon. Ralay answers his father by expressing concern about public opinion, in the form of the cautionary proverb: "No sooner has he taken a wife than he runs off and gets divorced" ["Il n'a pas plus tôt pris femme qu'il court divorcer"] (*Expérience*, p. 104). The narrator's rational analysis of the situation—that the two do not necessarily go together—again falls on deaf ears. When the narrator repeats his remark later to Rainipatsa, the latter finally understands, but to set him straight merely repeats Ralay's proverb, as if it needed no explanation. What is at stake is not the question of marriage and divorce, but the proverb that unites them inseparably, and as long as it is a question of the proverb, the narrator is wrong to dissociate them:

> Ralay didn't mean that a first hasty act was liable to lead
> to a second one: rather, he cited a fact which included both
> hasty acts, without being able to distinguish between them.
> As if he had said: And what do you make of the *hasty-act-*

of-getting-married-and-divorcing-right-away, do you ever
think about it? (*Expérience,* p. 105)[25]

Inasmuch as the proverb is formed of a particular immutable configuration of elements, which does not primarily *mean* and which involves mechanical memory, it is like the syntax or grammar of a language. To argue, as the narrator does, in a way that questions the set
composition of the proverb, is as futile and as incomprehensible as, for
example, disagreeing that in French an adjective agrees in gender and
number with the noun it qualifies.

It seems at one level that the narrator's difficulties are those en-
countered by anyone who has to deal with a language and culture
foreign to his or her own. The position of the narrator as an "outsider" is a paradigm of the ethnographer generally, and it is posed in
linguistic terms as a question of translation. Paulhan's difficulty with
proverbs is indeed, as he remarks on a number of other occasions, a
common problem of translation. Clichés in a foreign language always
strike us as more colorful, more concrete, more imaginative than corresponding terms in our own language. What we take to be quaint
and expressive is superficial and second-hand to the native speaker,
"just words." In bringing their linguistic dimension to the attention of
his Malagasy interlocutors, the narrator makes them feel quite uncomfortable, since he is in a sense exposing what needs to be kept
hidden for them to function *as* proverbs:

> I have recourse to the most unexpected metaphors: they
> seem to the Malagasies—as they do to me, come to think
> of it—as if they are said as part of a game [*par simple jeu*]:
> what's more, the interest of this game escapes them. (*Ex-
> périence,* p. 106)[26]

It is not that the narrator misses the point. Rather, he is too close
to the point for comfort. Hence the unease of the Malgasies he
questions:

> I found myself particularly disconcerted by the difficulty I
> had explaining to my Malagasy friends the cause of my
> discomfort. Their answers, even though they were full of
> good will, presented an awkwardness that was symmetri-
> cal to my own. (*Expérience,* p. 107)[27]

Once set in motion, the system of proverbs foregrounds its own specific linguistic constitution, while curtailing close analysis of its features. In posing the question of their meaning, and in treating them as metaphors, the narrator makes explicit what is kept implicit in the original. It is not just that they are demoted to mere sentences, but they become at the same time sentence and proverb, semantics and syntax, sense and influence. From the perspective of the native speakers, the continuity of the system of proverbs depends upon keeping this discrepancy hidden, which is why there is a double, symmetrical (though not identical) embarrassment. The natives' loss is also the narrators' loss, since he has a considerable stake in keeping the proverb, and the possibility of assimilating it, alive. For the natives, the resistance to making sense of the proverbs takes the form of a recontextualization, as if the proverbial expression did not stand out for special attention. This putting back into context works particularly well as a strategy, since the context will always provide the *raison d'être* of the proverb and can always be made to seem like a necessary, metaphorical relationship.

In reaffirming the primacy of the contextual, or the contingent, over the metaphorical, or the necessary, the efficacy of the proverb as imposition has been preserved, an outcome for which the narrator is as grateful as the native speakers. The most forceful argument always seems destined to win the argument about whether a proverb is *force* or *meaning,* and to decide the question in favor of the proverb rather than the *sentence.* Or, to reformulate it in rhetorical terms, the "meta-proverb" always functions as metonymy (context, contingency, just another proverb) rather than as metaphor (with its claims to totalization, to self-sufficiency, to freedom from context, etc.). It is a structural necessity of the system that metaphor be read as metonymy, even though the inverse, as the narrator demonstrates, is always possible. It is as if the narrator, as outsider, were structurally destined to eternal failure, since he *has* to translate, to read metonymy as metaphor, to isolate the proverb as citation, to add meaning to effect, to notice rather than ignore the discrepancy. Failure is not, however, the foreigner's exclusive prerogative: all native speakers are faced with the prospect of their proverbs falling flat. One can always say that it is "just a proverb": "Those are just words. . . . What are you talking about. . . . Leave us alone with your proverbs!" (p. 110),[28] and when used strategically in the context of a debate, this is potentially devastating:

> Everything then happened as if this misused proverb, forced
> to admit its status as a proverb, came to the aid of the opin-
> ion it was attacking, rather than of the one it was supposed
> to support. Its author had to invent some argument on the
> spot, some other proverb; even then, he would have diffi-
> culty avoiding the ridicule which had come from his ini-
> tial awkwardness. (*Expérience,* p. 110)[29]

If the narrator's predicament is now one he shares with the native
speakers, he has yet to experience failure from the "inside," which in
itself would hardly be an encouraging prospect or reward for his efforts. In any case, it is no longer certain that the division of inside
from outside is tenable, nor that the proverb can be assimilated. To continue would, it appears, involve either pursuing the complexities of
the problem that have come to light, or giving up the theoretical gains
in favor of a feigned success.

It is therefore difficult to know how to read the opening of chapter 3, and the second half of the essay:

> A few months go by. My language in turn begins to con-
> tain some proverbs. Of course, I usually quote them inno-
> cently when telling a story, "just for fun," yet I also man-
> age sometimes to introduce them into a discussion in which
> they come to my support. (*Expérience,* p. 111)[30]

The narrator has somehow overcome the insurmountable difficulties
of which he spoke just a little earlier in the essay; he is now on the
inside. He has managed to assimilate proverbs, and can use them
with a measure of success. There is a very definite "after" which
succeeds the "before" of the first half of the essay. Indeed, the sense
of temporal progression is underlined in the first sentence of this
second half ("A few months go by"). Yet despite asking the question,
"How did I manage to possess this beginning of knowledge *(ce commencement de science?),*" and giving some indication of the steps
involved, just how the passage from the first half to the second half
is realized is highly problematical, and is hardly something that was
in any way prepared. The ease with which this transition is negoti-
ated should not make us overlook its crucial importance. It is narrated with the greatest nonchalance, and yet it involves nothing less
than the passage which seemed impossible in the first half of the

essay: the possibility of going from "I quote them innocently when telling a story" to "I also manage sometimes to introduce them into a discussion."

The essay is more and more concerned with the precise nature of the relationship between the various sets of terms that have been brought into play in an attempt to account for the proverb. The necessity for a more precise articulation of what is at stake coincides in the essay with a reflection on the narrative organization of the essay in terms provided by the proverb. This is not simply a chronological moment whose occurrence we earlier anticipated when we considered the central transition of the essay. From the moment the narrator first asks the question of the proverb, it is in a sense already too late, he has already lost. This makes the narration of its recovery imperative, but the narration can never give us the proverb, since it is always either proleptic or retrospective. The proverb can least of all be simply cited; it can only be presented in the form of a representation, a mime, and although we are given literal, thematized versions of this mimicry in the latter half of the essay, the narrative is in fact concerned at every point with its own mode of representation.

This concern surfaces in the third section of the essay in a discussion of one of the narrator's "procedures" that helped him to speak using proverbs. The procedure in question involved forming an image of the character of the Malagasy people, which becomes ever more subtle and charming. The narrator acknowledges that he is making a fundamental error, but it is a common enough one, "that most travelers make" (*Expérience*, p. 113),[31] the error Paulhan refers to as the "illusion of the explorer" ("l'illusion de l'explorateur"). It consists of taking manifestations of Malagasy culture, particularly proverbs, as fine indications of a "Malagasy soul." However, this is precisely the kind of metaphorical misreading that prevented the narrator from speaking proverbs early on.

The narration continues from "within," as the narrator achieves almost native proficiency in speaking proverbs. The enjoyment of his success is, however, spoiled by a paradox, whose nature he then attempts to define more precisely:

> The more I hurry and force myself to be sincere, the more
> it seems to me that when I say a proverb, *nothing* happens:
> I mean, nothing of a linguistic nature, nothing that can be

expressed by relating it to this singular kind of sentence
named a proverb. (*Expérience,* p. 117)[32]

Once he has successfully broken through to the inside, and is apparently within the proverb, "*nothing* happens," just as when he was apparently "without" the proverb, it is also as if nothing happened when
he spoke ("I'm talking in a void" [p. 103], "no-one hears me"
[p. 104][33]). The distinction between a proverb and a sentence, as well
as the spatial and temporal metaphors of inside/outside and be-
fore/after, were all along, it seems, a lure; a handy but ultimately de-
fective narrative framework. As the narrator admits: "the very terms
in which I formulated and presented this worry are taken away from
me" (*Expérience,* p. 117).[34]

Whether or not it is successful, the proverb only comes into play
when there is an interference between two codes, since it necessarily
entails some kind of an interruption of language. It is neither identity (as success it is "nothing") nor difference (as failure it is also "nothing"), but it is the gap between two different figures of failure or success. What, we might ask, or rather where is the difference? How do
we get from one to the other? The essay conveniently offers us a literal answer to the question. At the very point of intersection, or of
interference, between the before and the after, at the precise center of
the essay, there is a blank: an ellipsis, a void, nothing. We cannot tell
the difference, because the narrator literally cannot tell, or narrate,
this difference. The focus of the narrative appears to shift towards
the end of the essay to what the narrator begins to call the "play of the
proverb" [*jeu du proverbe*], the play of differences whereby the proverb
continually appears and disappears. Since this involves accounting
for its production, the essay also, by analogy or by extension, tells
the story of the production and the uncertain status of the narrative
itself.

How are we to understand this relationship of analogy between
the proverb and the narrative about the proverb? The relation between thematized examples of the "play of the proverb," and the entire essay, is itself a question of no small importance.[35] If examples in
the essay have the same indeterminate status as the text itself, how are
we to read either one of them? Is the example an "actual" example,
introduced by a deictic "this is it!," giving us the "real thing," or is
it merely a simulacrum of a "play of the proverb," a "sentence which
I place skillfully" (*Expérience,* p. 123),[36] a convincing semblance of

spontaneity? To the extent that it determines its own status, it also determines its context, and by extension the status of the whole text. The same indetermination affects the text. Should we read it as a performative event or a constative statement? Whatever decision we make puts the example, so to speak, in its place. The text and the example seem to mimic each other, and to coexist in a state of permanent mutual displacement or usurpation. The connotations of parody or self-parody are undeniably present, and indeed it is precisely at this point that the question of irony is reintroduced:

> It is not easy to imagine in detail how the reversal, whose
> origin and effects we have just seen, can happen. Irony or
> humor can give an approximate idea of it. (*Expérience,*
> p. 122)[37]

The narrator then gives two examples that show orators who turn from their actual subject to the way in which they express it, and who attempt, like the narrator, to prove that what they are saying "is the case" *(c'est bien ça).* Unlike the earlier appearances of irony, when the narrator was mocking the seriousness surrounding the enunciation of a proverb, this irony is not merely a question of humor (or of the *effect* of irony). It is here both the putting into play and the suspension of the difference between meaning and saying, constative and performative. What this second irony suspends is the possibility of knowing whether one means what one says, and more pertinently, whether one can mean, or intend, to be ironic. The second irony ironizes the first irony—indeed, one could see irony as precisely the gap between the two—and as such the second irony is no longer simply a textual instance, and example of irony. Irony extends across the whole text in that this gap is everywhere—each example is "mis en abîme," and narrates this unnarratable gap, or *abîme,* or *rien.* When the Malagasies intimate early on that there is no place for irony, this is literally true. This is not just because it is a gap, such as the blank between the two halves of the essay, but because it is both everywhere and nowhere in the text. We can never tell whether the text knows itself to be ironic or not, since it could always be pretending not to know—which is, etymologically, what irony is all about: the art of feigning ignorance.[38]

Not the least of ironies of this text is that proverbs are taken to be deeply rooted in, and bound up with, common experience. The title of the essay sums up very concisely the equivocation that a close examination of the proverb brings to light; does the "experience" belong to the "je" or to the proverb? Are we dealing with an experienced disruption or a linguistic disruption? This question is exactly the kind of question that the "play of the proverb" can account for. The truly ironic disruption is between the "play of the proverb" and the text which attempts to account for it, between, in other words, the "play of the proverb" and *L'Expérience du proverbe*. What, then, is the relation between a proverb and a *récit,* between an unreadable text and the story, or the allegory, of this unreadability? [39] They in fact stand in a paradoxical synecdochal relation to each other. The proverb seems to contain within it, in its potential for disruption, the future possibility of the *récit,* and yet appears lexically as merely part of the narrative. The *récit* makes the proverb seem highly improbable, even impossible, when subjected to close scrutiny, but such an assertion cannot be treated lightly, since it may be telling a tale of its own impossibility. So that even though the *récit,* or allegorical narrative, appears to be what the narrator calls "a part of language used to establish that one can speak," it could very well be no more than a kind of proverb, inasmuch as it belongs metonymically to the rest of the language ("a *part* of language"). Thus the allegory of unreadability becomes "just" another unreadable text. Such seems to be the fate, according to de Man, of all allegories of unreadability: "Such an allegory is metafigural: it is an allegory of a figure (for example, metaphor) which relapses into the figure it deconstructs." [40]

Where does this leave Paulhan's "ethnographic" writings in terms of the history of French ethnography generally? A reading such as the one we have just performed effectively decontextualizes the essay, and shows it to be concerned as much with its own linguistic and narrative complexities as with the supposed object of its study. Through the detour of this decontextualization, however, we are able to recontextualize and rehistoricize the essay as an allegory of the very activity of ethnography itself, the complex negotiation of self and other, which is actualized in the drama of the proverbial joust. It is a mark of Paulhan's ability to exploit the resourcefulness of his own texts, and also an exemplification of the proverb's own metonymic capacity for recontextualization, that this essay resurfaces in another form as a presentation for the short-lived College of Sociology.

SACRED LANGUAGE

The College of Sociology represents an entirely different strand of French anthropology, one which has it roots in the theories of Emile Durkheim and Marcel Mauss around the turn of the century. Durkheim was writing in reaction to the sociological positivism of thinkers such as Auguste Comte, and attempted to conceptualize the sacred forces of "primitive" societies, which he sought to transpose in turn to the context of modern Western culture. He strongly influenced, in particular, the thinking of two of the founders of the College of Sociology Georges Bataille and Roger Caillois, who saw its project as a kind of resacralization of Western society. Paulhan was one of the chief supporters of the College's activities, publishing many of the lectures in the *Nouvelle Revue Française*. His role was chiefly that of a facilitator, and his intervention at the College on 16 May 1939 may be seen as nothing more than a kind of guest appearance. While Caillois and Paulhan, who both proposed theories of the sacred, seem to have been at opposite extremes of the spectrum, it is possible, I would suggest, to see a deeper complicity between them.

The work of both writers has its origin, in different ways, in the ethnology of the time. Caillois was a student of Marcel Mauss and Georges Dumézil, and a voracious reader of the ethnography and cultural history of the early part of the century. In his first work, *La Nécessité de l'esprit* (*The Necessity of the Mind*), he used the mythologies and beliefs of "primitive" societies as evidence for the universality of his theory of lyrical overdetermination. Paulhan's concerns were on the face of it far removed from those of Caillois and Bataille. While Caillois made a militant appeal in *Le Vent d'hiver* (The Winter Wind) for the "recalcitrants" *(réfractaires)* of society to form an elite community that would use its own power to subvert and regenerate Western civilization, drawing its inspiration from the sacred forces invested in similar privileged groups in "primitive" societies, Paulhan maintained that the sacred—which for him was manifest in the powerful "authority" of Malagasy proverbs—was within easy reach of everyone ("You don't need to go to Madagascar to have the experience of the proverb"). The crucial question of the "College of Sociology"—how can we resacralize Western society?—prompts diametrically opposed responses from Caillois and Paulhan: Caillois advocates a community of a select few purged of its weak, redundant elements, while Paulhan's solution is a utopian democracy, a "secret society" to which everyone belongs. A closer look at how the two writers elaborated their respective theories of the sacred, however, reveals in fact a deeper theoretical *rapport* between them.

Caillois's theory of the sacred is most thoroughly articulated in two of the lectures which he wrote for the "College of Sociology," "Le pouvoir" (Power), which Bataille presented in February 1938, and "La fête" (Festival), the text of which Bataille read in May 1939, which became in the two key chapters of *Man and the Sacred*, "The Sacred of Respect" and "The Sacred of Transgression." [41] Unlike Bataille, for whom the sacred offered a model of pure transgression, the mystical *sovereignty* of a kind of shamanism, Caillois was interested in analyzing the dynamics of the interaction between the sacred and the profane as it occurred in a wide range of "primitive" societies. In "The Sacred of Respect" Caillois stresses the sacred as a prohibiting force, one that functions as a means of preserving and regulating the social order. As Caillois shows, for example, in many Australian and North American Indian tribes, opposing clans have distinctly complementary and symmetrical prohibitions, and totemic emblems, such that what is sacred for one clan is profane for another, and vice versa, thereby allowing for a mutual exchange between the two.

According to Caillois, as societies become more complex, they lose this fundamental duality which is at the basis of their social structure, and the "sacred of respect" is transferred onto a single, sovereign power. In this evolutionary account of the genesis of political power, the crime of *lèse-majesté* becomes the most sacrilegious of all. Yet any society in which all of the forces are oriented towards its own preservation tends, in Caillois' theory, towards its inevitable decline, its decadence, and necessitates a period of regeneration and recreation:

> There comes a moment when an overhaul is necessary. A positive act has to ensure a new stability for an order. A simulacrum of creation is needed to renew nature and society. This is what the festival provides. [42]

The sacred force represented by the "festival" stands in dramatic contrast to the reverential awe that characterizes the "sacred of respect";

the dull continuity and repetition of everyday life is interrupted by an explosion of frenetic activity, its dispersion remedied by a paroxysm of intense, concentrated celebration in which the usual rules no longer apply. Caillois describes this period as a collective recreation of the world, a simulacrum of chaos that ushers in a renewed cosmos. And as he emphasizes, the disorder of the festival stands in a precise relation to the order of the normal course of life: "these sacrileges are considered to be as ritual and holy as the very prohibitions they violate. Like them, they can be called sacred." [43] The two antithetical forms of the sacred are thus inextricably linked, and indicate the fundamental trait of the sacred, its ambiguity.

One of Caillois's examples to illustrate this constant interplay between the prohibitive and the transgressive forces of the sacred is a Malagasy proverb, "The maternal uncle falls under the nephew's assegai," [44] which, as he points out, not only exemplifies the eternal conflict of generations, but also the struggle between the two fundamental elements, static and dynamic, of social life. Although it is open to speculation, it is unlikely that Caillois could have found this example anywhere other than in Paulhan's own translations and editions of Malagasy proverbs. By the time Paulhan had rewritten his *Expérience du proverbe* as the lecture "Of Sacred Language," he had already fully worked out his theory of terror and rhetoric in the 1936 *NRF* version of *Les Fleurs de Tarbes*. The analogy between Paulhan's articulation of an essential doubleness, or ambiguity, and Caillois's own analysis of the sacred, is not lost on either writer, and generates a brief exchange of letters between the two. Paulhan asks Caillois in October 1937:

> Do we basically agree? I mean: that the terrorist or the recalcitrant tends—whether he likes it or not—towards a power that he will have to one day assume. . . . And that this power [. . .] is expressed precisely by the very rhetoric which the terrorist rejected out of weakness. . . ? [45]

To which Caillois replies:

> Indeed, if one thinks about it, it contains a comparable reversal, at least formally, to the one in *Les Fleurs de Tarbes:* it's the same dialectic, applied by you to language, by me to social existence. [46]

Caillois is at the time less convinced than Paulhan of the coincidence of their respective projects. He continues: "The points of application are so dissimilar that one would have to stop there," and almost reproaches Paulhan for using Rhetoric as a means of recuperating and defusing the active dynamism of Terror. Both writers, however, recognize a fundamental ambivalence as the essential trait of the sacred. Caillois talks of "its fundamentally equivocal nature," [47] of the double impulse of fear and desire that it inspires. The two opposing yet complementary forces of the sacred act in league against the world of the profane, and at the same time function to preserve it. In the same way, the enigmatic status of the proverb derives from its continual metamorphosis from pure force into pure form. Proverbs could be said to exist in the mythic time of the festival, their wisdom and authority deriving from a primordial origin, while they at the same time restrain and preempt any originality. In effect, proverbs, or sacred language, act to both prohibit and make possible the renewal of ordinary, or profane, language. This triangular dynamic—in which two opposing yet mutually sustaining sacred forces work to perpetuate a third, the profane—characterizes both Paulhan's and Caillois's theory of the sacred.

Whereas Paulhan's sacred is available to the "first person to come along" (*le premier venu*), Caillois is at greater pains to trace its gradual dissolution, and reemergence, in the course of the history of civilization. *Man and the Sacred* ends by bemoaning the general spread of the profane across all facets of life in the civilized world, since it forces the sacred into more interiorized or private spaces. The sacred, according to Caillois, has lost its pre-eminence as a force that regulates the very rhythm and energy of social life, and has been replaced by pale imitations at best: "A general disorder is no longer appropriate: at best people tolerate its simulacrum." [48] In the first edition of Caillois's essay, before the war and in the wake of the Popular Front's adoption of paid holidays for the first time, this role appears to have been filled by the "empty" time of the holidays ("vacances"). After the war, however, Caillois revised the ending of the chapter on "The Sacred of Transgression"; in response to the question of what in modern life corresponds to the festival, Caillois states emphatically that it is not the social divisiveness and dispersion of vacations, but the concentrated energy and violence of war. Like the festival, war is a radical disruption of the continuum of everyday life; it is given an historical and, overtly or not, a religious justification in that it is seen as a necessary prelude to national and spiritual regeneration; it mobilizes the total energies of a nation; and the usual standards of civilized behavior are flagrantly overridden. Modern society appears to have substituted the grim dialectic of war and peace for that of the sacred and the profane. Yet Caillois also stresses the absolutely opposed functions and outcomes of festival and war; war exacerbates existing hostilities rather than suspending them, it fosters hatred and conflict rather than alliance and cohesion, it is a source of death and devastation rather than of renewed life and fecundity. He is led to ask himself what is responsible for this perversion of the originally recreative force of the sacred, and continues to see the gradual secularization of Western civilization as one of the principal causes, along with the emergence of vast nation states whose centralized power structures enable easy abuse of ever more sophisticated techniques of destruction.[49] This development in his theory of the sacred allows him at the same time to distance himself from the untimely similarity between Nazism and the program for social regeneration he had set out in *Le Vent d'hiver*. War is seen as an inevitable historical evolution that stands in exact opposition to Caillois's own abortive call for an organized movement to tap into the hidden sacred forces of social life.[50] The analogy breaks down precisely because war is no longer a simulation of chaos, but an actual orgy of destruction.

This shift of focus away from a political activation of the sacred, to a recognition of simulacrum as its very ground, in fact realigns Caillois's interest in the sociology of the sacred with his earlier studies of insect mimetism, and the later texts on the formations and images of stones. It also, perhaps unwittingly, confirms Paulhan's intuition of the deep affinity uniting their respective projects. While Caillois before the war adopted the stance of the militant "recalcitrant," wanting to go beyond Paulhan's apparent restraint in confining his theory to the linguistic realm, after the war he comes to realize that Paulhan had gone further than him in understanding how close their theories were. It is because the sacred is essentially a question of simulacra, of metaphor (or to quote Paulhan again, of "that rhetoric which the terrorist rejected out of weakness"), that it is socially, or politically, so effective.

So what can be made of Paulhan's swerve away from pursuing the political or theoretical implications of his work, into a more general problematic of linguistic and literary expression? Marc Augé has pointed out the limits of Paulhan's linguistically oriented comparison of Malagasy and French cultures in *Le Repas et l'amour chez les Meri-nas,* showing how Paulhan never quite takes the crucial step of using the model of language to explore the dynamics of cultural taboos.[51] What is significant in Paulhan's "ethnographic" writing is the shift, which we observed in particular with *L'Expérience du proverbe,* to the narrative form of the *récit,* which assessments of Paulhan's writings do not normally take into account. Far from being a simple evasion, by a turn towards the fictional, of the methodological or political complexities of ethnography, the *récit* allows Paulhan both to engage with the practice of ethnographic writing, and to read in a sense beneath its surface, beyond the commonplaces of colonialist textuality. *Aytré qui perd l'habitude* (Aytré Who Gets Out of the Habit) does just this.

Written while Paulhan was in Madagascar, *Aytré* is in fact based on an actual unsolved murder case. Aytré, a colonial sergeant, is assigned to keep the log of the journey which he makes, together with two other Frenchmen, Guetteloup and an adjutant, escorting three hundred Senegalese women across Madagascar. He begins by simply recounting facts, such as the distance they cover, or the supplies they are low on, but the more he writes, the more attentive he becomes to Malagasy culture. His log is slowly transformed into a more searching personal journal, in which he "gets out of the habit" of seeing things as he is supposed to. As he says at one point: "The strangeness of things in Madagascar corresponds to the strangeness of men." [52] His language reveals an increasing sensitivity to the lot of the Malagasies, and by the end of his journal he begins to question (and reverse) the hierarchy of the colonizing culture as civilized and naturally superior to that of the colonized. Aytré's log/journal is itself framed by two chapters which are narrated by the adjutant, who comments upon Aytré's writing, and who informs us of the murder of a French woman, Raymonde. We never find out who in fact murdered Raymonde, but the adjutant seems intent on proving that what he sees as the gradual "disintegration" of Aytré's log is evidence of the latter's guilt. However, the adjutant's language, in contrast to Aytré's clear-headed and increasingly politically aware narration, is far more troubled and incoherent. He admits to stealing from Raymonde, and even though Aytré seems to have been charged with her murder, we are left with a strong sense of suspicion about the credibility of the adjutant's version of the events. As he writes in the last chapter, for example: "Aytré was no longer enough for himself. I recognize signs put there for my benefit; they don't really mean: hair, sun rays, inquiry—but they mean this other thing which has now been added to everything else that is happening to me, and even to my memories, thereby undoing them" (*Aytré*, p. 95).[53] At one level an intriguing murder mystery, this *récit* could also be read as an allegory of colonialism (through the representative colonial subject of the adjutant) cracking under the strains of its own system, the breakdown of an arrogantly Eurocentric view of the world when it tries to understand the strangeness of the culture and people it is attempting to "civilize."

Paulhan was never to return to Madagascar, just as he was never to finish his thesis on the semantics of the proverb. This was not due to any loss of interest on Paulhan's part, since he in fact produced plan after plan, and hundreds of pages of different manuscript versions. One is left to surmise whether there was not something interminable about the very enterprise itself, which continually generated more narratives, and seemed propelled by a kind of metonymic imperative always to analyze one more example. The inability to end testifies as much to the stuttering repetition of narrativity which Paulhan found himself caught in when he tried to draw some universal conclusion from his experiences, as to his unwillingness to leave behind the particularity of his experience, to translate it, and thereby to lose it. The tension of this dilemma—caught between generality and particularity, theory and observation, *récit* and proverb, self and other—is everywhere inscribed in Paulhan's texts that come out of his time on Madagascar, and it indicates the acute—and perhaps premonitory—sense Paulhan had of the dilemma facing all ethnographic narration.

U N D E R W R I T I N G
T H E
P E R S O N A L

Modesty and the récits

*The danger of modesty: being too attracted to the
person who admires you. (But what if it were only a
ruse to invite this admiration?)*

"Do you love me?" Maast asks.

"Yes."

*"But do you love me even more? Remember that I am
modest, and unsure of myself, and not very demanding.
And that, well, we cannot love each other unless you
give a little more of yourself than I can give of myself."*

Modesty, a bad ruse.[1]

Autobiographical fragment,
15 December 1926

*I have always avoided, insofar as I was able to, adding
one more personal view to all those which are already
around in the world.*[2]

II, Introduction, 1967

commonly accepted view of Paulhan's work is that his evolution as a writer follows a recognizable trajectory, beginning with his Malagasy texts, passing through the "formative" stages of his semi-fictional, semi-autobiographical *récits,* before flourishing in the public garden of Tarbes with his "mature" theoretical texts.[3] We saw, in reading his texts from the Madagascar years, that Paulhan was clearly drawn to the short narrative form which the French term a *récit.*[4] This occurs in *L'Expérience du proverbe* as a move from an account of his personal experiences, to a narrative which attempts to negotiate the very process of narrating the personal. A *récit* such as *Aytré qui perd l'habitude (Aytré Who Gets Out of the Habit)* seems to follow naturally from the studies of Malagasy proverbs, and indeed once Paulhan returned to France in 1910, his first writings were mostly *récits,* composed around the First World War, or just after it. Critics have also tended to regard these texts as essentially autobiographical, and their status as autobiography is hard to deny, given that Paulhan almost always narrates in the first person, and often states that the narratives have their origin in actual experience.[5] What I would like to do in this chapter is to explore the autobiographical, or more precisely the personal, within Paulhan's early *récits,* keeping in mind the unprecedented interrogation of the relationship between language, the self and the world then taking place in French literary history. This included the influence of Freudian psychoanalysis, the emergence of Surrealist literature and art, the beginnings of the Modernist movement, and Proust's major rethinking of the interaction between self, time, memory and narrative. I would suggest that while Paulhan's *récits* do give us some insight into Paulhan's life, their real significance lies in what they have to tell us about the process of narrating the personal. Although his narrative style goes very much against the grain of the radically disruptive writing practices of Surrealism or Modernism, the originality of the *récits* lies in the understated quality of their effects (compounded by Paulhan's own insistence on their modest literary value), which are all the more powerful and far-reaching for their subtlety. The *récits* provide the best place to read Paulhan's language, and his anxious reflection upon language, which looks forward beyond his time, revealing what one might call a post-modern linguistic sensibility. Within my study of Paulhan's work in general, this chapter will also serve to underline the importance of being keenly attentive to Paulhan *the writer,* and not simply Paulhan the influential editorial presence, or the unorthodox literary theoretician.

JEAN PAULHAN AND JACQUES MAAST

It seems easy enough to identify Paulhan with his character Jacques Maast, who often assumes a first-person narrative position in the *récits,* and who appears throughout Paulhan's texts with enough regularity for us legitimately to hypothesize that this is simply a pseudonym. Indeed, not only is Maast a commonly recurring character in Paulhan's *récits,* but Paulhan himself used the name Maast to sign articles published in Resistance journals during the Second World War. Maast is in fact the name of a small village in Northern France where Paulhan spent a period of time during the First World War, and where he allegedly met his future second wife, Germaine Pascal.[6] In the *récits* themselves the village is not named as such: *Le Guerrier appliqué (The Diligent Soldier)* takes place near St. Denis, and it is purportedly composed in Bois St. Mard. Likewise, *Progrès en amour assez lents (Progress in Love on the Slow Side)* states that it was written in Velleminfroy, the village in the *récit,* although other drafts also name Colombey-les-Belles, Breuches, Marseille and Tarbes. Furthermore, at different points in his career, Paulhan adopted other pseudonyms: Jean Guérin was the one he used most frequently, as a "chronicler" in the pages of *Nouvelle Revue Française,* but he also signed several texts as Lomagne, and as Just.[7] Both the geographical location and the location of the writing subject are thus equally unstable, and the name Maast serves metonymically to ground at the same time the writer, the place of the events, and the act of writing (whether fictional or autobiographical).[8]

The recent publication of the previously unavailable autobiographical writings by Paulhan—mostly personal diaries and notebooks he kept throughout his life, and which are often the place where he drafted early versions of published material—has revealed just how close the *récits* are to the actual events of Paulhan's life.[9] Paulhan recounts, for example, the episodes of *La Guérison sévère*

(The Severe Recovery) almost word for word as they appear in the published *récit*. He was indeed critically ill with pneumonia, and his illness occurred at the time he was beginning to leave his first wife Sala Prusak for Germaine Pascal. The characters are given different names, but we can connect the dots without too much difficulty; if Jacques Maast is Jean Paulhan, then Juliette is Sala, and Simone is Germaine. The transition from *Progress in Love on the Slow Side* to *The Severe Recovery* seems to suggest a definite continuity; at the end of *Progress in Love on the Slow Side* Jacques is being overtaken by a fever, which he then succumbs to fully in *The Severe Recovery*. However, several subtle changes occur in the passage from autobiographical writing to *récit,* and these inconsistencies are all the more telling for being relatively minor. If Sala is the Juliette of the *récit,* then he had *already* met her in 1911 (the year they married), whereas in *Progress in Love on the Slow Side* Jacques meets Juliette for the first time during the First World War. In *The Severe Recovery,* Jacques is already married to Juliette, and has an affair with Simone in Thénissey, on the way to meet Juliette. The ending of *The Severe Recovery* —Jacques' reconciliation with Juliette—seems to mark the end of his relationship with Simone, whereas Paulhan in fact left Sala Prusak for Germaine Pascal. The circumstances of the love affair do not quite match up either. In *Progress in Love on the Slow Side* Jacques first meets Juliette and Simone (who seem to be good friends) at roughly the same time, in Velleminfroy, while in *The Severe Recovery* Jacques had met Simone rather secretively (at least according to Juliette) in Thénissey. The slight mismatch between the actual events of Paulhan's life and the events of his *récits* is carried further in an interesting twist, which is that in his "private" account, the women are *already* fictionalized as Juliette and Simone. Indeed, the closer we get to Paulhan's "real" self, the more insubstantial or virtual it seems to become. This is the case in different ways for all of the "autobiographical" *récits,* where the self is often a kind of absent (indifferent, distracted, or abstracted) self, or an altered one (Jacques is delirious, or dreaming). For all the narrator's earnest sincerity in *Progress in Love on the Slow Side* ("I'll make my tale as plain as possible" [10]), the revelation of a "true" self is not what the autobiographical texts appear to be ultimately most concerned with. In fact it is "the simplest things," to quote Jacques, which are the most difficult to explain. If a *récit* such as *The Severe Recovery* is

read as a continuation of *Progress in Love on the Slow Side,* it is less in terms of an autobiographically (or even fictionally) consistent chronology, than as a prolongation and continued pursuit of the narrative and linguistic enigmas which are the focal point of all of Paulhan's *récits.*

I'd like to turn my attention for a moment to *The Severe Recovery,* reading it as an example of the way in which this shift occurs, from an autobiographical recovery of the self and its circumstances to a reflection on the very process of narrating the personal. The *récit* is divided into three sections. In the first, Jacques presents his hallucinatory thoughts during his sickness, but they are accompanied by a more lucid commentary, presumably from after his cure; in the second, Juliette narrates the sickness from her point of view, and discovers evidence of his infidelity to her; in the third, narrated again in the first person by Jacques, there is a violent resolution between them, and Jacques gets over the worst of his illness. The revelation of his infidelity tests the love between Jacques and Juliette to its limits, and it may be read thematically as the final stage in the progress of Jacques' love. Just as in *Progress in Love on the Slow Side* love is equated with a dangerous kind of letting go, the analogy with sickness is clear, and a "severe" cure is called for in order to put a halt to this potentially fatal abandon. The transformation this involves is by no means that simple, of course. The first chapter, "Maladresse à se guérir"("A Bad Job of Recovering") is a series of hallucinatory descriptions marked by a kind of fluid continuity, seen at first as something of a triumph of vigilance through the sickness:

> I have not stopped keeping track of my thoughts since the beginning of this illness. It is surprising that they should have remained exactly the same throughout, when my body was changing so much. (*Guérison*, p. 48)[11]

Later on, however, this impression is corrected from the "healthy" perspective of Juliette and the doctor, who "translate" Jacques' thoughts for him as simply the product of a delirious mind. This translation, or interpretation, suggests that the passage from sickness to cure requires the distance of a process of reading, or of self-rereading, although this process is certainly not self-evident. The question of reading is broached with a degree of uncertainty and hesitancy in *The Severe Recovery*:

> I have not stopped keeping track of my thoughts, but there
> came a time when I wanted to benefit from them. I don't
> know how this transition happened: perhaps it was the ef-
> fect of a familiarity which is easy to take advantage of. Or
> even . . . But I am hardly able to talk of these things which
> are not only about me. (*Guérison,* p. 50)[12]

How is Jacques in fact cured? The decisive moment comes when Jacques, possibly by unconscious design, allows Juliette to find the evidence of his infidelity: a flower, a black knotted ribbon, and some letters from Simone. They are all given over to Juliette, who burns the flowers and the ribbon, but not the letters. The reason for this, Jacques conjectures, is "perhaps that it was impossible to be mistaken about those letters from Simone—whereas the flower and the bow, she thought, are signs" (*Guérison,* p. 62)[13]. The reconciliation is made through an exchange in which Jacques concedes his fault in return for the pain caused to Juliette by his betrayal:

> it seems to me that she is henceforth taking responsibili-
> ty, in return, for my slowness, for so many wasted ideas,
> whose lack I feel strongly today—and for my initial awk-
> wardness in defending myself against the ease which one
> takes in dying. (*Guérison,* p. 62)[14]

Jacques' lucid, retrospective commentary on his own dream narrative is apparently aligned with Juliette's account of Jacques' sickness, and suggests a definitive separation between delirious writing and rational, objective interpretation, or between writing and reading. Yet we cannot say that Juliette's *récit* is entirely reliable, since as she gets closer to the heart of Jacques' secret, her state of mind resembles his more and more:

> My despair did not get any greater: but it seemed to go
> into my body. During all the days that followed, I had vi-
> olent contractions and dizzy spells that were so frequent I
> could no longer remain standing . . . my thoughts became
> confused . . . I could see waves in the blue paper of the
> window panes. (*Guérison,* p. 58)[15]

Juliette appears to be contracting some of Jacques' symptoms, and is clearly beginning to hallucinate. Yet could we not say that Juliette's assimilating Jacques' sickness is a kind of reading, just as Jacques' delirious narrative is a kind of writing? Jacques and Juliette are in fact inextricably bound up in a shared predicament at the heart of their suffering (in which fever and love come together), namely, that there is, literally speaking, a text to be read: the "evidence" of Jacques' infidelity.

Juliette, however, seems to have a great deal of trouble reading this text. How can we understand her decision to burn the ribbon and the flowers, and yet keep the letters? The letters are *so* incontestably compromising that she doesn't even bother to read them—they are only significant insofar as they point deictically to the flower and the ribbon as being themselves infinitely more meaningful. If we are to take Jacques at his word, the flower and the ribbon are completely unrelated to the affair with Simone, yet this reinforces rather than diminishes Juliette's need to destroy them. Jacques himself seems readier to face death than to face reading (indeed Juliette is always deploring his indifference to death). For a while, he has the opportunity to burn the letters himself, but does not do so:

> But something else occurred: everything happened as if I had wanted to prepare Juliette for the moment when she would read the two letters. (*Guérison,* p. 61)[16]

It is in fact consistent with his state of mind that he would not burn them, since as far as he is concerned there is no danger in his indifference. The danger arises precisely at the moment of reading. Reading is potentially catastrophic, and yet it is also the necessary passage, the cure. According to Jacques, the cure is made possible by the "useful inscriptions" with which he covers the walls, and which he repeats endlessly. Throughout *The Severe Recovery,* the severity of the cure (i.e., the violence of the passage from indifference to caring) and the *effort* of the *récit* are tied to inscription:

> (Jacques) "It tires me to write all these events." (*Guérison,* p. 49)

> (Juliette) "I thought I saw these words written on the wall, or on the bedcovers. I called to them, I took ahold of them. I immersed myself in them—but for half an hour at the most, then I was exhausted." (*Guérison,* p. 56)

> (Jacques) "I remember that the effort of writing seemed
> to me abnormal or unpleasant." (*Guérison*, p. 53)

> (Jacques) ". . . the useful inscriptions . . . certainly had a
> profound effect on this severe recovery, and they them-
> selves joylessly created it in their own image." (*Guéri-
> son*, p.53)[17]

Writing and reading are thus essential in bringing about Jacques' cure, and in unlocking the secret of the *récit;* yet they also introduce a kind of narrative anxiety that is not dispelled, and that nudges the text ever further away from being simply a piece in the autobiographical puzzle of Paulhan's life.

How does his writing differ from that of his contemporaries? Paulhan is not undertaking a vast autobiographical project like Proust's or Gide's, which involve, in different ways, a rich and complex interweaving of life and textuality. Nor is his writing radically innovative in terms of narrative form or style, like the experimental writing of the Surrealists, the Cubists and the early Modernists, with whom he was after all working closely as an editor. Insofar as they present Paulhan as a young man, still at a rather impressionable age, the *récits* might be aligned with the early Surrealist autobiographies, such as André Breton's *Nadja,* Michel Leiris' *Manhood* and Roger Caillois' *The Necessity of the Mind,* all of which Denis Hollier has characterized as "works of an insolent immaturity."[18] Yet Paulhan's writing is precisely *not* "insolent" nor—I would argue—"immature." This raises the question both of Paulhan's language and, again, of the status of his *récits* in relation to his later work. Does Paulhan really leave behind the "personal" (that is, the private self which he perhaps too hastily, "immaturely," revealed through his *récits,* or at least used as their pretext)?

Not only does Paulhan constantly make his "private" self available to the public through interviews, letters, essays and anecdotal narratives, but even his theoretical texts are framed, or constantly interrupted by personal interventions. *La Peinture Cubiste (Cubist Painting),* for example, begins with a casual discussion between the narrator and his doctor about a painting seen in a gallery window; *Les Fleurs de Tarbes (The Flowers of Tarbes)* ends with the famous "Let's just say I said nothing"; and *Clef de la poésie (Key to Poetry)* (arguably Paulhan's most abstract and impersonal text), ends with the claim that "I was the discovery I was making," a kind of folding back of the text upon itself which we also saw in *L'Expérience du proverbe*, with the double valence in French of "expérience" as both an objective scientific experiment, and a subjective, personal experience. This movement from an initially objective analysis of a problem, to the sudden (often surprised) personal implication within the problem, is very characteristic of Paulhan's texts. It creates an unstable, volatile textual space, in which the borders between "theoretical" texts and personal narrative become difficult to determine. Paulhan's texts constantly merge into each other, producing a kind of intertextual symbiosis that is all the more pronounced in that he is constantly rewriting them. Could we conclude, then, that all of Paulhan's texts are in a sense fundamentally autobiographical?

In his essay "The Ease of Dying" Maurice Blanchot makes a suggestion along these lines about Paulhan's writing when he states: "I almost think . . . that Jean Paulhan wrote nothing but *récits*, or always in the form of *récits.*"[19] This affirmation of Paulhan's propensity for short, personal narratives quickly gives way however to a suspicion that the term *récit* —like Paulhan "himself"—is not what it at first appears to be, a suspicion confirmed by the rest of Blanchot's essay. Blanchot does not mean that the *récit* functions as an autobiographical "screen" which would serve both as a surface onto which Paulhan projects his life, and as a cover to hide his "true" self; what Blanchot does in calling all of Paulhan's texts *récits* is to unite the personal, fictional writings with the theoretical essays, in a critical gesture as astonishing for its insight as it is simple. It forces us to rethink our understanding of the term *récit*, and provides a double clue as to the neglect from which Paulhan's texts have suffered until recently: the "personal" texts are too frustratingly elusive, while the "theoretical" texts are too personal, too light-hearted to be taken seriously. To approach the problem from a different angle, as Blanchot does, is to recognize the philosophical importance of Paulhan's theoretical writings when read *as récits*, that is in terms of a "narrative practice" ("une pratique narrative") ("Ease," p. 127), which in turn allows us to read within the autobiographical *récits* many of the theoretical concerns which preoccupied Paulhan from the 1920s until his death in 1968.[20] Paulhan often refers to these concerns as the "enigma of language," or the "mystery in literature," and since the exposition of the problem takes as its most readily available evidence the language at hand— that is the language *of* the texts themselves—the early *récits* not only anticipate the explicit themes and questions later articulated by Paulhan, but also the narrative performance, which is so crucial to understanding the textual dynamic. What, then, of Paulhan's language (which Blanchot, curiously, spends very little time discussing)? I'd like to look more closely at the language in one of these *récits, Progress in Love on the Slow Side,* not so much in order to perform a stylistic analysis, but so as to demonstrate the ways in which language is crucial to an understanding of their very narrative/theoretical process (what Blanchot calls, in that most untranslatable of French terms, "la démarche"[21]).

On an initial reading *Progress in Love on the Slow Side* seems to hold no surprises; as a story, it is about precisely what the title announces. Jacques Maast, a French soldier on leave from the front during the First World War, finds himself in a small village, Velleminfroy. He narrates, in the first person, his experiences during the few days he spends in the village, and the narrative is centered around what one might call a sentimental or, more explicitly, a sexual education. He recounts his erotic adventures with three girls from the village: Jeanne, Juliette and Simone. Jacques Maast is set apart from the other male characters by a tendency to reflect very self-consciously on life, a trait which prevents him from achieving the kind of easy, spontaneous success his fellow soldiers have with women. Yet paradoxically, what he had taken to be a flaw or failing [*défaut*] (at the end of chapter 5 he states: "One should put a similar failing at the beginning of these tales: a failing in love, to be precise" [*Progress,* p. 21])[22] turns out to be precisely the quality which makes his prowess as a lover much celebrated by the end of the tale. This surprise reversal of events is typical of Paulhan, and in *Progress in Love on the Slow Side,* it becomes the decisive turn of events; as the narrator says: "What to do, in life, with a failing? One has to wait for it to become a quality" (*Progress,* p.47).[23] If Jacques' experience can be said to be an education, it is as much in the *language* of love, its familiar or commonplace expressions, as in its acts, and the progression towards this particular linguistic competence is marked by each of Jacques' successive relationships. With Jeanne, it seems as if there is no need for language: "In short, I was satisfied that everything between Jeanne and me happened spontaneously, without words, or almost so" (*Progress,* pp. 9–10).[24] This spontaneous, unspoken desire is placed in an ordered homology which attempts to prescribe the development that

Jacques's education will follow: "It seemed to me more honest thus to assign (I told myself) each thing to its place: acts to things having to do with desire, and words to things having to do—my God—with the soul" (*Progress,* p. 21).[25] Words are said to express the soul, just as acts are said to express desire, and the need to keep language and desire apart ("each thing in its place") is as much a need to keep language uncontaminated by desire. In terms of the narrative itself, it acts to preserve the capacity of language to convey meaning, to express an inner state, and thus, more significantly, to express what happened—to narrate or to tell the tale of desire and its progress.

However, the narrator also wants his language to be *like* an act—a kind of performative—and it is because of this unavoidable interaction between, or crossing over of, language and desire that the neat scheme is upset in the ensuing affairs. The affairs with Juliette, then Simone, are marked by an increasingly dense linguistic mediation. Language begins to stand out, to embarrass, to get in the way of love. The narrator starts noticing Juliette's speech mannerisms first of all, when she says to him: "I am proud to have inspired love in you" (*Progress,* p. 23), upon which Jacques thinks to himself: "It's clear that a word like *inspire* could separate us more than anything else" (*Progress,* p. 24).[26] Simone's language is even more contrived, and communication between her and Jacques is fraught throughout with misunderstandings:

> As I told her the first night with a modesty which was perhaps awkward:
> "I'm the one you prefer, aren't I?"
> She replied with irritation:
> "What's that supposed to mean? How many boyfriends do you think I have?"
> As I didn't say anything, she went a little further, and added:
> "I want you to know that I have never given myself to anyone before you. Don't doubt it."
> And these differences within her language ended up embarrassing me. (*Progress,* p. 37)[27]

The question of her sincerity comes up at several points, and her reply is always one of angry denial:

"Why are you asking me this? Do you think I have ever
lied to you? I want you to know that my words are all sincere, and in no way deceitful."

Then everything must come to a halt, and I no longer
remember what I was going to say. Why does she talk like
a book? (*Progress*, p. 37)[28]

The irony is that this indignantly "sincere" disavowal should be
couched in rather stiff and artificial language, and the narrator's dis-
comfort is all the greater, since Simone's language resembles, more
and more the language of the *récit* itself. So much so, that we could
well remove the quotation marks around her speech, and fuse her
narrative with the narrator's. The narrative instability of the *récit* is reflected in Simone's multiple registers: she breaks into song, commu-
nicates via letters which are as "bookish" as her speech, teases Jacques
during their conversations, and is always "full of stories." Not surprisingly, her sincerity—which presupposes precisely a correspondence between "the soul" and "words"—becomes less and less important to Jacques. He says of her after a while: "Despite her
awkwardness, I still like this search for beautiful phrases, and this effort of Simone's" (*Progress*, p. 39),[29] and as this particular episode
draws to a close, he remarks: "Her facility for lying here added so
much to her finesse, which I think is new, and invented just for me"
(*Progress*, p. 42).[30] Thus, her "awkwardness," at first grouped together with "insincerity" and "failing" as undesirable traits, ultimately
becomes on the contrary extremely appealing.

If the narrator's aim is to nurture a linguistic competence that
would supplant or transform his incompetence, this involves crossing the boundary separating language and act, since he wants his language to be as effective as an act. The hoped-for conflation of language and act that would repair the disruption of the initial homology
gives rise in turn to further complications. Not only does the language
in the love affairs become increasingly complex and unstable as the narrator's desire progresses, but desire itself is turned aside, perverted *by*
language, which has its own seductive power ("I like this search for
beautiful phrases. . . ."). The question then becomes one of reconcil-
ing desire as an act with desire as a performative, or as a *speech act,*
to borrow J. L. Austin's term.[31] In terms of the effectiveness of Simone's language, and by implication the narrator's too, the story she
circulates of her exploits with Jacques is clearly successful performa-

tiv**t**ly. It has the effect of making Jacques' reputation as a lover, and of setting in motion again the Jeanne–Juliette–Simone cycle. Yet at the same time this success is due to a circulation of stories that are no longer within the narrator's control. Jacques acknowledges this more troubling aspect when he says towards the end:

> Clearly favorable, this reputation, to my surprise. Favorable, but worrisome, and I began to wish that a military order would come at any moment to tear me away from this garden of delights. (*Progress*, p. 47)[32]

The narrator backs away from this glimpse of disorder, as desire threatens to spiral out of control.

The narrative instability generated by language is very much present throughout, and is manifested in the constant uncertainty about the status of the *récit* that is being narrated. The tale is continually punctuated by meta-narrative asides such as the following:

> Now that I look back on these adventures, which have merged together, I'm surprised that they are so simple. Their greatest quality is, no doubt, the fact that they happened to me: it's also the most difficult one to explain: but I'll try, I'll make my tale as plain as possible. (*Progress*, p. 16)[33]

This passage takes the form of a promise ("I'll try"), and of a promise to be sincere ("I'll make my tale as plain as possible"). Promises are essentially future-oriented, and these moments of narrative uncertainty are often proleptic rather than retrospective. The concern is less "what happened" than "how will I be able to tell what happened?" ("I don't usually have the thoughts, or the voice, that would allow me to say, like Duffy: I did . . . I was in . . ." [*Progress*, p. 29][34]). These moments of self-conscious reflection on the act of narration take the form of a parabasis, that is both literally an authorial intervention, and rhetorically an interruption of the discourse. They should reveal an authoritative first person narrator, but they could hardly be further from providing this kind of assurance. As such, they are examples of the narrative figure that Gérard Genette in *Figures III* coined paralepsis—the act of giving what one properly speaking does not "have" to give—which he opposes to paralipsis, when one says what one claims not to be saying, or does not offer what one is in fact offering (as, for example, in the phrase "Not to mention . . .").[35] One such example of a para*leptic* parabasis is the following passage:

> What's more, I am not quick and I need adventures to happen to me more slowly than they do to others.
>
> The rest would have to be written in a different way, with different words, or rather, with something other than words.
>
> But that is just where I am wrong. Quite the opposite: it must be written in exactly the same way—pretending that the passage I spoke of doesn't exist at all, but that everything follows and is woven together into one [. . .] .
>
> So I will tell it, in the same way. However, you must try occasionally to imagine this effort, underneath the story. (*Progress,* p. 33)[36]

However hard the narrator may try to tell us that he has opted for a seamless narrative, the actual evidence of the text, particularly at such points as these, tells us otherwise.

But what of the enigmatic "rest," and of the effort we are invited to look for "underneath the story?" It seems we are confronted with two modes of writing. The one would be adequate to the complexity of the narrator's experience, to his own perplexity, a strange writing to which he alludes but which he shies away from. The other amounts to a sort of cover-up, insofar as it hides (somewhat dishonestly) the discontinuities, the uncertainties with a homogeneous text in which "everything flows and is woven together into one." We have seen that the claim to this second mode of writing is denounced by its own performance, and we are left wondering what kind of writing we are given, and how to "take" it.

If the very process of writing unsettles the narrative, we as readers are equally thrown off balance as we attempt to read. The syntax of *Progress in Love on the Slow Side,* and of Paulhan's writing in general, is always slightly odd. One constantly has the sense that something is not quite right, although it would be difficult to point to anything very definite. Words are a little out of place, but never so much that the sentence is grammatically incorrect. We often find dislocated, isolated infinitive verbs at the end of sentences, and the syntax is often too elliptical, or too diffuse, in relation to what it is expressing.

For example, when Jacques and his companions are playing together with Simone and her friends on the swings, the narrator says:

> So we swung them three times, and we were swung twice, except Duffy, who remained sitting on the ground, without being stubborn, but with indifference. (*Progress*, p. 14)

> Nous les balançâmes ainsi par trois fois, et nous fûmes balancés deux, sauf Duffy qui restait assis par terre sans y mettre de l'obstination, mais avec indifférence. (*Progrès*, p. 52)

This sentence is very typical of the limping rhythms, the discontinuous syntax, and the kinds of imbalances one finds in Paulhan's writing. The use of both simple perfect and imperfect tenses emphasizes the disjunction between the first and second halves of the sentence. The punctual action of swinging and of being swung contrasts sharply with Duffy's non-punctual passivity. There is in fact a chiasmus involved in the second half of the sentence between action and inaction. Whereas one might expect the "without" to go with the inactive "indifference" and the "with" to go with the more potentially active "being stubborn," they are in fact reversed. The sentence might be said to swing back and forth between activity ("we swung them," "being stubborn," "with") and passivity ("we were swung," "Duffy, who remained sitting on the ground," "indifference"), and the imbalances, like the "three times"/"twice," refuse to come to rest or to resolve themselves.

This sense of language having been knocked "off balance" is particularly acute where the question of time is concerned. The temporality of the *récit*, whether considered grammatically or diegetically, is profoundly unstable. The time of narration is never distinguished from the time of the events narrated (the narrator now seems to be still living the events of the story, now looking back on them as if they had already happened), and the verb tenses constantly shift from the simple past to the present, to the imperfect, and to the present perfect without any respect for chronological consistency. If the language of the *récit* is so constantly "out of synch" with the events it narrates (or with itself *as* an event), we may justifiably ask whether there is any progress at all in this tale, and if so, what form it takes. In Paulhan's elliptical syntax there is often no more than the suggestion of a grammatical conjunction, and connections between clauses and sentences are often made *disjunctively*. The narrative seems suspended somewhere between continuity and discontinuity, and the language of the *récits* never seems to "get going." How can we measure the narrative progression, then, since linear time seems to lead us nowhere, and circular time soon becomes unpleasantly vertiginous. The title in French provides an important clue to the nature of the progress in *Progress in Love on the Slow Side: Progrès en amour assez lents*. The "assez lents" could be read as both "rather slow" and as "slow enough." In the second case, slowness is positively valorized, a reading which is confirmed by several statements in the narrative to this effect. For example, the narrator says at one point: "As for me, if I get to things later, at least I know fairly clearly how I got there" (*Progress*, p. 36), and: "Everything happens to me as if I had found a life that was *already* too far along." [37] If life is already "too far along," or too fast (one is always ahead of oneself), then there is clearly a need to slow down, and wait until one (or language) catches up with oneself (or itself). This is worth the wait in the *récit*, since it permits the all-important reversal to take place: "What to do, in life, with a failing? One has to wait for it to become a quality. Patiently, if possible." (*Progress*, p. 47).[38] This patience, or passivity, indicates that the progress of the tale is measurable less in terms of acts or actions than of patience and passions.

Just as the narrator is always waiting for passion, so the narrative itself seems to hang in the air. It is neither the homogeneous text in which "everything follows and is woven together into one" nor the "different way," which would require "something other than words," but the tension between the two. The stylistic imbalances make possible the performance of this textual balancing act, and its discontinuities allow for its continuity, its progress. Just such a discontinuous continuity would at the same time connect this *récit* to *The Severe Recovery*, and sever this connection. The tension between continuity and discontinuity again highlights the inadequacy of taking the *récits* as autobiographical. Their quirky language, their textual awkwardness, are not just stylistic features which could be read, in a sense, as Paulhan's "signature," but they are intimately bound up with the process and progress of the narrative itself.

This movement has been masterfully theorized by Blanchot in "The Ease of Dying." For him, the movement of a *récit* is "simply" the continuity of a narration. A tension is set up and sustained between the simplicity of the motivating "force" of the *récits* and the duplicity of the *récits* themselves, their particular self-reflexive quality, a kind of self-searching which is also a "search for the movement of the search" (*Ease of Dying*, p. 124).[39] If this paradoxical structure—whereby the duplicity of the *récits* is the guarantee of the simplicity of their "secret"—is true of the *récits* such as *Progress in Love on the Slow Side* or *The Crossed Bridge,* insofar as they are animated by this "search," then it could be said to hold true for all of Paulhan's texts, which have an invariably single-minded motivation. The moment of "revelation" of so many of Paulhan's texts comes with a reversal we saw to be operative in *L'Expérience du proverbe,* for example, and Blanchot goes so far as to wonder: "is not this secret the mysterious 'fact' of reversal. . . ?" (*Ease of Dying*, p. 128).[40] Blanchot points to the restraint, or *modesty* of Paulhan's language as a means of guaranteeing the continuity of the *récits*. Rather than being simply an indication of the style, tone, or semantic value of Paulhan's *récits,* modesty is a condition of their possibility, since it guarantees the continuity of the reversals, and is described by Blanchot as a kind of survival technique. What would it mean, then, to read the modesty of Paulhan's texts? It is worth reflecting for a while on the question of modesty, obviously a crucial term when discussing Paulhan's language.

MODESTY, MANIA AND OTHER WOR(L)DS

Among Paulhan's original manuscripts are a wealth of documents, many of which have now been published, that give us a considerable insight into Paulhan's more private self. There are first of all the vast collections of letters he exchanged with many of the authors he helped to publish, which form one of the most important correspondences in French literature this century; there are radio interviews[41] and journal interviews;[42] diaries, notebooks, scraps of papers containing outlines for books, ideas, and random observations. In fact, we do not have to look very far before we discover a surfeit of information about Paulhan, most of it carefully organized and filed away by Paulhan himself. One set of documents which are particularly intriguing in this respect is a series of scrapbooks kept by Paulhan, in which he pasted anything that appeared in print relating to himself (articles written by him, articles about him, or anything which he used in some way or responded to).[43] In these press cuttings, mentions of his own name are invariably highlighted. How does one read these scrapbooks? What do they tell us about Paulhan? Do they reveal someone who was acutely aware of his own presence on the literary scene, and of the pervasiveness of his own influence (real or imagined)? At the very least, they beg the question of Paulhan's celebrated modesty. But what is modesty, and how can it be measured? And what is modesty when considered as a linguistic or textual problematic? Paulhan would seem, in his unemphatic style, and his continual insistence on the everyday, to be an exemplary "modest" writer. A text that explicitly thematizes this question is a short prose piece, "Manie," from a collection entitled *Causes célèbres (Famous Cases),* written by Paulhan during the Occupation, but signed, significantly for us, with the name Maast.[44] Each of these short texts is composed as a kind of intellectual exercise; they are all the same length, and are each based on a paradox. In "Manie," this paradox seem to be the way the mundane can surprise us, or the freshness one can find in the routine of everyday life. The text of "Manie" reads as follows:

> After twenty years of marriage, we have all of a sudden adopted a new habit: just as we are falling asleep, we nestle together. Sometimes she turns her back to me, and I move my knees up under her bended knees. With one hand I hold her shoulder, with the other, her hips. Or else she sleeps lying on her back, in which case I hold her with my left arm under the small of her back, while slipping my right arm under her neck. This is how the nights go by.
>
> Today is Tuesday the 22nd of August. When I got up, I was surprised to find the transom half torn out of the window by the storm. In place of the piece of wood, you can see a tree, so close that you want to tell it its name. I recognized our oak tree.
>
> I woke Manie up to show her the tree. She was as surprised as I was. Before breakfast, she wanted to try the rapidex, which we bought yesterday. It's a furniture polish which will let us wipe away the marks I made on the table

(Manie claims) when I put dishes down on it that were too hot.

The result was not conclusive. However, the marks seem to me more pleasant to look at.

Not much news in the newspapers: cracks in the economic edifice of the country have supposedly been spotted. Yes. The funeral of a certain Monsieur Dessaulle, once sentenced for polygamy, was attended by the five wives of the deceased. It is apparently possible to make a small fortune raising animals—little ones, I assume, but who knows?—whose name the advertisement does not give.

Before going to work, I asked myself if my life was delightful. Not delightful; rather, full, considerable. Another word.

I have several reasons for naming her Manie. First of all, her name is Germaine, from which I got Maine. Then, it is true that love is a mania, I do not think of her with reason.

Not to mention that it is wise to give things, and people, their most modest name.[45]

The text presents a sketch of the fairly ordinary life of a couple whom we take to be Paulhan and his wife, Germaine, although it is narrated with surprising lightness and vivacity. Even after twenty years of marriage, it appears that the most commonplace activity can be a source of wonder and renewal, and the whole text thematizes the renewal to be found *within* habits. In "Manie," this regeneration is a literal—albeit somewhat banal—*reawakening,* after a description of how the narrator and his wife now habitually *fall asleep.* Linguistically, the text is thus also about restoring dead (or sleepy?) metaphors to their original liveliness. There is nothing particularly striking about the language, unless we are (paradoxically) struck by its very ordinariness, but it possibly suggests that metaphorical language is a means of access to the extraordinary through the ordinary. As the last paragraph states, the text is also about the importance, or wisdom, of naming modestly, appropriately, or properly. The last line—"Not to mention that it is wise to give things, and people, their most modest name"—is often quoted in the context of discussions of Paulhan's modesty, and modesty is a good term to use in talking about the language of the text. Etymologically (from "modestus") it has to do with keeping measure, exercising moderation, staying within bounds, not exceeding a given frame of reference. This can be seen, for example, in the routine nature of the description of the start of the day; more generally, the text appears to exemplify the very principle of modesty it advocates. For example, the narrator asks himself before going to work "if [his] life was delightful. As if "delightful" were too excessive a word, he answers himself: "Not delightful; rather, full, considerable." When he discovers the damage caused to the window by the oak tree which has been uprooted by the storm, his instinct is to domesticate it by naming it: "so close that you want to tell it its name." The bad economic news is downplayed by attenuating it grammatically to the point of rumor, and by assimilating it with other amusing *faits divers*.

The greatest pressure in the text to conform to its own linguistic imperative comes, however, with the question of the name of the narrator's wife, Manie, whose "proper" name—Germaine—was in fact the name of Paulhan's wife. He gives "several reasons" for re-naming her Manie. What are we to make of these reasons? It seems natural enough, to begin with, that since "it is true that love is a mania" and "I do not think of her with reason," that he should choose this name. But what kind of "reasons" are these if they rely on an *absence* of reason? It makes no sense that the narrator should first name his wife Manie—hardly a "modest" name—and then have the name motivated in retrospect. There is moreover no reason why Germaine should necessarily lead to Manie. The name could equally well have given, for example, "Aimée," "Amie," "Mariée," "Gamine," or "Ma Reine." These "reasons" thus reveal themselves on some level to be very unreasonable and they disturb our sense of the "modesty" of this text. In reading the text more attentively, its more disruptive features, which cannot be covered over for long, come to the fore. These elements all disrupt the smooth surface of this picture of domestic happiness, break outside the closed frame of its reference, as well as its linguistic economy. On a purely thematic level, there is the violent irruption of the tree into the couple's cozy interior. And if we pause to reread the opening lines again—"After twenty years of marriage, we have all of a sudden adopted a new habit"—it dawns on us what is awry. Habit is not something which can be acquired "all of a sudden." Or if it is, then it can be lost just as suddenly, and with it, the sense of reassuring continuity which is the very condition of possibility of habit.

The paradoxical reversal of habit and sudden change brings into focus the principal rhetorical operation of the text, and possibly of all the *Causes célèbres,* that is, metalepsis, or the reversal of cause and effect. The naming of Manie can be read as a sort of metalepsis, since this term is often used, in classical rhetoric, to describe the inversion of the metonymic relation between name and thing, in which the thing (cause) would, once the inversion has taken place, be determined by the name (effect). On one level her name is determined according to a logic of predication ("love is a mania, I do not think of her with reason"), but on the level of the letter it is possibly determined as a purely textual effect. The reversal of the normal order—the name Manie as an anagram ought to make sense only *after* it has been semantically motivated—is precisely the kind of inversion that metalepsis can account for. It could likewise explain the reversal of habit and sudden change that comes at the beginning of the text. There are, however, other names in the text which have to be accounted for. There is, for example, the polygamous Dessaulle, as well as one name over which we are in danger of passing all too quickly; the name of the furniture polish used by the narrator, the "rapidex." All of the conflicting tensions of the text seem to come together in this name. It both exemplifies the movement between proper and common name (the brand name of 1940s furniture polish in France becomes the common name "le rapidex," just as we often refer to all paper tissues as "kleenex," for example, and it allows for the onomastic pun linking the proper name Manie to the abstract noun "manie") and also serves as a kind of domesticating force, covering over the marks left as a result of domestic accidents, and thereby reasserting the language as something reassuringly "appropriate" or modest.

Modesty, as we have considered it until now, implies a relation of adequation or appropriateness. However, it is also often thought of as meaning less than adequate, as an *under*statement or litotes. There is a paradox with modesty, which is that the moment the claim is made to modesty, in other words, the moment modesty names itself, it is already something of a boast, it already takes the form of self-recognition, of self-congratulation, and is anything but modest. Paulhan himself remarks on precisely this paradox in "La demoiselle aux miroirs" ("The Mirror Maiden"):

> People made fun of the preacher who used to say: "No-one's a match for me when it comes to modesty." But we

> should point out the paradox behind the joke: that is, it is
> a contradiction to be modest, and to *know* one is modest
> ... thinking of oneself as proud is a gesture of modesty,
> thinking of oneself as modest, a gesture of pride.[46]

The claim to modesty is always necessarily excessive to what is being stated. Indeed, it is a hyperbole, or a "mania" of sorts. The text is thus always both deficient to itself (as a modest description) as well as always in excess of itself (when read in terms of its poetics), always both litotes and hyperbole, modesty and mania, but never able to coincide with itself, to be modest in the sense of adequate or proper. Paulhan's "modest" language is never what it appears to be, and carries within it its own excess, or "mania."

If "Manie" exemplifies Paulhan's fascination with the everyday, and with appropriately inexcessive language for the routine nature of daily life, it also subverts the very modesty it espouses, suggesting something beyond the surface evidence of the apparent world. In "Le Clair et l'obscur" ("The Clear and the Obscure") he talks of this "beyond" as an "other world": "As if our world were side by side with some other world, which is normally invisible, but whose intervention, at decisive moments, was alone able to save the former from collapse." [47] If "our world" is the world of the everyday, the waking world in all of its apparently reassuring self-evidence, could we equate Paulhan's "other world" with the world of dreams, which he was also constantly drawn to? The attraction of dreams for Paulhan was certainly not the same as it was for the Surrealists. He was not interested in the process of uncovering an unconscious world, and revealing its hitherto unexplored riches, the exotica of the human mind. Rather, dreams provide another illustration of the same contradictory narrative process, such that, as Blanchot points out, dreaming and narrating for Paulhan amount to the same thing:

> If everything is a *récit*, then everything would also be a
> dream in Jean Paulhan's writing, until one is awoken by
> darkness, in the same way that writing is like a dream, a
> dream so precise, so prompt in revealing itself, in solving
> the enigma, that it never stops reinscribing the enigma into
> the dream and, consequently, *revealing* itself as enigmatic.
> ("Ease," p. 123)[48]

How, then, do we read a *récit* which *is* a dream narrative, *Le Pont traversé (The Crossed Bridge)?*

The *récit* presents itself as a series of dreams the narrator has over three nights. Thanks to what the dreams tell him, there is ultimately a successful reconciliation between an "I" and a "you," both unidentified (they are most plausibly Paulhan and Germaine Pascal, or Jacques and Simone). The details of what caused the strife in the first place are unclear, although one might say that the *récit* is the hidden secret of *The Severe Recovery* in more ways than one. It makes a fleeting, but significant appearance in the following passage, which is from one of Jean Paulhan's diaries:

> Juliette imagined that I was attached to the first mud-splattered page of *The Crossed Bridge* for some reason. "I find it dirty, I find it ugly, I find it a memory for you. . . ." She took it and tore it in two.[49]

The status of this fragment is extremely problematic. One of Paulhan's fictional characters (Juliette) discovers a copy of one of Paulhan's stories (or its "first mud-splattered page," an elliptical detail which evokes an entire scene we can only imagine, as it is never described), and sees it—like the letters in *The Severe Recovery* which Juliette also does not read—as a sign of Jacques' infidelity. Her erroneous presumption of Jacques' (Paulhan's?) "attachment" to the book (erroneous, that is, if we believe the narrator, but why should we?) seems to imply that Jacques is in fact totally *indifferent* to its fate. What if this indifference, however, were merely feigned, a clever ruse? But then why would Paulhan "himself" need to write this down in his personal diary, what *difference* would it make to him? We are soon lost in a hall of mirrors, trying to grasp the simple facts that underlie this tale. In fact, the anonymity of the characters again confirms that the question of referential verifiability is not the most important aspect of this *récit*. Despite the image of the bridge as a metaphor for a successful passage, it is perhaps the most opaque of all of Paulhan's texts, yet paradoxically the one which is the most intimate of dialogues between Paulhan and "himself." The dream narratives are framed by the narrator's commentary, explaining them to the addressee of *The Crossed Bridge*, although they are in fact "self-addressed": "No sooner had I made the decision to look for you, than I answered myself with an abundance of dreams" (*Crossed Bridge*, p. 63).[50]

The dream narratives themselves are remarkable for the precision of their descriptions, the clarity of their details, and at the same time their extreme opacity, even (or perhaps especially) to the narrator. "It is strange," he comments after the first night's dreams, "that one should take, being alone, so many precautions and images in order to talk to oneself" (*Crossed Bridge*, p. 67).[51] Indeed, many of the scenes of the dreams dramatize this difficult dialogue between self and self (there are several twin-figures that the dream-narrator tries to approach), and as they seem on the verge of producing a moment of self-understanding, or self-recognition, they dissolve: ". . . the dreams stopped just when they were about to be resolved in a pure feeling" (*Crossed Bridge*, p. 63). All that remains for the narrator is ". . . the feeling by which one appears to oneself to be melting" (*Crossed Bridge*, p. 68).[52] Despite the successful reconciliation which is the ultimate consequence of the dreams ("From my dream I had invented another self-assurance, and this bridge between the two of us crossed" [*Crossed Bridge*, p. 75]), the narrator is left with a feeling of inconclusiveness, that the *real* meaning of the dreams is still just out of reach: "You will see," he says at the end, "more things than I can name" (*Crossed Bridge*, p. 75).[53]

The bridge is a metaphor for the shuttling of meaning back and forth between the conscious self interpreting his dreams, and the dream self speaking to its other self in images. Neither of these selves has the whole picture, and each self is at the same time the other's "other," with no particular priority being given to the unconscious self or the conscious one. The "strangeness," or inaccessible otherness, of the *récit* is just as much on the side of the conscious world as the unconscious, as the narrator himself comments at one point:

> It is accepted that we perceive real things clearly, and dreamed things in a confused fashion. This opinion hinges solely on the assumption that we have the former at our disposal—so that it is easy, whenever we wish, to make them clear. But if we ignore this practical aspect, real objects surprise us by their confusion. (*Crossed Bridge*, p. 72)[54]

To put it another way, if the back-and-forth movement between the real world and the dream world is based on the presumption that the dream world is "further away" than the real world, then the surprise might be said to come from the chiasmic reversal of real world/dream world and proximity/distance. This lays a different emphasis on the metaphor of the title of the *récit*; it is not just a bridge, but a *crossed* bridge. Paulhan (or rather the narrator) brings this into clearer focus in an endnote to the *récit*. He replies to an objection (by Mme de Genlis, whom he quotes) that it is incorrect ("*impropre*") to say "to cross an bridge" ("*traverser un pont*"), since there is no notion of resistance to be overcome, of an obstacle to be crossed. As Paulhan writes:

> This word would therefore have been rejected if it hadn't seemed that its very flaw brought out all the more clearly the kind of confusion that could be seen as a particular feature of the events recounted above, and this confusion is such that the ideas or feelings naturally designed to bring us closer together, in their turn became a reason for moving further apart. (*Crossed Bridge*, p. 76)[55]

The double valence of "to cross," used both in the sense of crossing a forest, and going over, or through, thereby connoting both freedom of movement and the existence of an obstacle to this movement, makes it an ideal word to demonstrate the complication at the heart of this tale, and by extension, of the other *récits* as well. It is because of its imperfection, its *défaut*, that "to cross" is paradoxically the best word to express the combination of opacity and lucidity that characterizes the dream, being both a means to an obstacle, and an obstacle to that end, the thing you cross over or through. The "coming together" (not only of two shadowy subjects, but also of the narrator's conscious and unconscious selves, and more importantly of language and what it tries to express) is at the same time a "moving further apart."

If the reversibility of the chiasmus in this *récit* makes the obscure transparent, and works to defamiliarize the seemingly familiar, it can also, of course, work the other way round. This is how we might see the *récit Lalie*, which is markedly different in theme and tone from Paulhan's other *récits*. It is not autobiographical (although it was written for the daughter—named Lalie—of a friend of Paulhan during the First World War), but it is concerned with a similar doubling or multiplication of selves that we find in some of the dreams in *The Crossed Bridge*, and in the process of trying to unravel Paulhan's fictional self from his "real" one. *Lalie*, too, is a story about love; Lalie, the young girl who is the main character of the story, gradually finds herself being drawn into a magical, fairylike world of "ladies-of-the-well," "men-of-the-woods" and "poppycocks" ("coquecigrues"). She moves back and forth between the brutish, skeptical world of Nicolas, and the "other" world of the strange creatures in the wood, and at the end of the story turns her back on the traditional life in the town which remaining Nicolas' girlfriend would inevitably lead to. The two worlds lie "side by side," or rather the fairy world is "within" the everyday world, and she learns to get through to it by a process of willful self-distraction:

> She is singing a little tune, and in order to trick time, she imagines that she sees sheep jumping over a fence. . . . Lalie keeps on imagining: after the sheep, the herd of cows and their black dogs, then the foxes, the squirrels, the frogs. Something moved in the grass. This time it is the long chain of the ladies-of-the-well. (*Lalie*, p. 104)[56]

This distracted self recalls the other selves (or nonselves) in Paulhan's *récits,* particularly *Progress in Love on the Slow Side,* which are variously figured as absent participation, absolute passivity, indifference, and amorality. Both Jacques Maast and Lalie are most keenly attentive to the "other" world when they are most distracted, and it is perhaps significant that at these moments in the *récits* we often find the most precise lyrical descriptions. These descriptions seems curiously suspended within the narrative, unrelated to the events of the *récits* except to mark the pure visual pleasure of the absent narrative subject, as if the *récit* were most powerfully present at these moments of narrative absence. Toward the end of *Progress in Love on the Slow Side,* for example, Jacques is waiting for Simone, and we read the following:

> I wait, and the first few moments are light ones; I enjoy seeing a field of alfalfa on which there are so many white butterflies, all alike, that they seem to be attached to each other by threads, like a giant cloth which floats up and dips down in a thousand places. (*Progress,* p. 40)[57]

The attentiveness to details of nature, and the subtle, precise lyricism of passages such as this one is a feature of Paulhan's language in the *récits* that many readers overlook, perhaps because they occur precisely when "nothing" is happening. Yet this attention within distraction could be read as confirming Blanchot's remark that "this vigilance is the 'subject' of the experience" ("Ease," p. 133). If the movement between this world and the other world can be seen as the interdependence between vigilance and distraction (which functions as an endlessly reversible chiasmus), then what would it mean to posit, as Blanchot does, attention as a kind of subject beyond subjectivity, a narrative vigilance that would watch over the movement between vigilance and distraction? This non-subjective vigilance would be nothing other than the writing of the *récits* (or as Blanchot will say, "l'écriture-lecture"—"reading-writing"), occasionally taking the form of the impersonal pronoun "on" in the French text—with the same subjectless authority that characterizes proverbs—and like the "poppycock" in *Lalie,* now appearing, now fading back into the natural surroundings from which it had emerged.

In psychoanalytic terms, if this "other" world is coextensive with dreaming as an unconscious dimension of the human mind, this vigilance would be the distracted-yet-vigilant dreamer-narrator. In several playfully naïve remarks on Freud, Paulhan criticized psychoanalysis for wanting—as he saw it—to explain the unconscious solely from the perspective of the conscious mind. When asked in an interview with Robert Mallet in 1952 whether Freudian psychoanalysis was at the origin of *récits* such as *The Crossed Bridge,* Paulhan answered that he was generally suspicious of its claims to demystification: "If our unconscious is as crafty as Freud imagines, how could it not keep trying to change languages: for example, invent new signs, change the meaning of the old ones? It's this kind of operation I had wanted to catch in action." [58] How, in other words, does one prevent dreams from becoming, as Paulhan puts it in an autobiographical fragment from the last years of his life, "the least secret thing in our lives?" [59] Although Paulhan never gives any indication that his understanding of Freud's theory goes much beyond the popular opinion that it is simply a matter of interpreting the hidden sexual meaning of symbols, his critique (which he elsewhere modestly claims is simply "a reservation about one aspect of Freud" [60]), nonetheless represents a highly original understanding of the relationship between narrating and dreaming. Paulhan's concern, traversing all of his texts but perhaps best exemplified in the early *récits,* is never to stop "reinscribing the enigma" of language (and dreams) within the text which attempts to account for this enigma, to keep the secret part of himself secret (even while revealing it).

CODA: PROGRESS IN LOVE?

The particular constellation of love, dreaming and narrating, which is so crucial to the psychoanalytic frame of reference, continued to obsess Paulhan. In diary entries from the last few years of his life he returned to *Progress in Love on the Slow Side,* and continued to rework passages from it, particularly its more explicitly erotic scenes, as if it still held some inaccessible secret, not so much within the words he had written as a young man, but in the continuing act of writing and rewriting it. If we picture Paulhan in his later years endlessly captivated by his own early love stories, how do we see this image, now that Dominique Aury has revealed herself to be the author of the *Story of O,* the sado-masochistic erotic novel she wrote in 1954 under the pseudonym of Pauline Réage to "ensnare" Paulhan, knowing his taste for pornography? Her ploy worked, Paulhan helped publish the novel, writing "Le Bonheur dans l'esclavage" ("Happiness in Slavery") as an introduction to it, and Dominique Aury, who had been his secretary at the *Nouvelle Revue Française* since the journal reappeared in 1953, remained Paulhan's lover until his death. How do we read Paulhan's involvement with the *Story of O* in the light of this revelation? It appears to confirm the rather distasteful attitude which was apparent at points in *Progress in Love on the Slow Side,* which Jacques Maast prefers to call "amorality" (a typical comment is the following: "It is strange that I should desire a woman, not so much in proportion to how much she pleases me, but on the contrary, and in order that I might look down on her a bit"[*Progress,* pp. 3–4).[61] It suggests also that Paulhan's critique of Freud, and his interest in pornography, is part of a wider mystification of sexuality and sexual relationships, which serves to mask the prevailing dynamics of power within sexism, which clearly stood to benefit someone with Paulhan's position of authority. While there is something quite disturbing about Dominique Aury's willing submission to Paulhan's intellectual as well as sexual authority, the act of seduction was clearly Dominique Aury's gesture alone. What is perhaps more intriguing is to think of Paulhan's response to the "love letter" which Aury claimed the *Story of O* was. If she wrote it as a private letter to one man, and wanted it to be kept secret (or at least her anonymity preserved), Paulhan did respect this wish, but took it upon himself to share the book for its literary qualities. Everything about this venture must have delighted Paulhan; aside from the subject of the novel itself, here was a secret, which he was able to keep, but which he was able at the same time to publish, allowing it to circulate, and its notoriety to grow, all the while knowing full well its provenance. To Aury's gesture of seduction, attempting to "enslave" Paulhan through the account of her own fantasies of sexual enslavement, Paulhan replied by setting the text free, releasing it to the public in a gesture of liberation designed to reaffirm the text's mystery, knowing how pornography can rid sexuality of its secrets, and consequently, of its passion. In an interview with Madeleine Chaptal in 1967 for *L'Express* on the question of love, the interviewer asked Paulhan what he saw as the difference between love and eroticism. He answered as follows: "Yes, they're very different: eroticism is love after reflection. It's love without anything surprising about it. I would rather be for surprise, for surprises. It's an opinion concerning love. I prefer the kind of love one cannot speak of." [62]

We might read into this comment a veiled reference to his affair with Dominique Aury, although we will never know. What it does show is Paulhan in 1967 (but who is really writing or speaking here?) tirelessly affirming an essential mystery of love, just as he did when he wrote his *récits* some fifty years earlier. This we should read as exemplified not by Nicolas's love for Lalie, but rather Lalie's love of the mysterious other world itself.

3

BLANCHOT READING PAULHAN

"Nous nous souviendrons de ces jours."
("We will remember these days.")

Letter from Paulhan to Blanchot,
May 1940

WHO SAID ANYTHING ABOUT TERROR?

How do we read the "encounter" in the 1940s between Jean Paulhan and Maurice Blanchot? Ever since Jeffrey Mehlman brought Blanchot's early pro-fascist journalism in the 1930s out into the open, the fate of the critical reception of Paulhan's *Les Fleurs de Tarbes, ou la Terreur dans les Lettres (The Flowers of Tarbes, or Terror in Literature),* which first appeared in book form in 1941, has become almost inseparably linked to Blanchot's reading of it, "Comment la littérature est-elle possible?" (How is Literature Possible?)[1] There is little doubt that the "encounter" between Blanchot and Paulhan was an extremely

77

significant one. Blanchot's reading of Paulhan's book (coincidentally or not, but that is the question I would ultimately like to address in this chapter) occupies a rather crucial place in the shift in Blanchot's career from being an apologist for a certain form of right-wing political ideology during the 1930s, to his more celebrated role as a fiction writer and literary critic from the 1940s onwards.

The question of the extent to which this encounter between Jean Paulhan and Maurice Blanchot was an "occasion," which allows us to interpret the transition and transformation of Blanchot's early writing career, has been addressed in ways which have led to Paulhan's texts being appropriated and reinscribed, to a number of different theoretical ends. Jeffrey Mehlman, for example, has attempted to link the timing of Blanchot's privileging of the essential silence or nothingness at the heart of the literary enterprise to Derrida's (and by extension Deconstruction's) supposed evacuation of politics and history from literature: conscious forgetting as a way of covering over its guilty origins, with Paulhan being described as one of the chief instigators of this political "amnesia." [2] Allan Stoekl, in his book *Agonies of the Intellectual,* has read the work of both Paulhan and Blanchot within the context of a twentieth century intellectual ancestry in France going back to Durkheim.[3] One of the main difficulties in writing about this encounter has come about as a direct consequence of Mehlman's intervention. His reading of Blanchot's career is based in part on a consultation of the correspondence between Paulhan and Blanchot. When Mehlman's article appeared in French in *Tel Quel* in 1983, Blanchot reacted by categorically denying Mehlman's claims, and forbade any further access to his correspondence with Paulhan. Although this puts any subsequent commentary somewhat at a disadvantage, it does not really alter the thrust of my own reading. What I would like to do is to take a closer look at the "encounter" between Blanchot and Paulhan, which I take to be one of the crucial events of French twentieth century intellectual history, and to broaden its historical frame of reference beyond Blanchot's reading of *Les Fleurs de Tarbes,* by including Blanchot's later, and equally important essays, "Le Mystère dans les lettres" (Mystery in Literature) and "La Facilité de mourir" (The Ease of Dying). In other words, I would like to *keep reading,* and this act of reading on, as we shall see, will produce a new twist on the questions which both Paulhan and Blanchot engage; questions of history, of reading and writing, of their temporality, and of their occasions.

If *Les Fleurs de Tarbes* can be said to have a historical context, then it is in its oblique intersection with several intellectual currents of the 1930s and 1940s in France. The concept of terror had been revived in France in the 1930s thanks largely to Jean Hyppolite's *Genèse et structure de la Phénoménologie de l'esprit de Hegel (Genesis and Structure of Hegel's Phenomenology of Mind* [1946]) and Alexandre Kojève's *Introduction à la lecture de Hegel (Introduction to the Reading of Hegel* [1947]). The French "discovery" of Hegel was largely due to the courses given by Kojève during the 1930s. His anthropologized version of *The Phenomenology of Mind* was based on a narrative subtext to Hegel's book that went from the events of the French Revolution to the First Empire; Napoleon's march into Jena is interpreted by him as a literal "end of history." As Vincent Descombes puts it: "Kojève bequeathed to his listeners a *terrorist* conception of history." [4] This became an important motif in the philosophy of the period. Merleau-Ponty, for example, wrote a book entitled *Humanisme et Terreur (Humanism and Terror)* in defense of the Soviet Communist party, and Sartre focused on the period of terror in his analysis of the French Revolution in *Critique de la raison dialectique (Critique of Dialectical Reason).*

This motif was carried over into the realm of literature: Queneau's novels of the 1930s and 1940s are clearly marked by Kojève's reading of Hegel, and Sartre gave an extensive analysis of the change in the relation of the writer to society after the French Revolution in *Qu'est-ce que la littérature? (What is Literature?),* in particular in the section entitled "Pour qui écrit-on?" (For Whom Does One Write?).[5] Blanchot's response to Sartre's text was "Literature and the Right to Death," which takes the form of an ironic commentary on both Kojève's and Hyppolite's readings of Hegel, and is at the same time an implicit debate with Sartre on the question of the "literariness" of literature.[6] Sartre's question—"What is literature?"— seems rhetorical, since he at any rate is very clear as to what literature is, or should be. It is certainly no accident that Blanchot should first take up the question, prior to Sartre's politicized promotion of committed literature, by way of Paulhan. Paulhan's entire *oeuvre* might be said to constitute an extended answer to this one question about the specificity of literature. Toward the beginning of *Les Fleurs de Tarbes,* Paulhan poses the question explicitly as "this childish question: 'What is literature?'—childish, but which we spend a lifetime avoiding." [7] The title of Blanchot's essay on Paulhan's book —

"How is Literature Possible?" [8] —is, quite literally, a meditation on Paulhan's "childish" question.

As early as 1955 Paul de Man noted the theoretical complicity or solidarity between Paulhan and Blanchot in a configuration that included, significantly enough, Mallarmé and Hegel:

> For Mallarmé, poetic nothingness assumes the form of a concrete and specific choice, one that continues to obsess him: "namely, if there is occasion to write" [à savoir, s'il y a lieu d'écrire]. Fifty years later, Maurice Blanchot entitles an article on Paulhan's *Fleurs de Tarbes* "How is Literature Possible?": these two names—Paulhan and Blanchot—taken together ["unis de la sorte"]—sum up a whole historical period and a present situation.[9]

In this essay, the main portion of which is a reading of Mallarmé's "Une dentelle s'abolit," de Man traces a line from Hegel through Mallarmé to Paulhan and Blanchot, although this trajectory is in no way intended to suggest a historical series of influences. If anything, it complicates the notion of a movement that goes from origin to derivation, since according to de Man, Mallarmé and Hegel reach similar conclusions quite independently.

The article alluded to by de Man was the first piece of literary criticism that Blanchot published outside the context of journal reviews —although this is where it first appeared[10] —and it might be said that while it was a significant event as far as Paulhan criticism goes, Blanchot owes Paulhan a certain contingent debt, one that is entirely different from the kind of gratitude felt by most of the writers whom Paulhan had helped to publish. It is certainly true that the appearance of *Les Fleurs de Tarbes* in 1941 was considered an event of great significance by Blanchot, and in the first of the articles in the *Journal des Débats* he made the claim, edited out of the subsequent versions, that Paulhan's book was one of the most important works of contemporary literary criticism.

Paulhan had been promising his book ever since he first mentioned its imminent appearance in a letter to Francis Ponge in 1925.[11] An earlier, abbreviated, version was published in serial form in the *Nouvelle Revue Française* from June to October 1936, but sections of it were reworked elsewhere prior to the 1941 edition.[12] The work is privileged by Paulhan himself as a kind of cornerstone, since he mentions it almost obsessively in his correspondence from the 1920s to the 1940s, although he never produced its promised sequel, *Le Don des langues (The Gift of Languages)*.[13] Yet *Les Fleurs de Tarbes* is not just an assembly of previously unconnected parts, since it also takes up questions already addressed in texts such as *Jacob Cow le pirate, ou si les mots sont des signes (Jacob Cow the Pirate, or If Words are Signs)*, *Entretien sur des faits divers (Conversation About Miscellaneous News Items)*, and "La rhétorique renaît de ses cendres" (Rhetoric is Reborn From Its Ashes). It analyzes, in perhaps the most extensive and elaborate manner of all of his texts, the tension which is without question the most tenacious of critical commonplaces associated with the name of Jean Paulhan; the tension between terror and rhetoric.

Paulhan's understanding of rhetoric is, on the face of it, fairly traditional. Indeed, rhetoric for Paulhan is necessarily on the side of tradition (he also refers to it as "la Maintenance" [*Fleurs*, p. 183]), and it goes hand in hand with a conviction that language is in no need of change. In his *Traité des figures (Treatise on Figures)*, a commentary on du Marsais' *Traité des tropes (Treatise on Tropes)*, Paulhan discusses the eighteenth century obsession with classifying figures and tropes, and sees the attraction of such a stable catalogue of figures as also being the appeal of the rhetorical figure itself, which he always identifies with the commonplace ("lieu commun" in French being a more neutral and specifically linguistic term than "commonplace" in English). *Les Fleurs de Tarbes*, however, presents itself on a first reading as an extensive survey of an opposing tendency within literature, which Paulhan calls *la Terreur*.

Terrorist writers, according to Paulhan, espouse continual change and renewal, and vigorously denounce rhetoric's codification of language, its tendency to stultify the spirit and banalize human experience. *Les Fleurs de Tarbes* appears to support, through a long series of proofs, the Terrorist conception of literature and language. As Jean Paulhan states in a letter to Maurice Nadeau, what he was trying to do in *Les Fleurs de Tarbes* was not so much to elaborate a theory of literature, or to make an outspoken personal statement on the place of literature in society, but simply to collect, catalogue and "measure," almost as a statistical, quasi-scientific exercise, the critical assessments which had dominated discussions of literature over the previous 150 years or so. It should be said that these are taken mostly (although not exclusively) from French literary critics, whence the obscurity of many of the references for an anglophone reader. Paulhan finds examples of a terrorist denunciation of rhetoric in, for example, Gourmont's condemnation of "moral clichés," or Albalet's scorn for "picturesque clichés," or Flaubert's ironic *Dictionnaire des idées reçues (Dictionary of Received Ideas)*. Later on, he invokes 19th century French critics, such as Taine (who saw Racine as "the epitome of verbosity" (le comble du verbalisme), Renan (for whom the entire classical literary tradition was "an abuse of rhetoric" (un abus de la rhétorique), or Brunetière (who was equally dismissive of Malherbe's poetry for similar reasons). Paulhan's own argument turns around the notion of literary originality and authenticity, and of the dangerously seductive "power of words" (pouvoir des mots). He extends his discussion beyond the realm of literature, to encompass popular journalism (the clichés of the time being, for example, "ideological warfare," "the youth of today," "freedom," "popular opinion," etc.). Henri Bergson is seen by Paulhan as the most powerful "anti-verbalist" critic of the first half of the twentieth century, and is described as terror's own philosopher. Bergson's challenge to literature is "without a doubt the most serious reproach of our time: this is that the author of commonplaces gives in to the power of words, to verbalism, to the hold language has over it, and so on." [14]

The opposition between terror and rhetoric appears, then, to polarize two conflicting ideologies of expression; the aspiration toward originality on the one hand, and on the other, the attraction to the stability of the commonplace. Paulhan's predilection for the commonplace has led many commentators to think of Paulhan as a literary "conservative." It certainly seems that Paulhan's book ends up being nothing more than a scrap book of commonplaces or citations (somewhat akin to his anthology of Malagasy proverbs, or indeed his own "autobiographical" scrap books), and that he revels in exposing the naïveté of the terrorist at every turn. Despite the provocative connotations of the term terror, we will have to reserve judgment on how Paulhan situates himself with respect to its ideology. He says early on: "It's not that I find the mystical possession of the intellectual ("savant")—nor in earlier times the revolution—in the least bit contemptible. Far from it. I'm just suspicious of a revolt, or a dispossession, which comes along so opportunely to get us out of trouble." [15] It seems, thus, that it is not the ideology of terror *per se* which Paulhan takes to task, but rather the claims it makes for itself. We might begin by looking at the reason for Paulhan's choice of this particular term.

Les Fleurs de Tarbes contains only the vaguest of allusions to the period of bloody executions of 1793 and 1794 that were carried out by the Comité de Salut Public (Committee of Public Safety), as the revolutionary government attempted to purge its enemies and hold on to the political ground it had gained. This one explicit reference occurs early on in the book, towards the end of the section entitled "Portrait de la Terreur" (The Portrait of Terror), and is worth quoting in its entirety:

> We call periods of *Terror* those moments in the history of nations (which often follow some famine), when it suddenly seems that the State requires not the ingeniousness of systems, nor even science and technology—no-one cares about any of that—but rather an extreme purity of the soul, and the freshness of a communal innocence. Consequently citizens themselves are taken into consideration, rather than the things they do or make: the chair is forgotten in favor of the carpenter, the remedy in favor of the doctor. Yet skillfulness, knowledge and technique become suspect, as if they were covering up some lack of conviction. The representative Lebon decrees, in August 1793, that the revolutionary tribunal of Arras will begin by judging those prisoners who are "distinguished by their talent." When Hugo, Stendhal or Gourmont talk about massacres and slaughters, they are also thinking of a kind of talent: the kind which appears in flowers of rhetoric. As if the mischievous author—taking advantage of the effect *already* obtained by this arrangement of words, that literary device—were happy to construct, out of bits and pieces, a beauty machine, in which the beauty is no less displeasing than the machine.[16]

Terror seems to stand not so much for the historical events themselves, but synecdochally for the Revolution, or rather for a decisive turning point in French history, and more specifically in French *literary* history. It underlines the shift Paulhan finds in French literature from pre-Revolutionary Classicism, when writers submitted happily to the various rules imposed by traditions of genre and rhetorical composition, to Romanticism, whose "terrorism" consisted in abandoning accepted literary form in search of a more authentic, original expressiveness. In terror's violent overthrow of rhetoric, the priority of language over thought is completely reversed. As Paulhan puts it in a short commentary following *Les Fleurs de Tarbes*:

> Thus linguists and metaphysicians have at times (with the Rhetoricians) held that thoughts were derived from words, at other times (with the Romantics and the Terrorists) words from thoughts.[17]

For Paulhan, however, the rift between the two opposing concepts of literature is by no means confined to this one turbulent moment in French history, since the persistence of the antagonism between "terrorists" (writers such as Rimbaud, Apollinaire and Eluard) and "rhetoricians" (Paulhan's examples include Théophile Gautier, Valéry and Léon-Paul Fargue) is an indication that we are confronted with a question that cuts deeper than its particular, historically determined manifestations.[18]

The interest for us, as readers of *Les Fleurs de Tarbes,* is to see how this tension itself gets played out. According to "terrorist" writers, an excessive concern with language inhibits the potential of literature to be what it is capable of, given its infinite creative possibilities. Terror is literature that rejects literary commonplaces and conventions in an attempt to accede to pure, authentic expression (Paulhan is fond of citing Rimbaud's rejection of the "poetic old-fashionedness" (vieillerie poétique) of his literary predecessors). For Blanchot, the multitude of guises in which terror appears in *Les Fleurs de Tarbes* can be generally divided into two types: those who would like to bypass language altogether ("Art consequently has only one objective: to bring to light this inner world, while keeping it untouched by the crude and general illusions with which an imperfect language would dishonor it" [*Faux pas,* p. 95]) and those who are intent on cleansing language of its impure and outworn expressions, "making sure that they rid language of everything which could make it look like ordinary language." [19]

After spending the first half of *Les Fleurs de Tarbes* confirming the validity of terror's arguments, Paulhan then spends the second half unmasking their futility by showing that terrorists are the victims of an optical illusion ("we only enter into contact with literature, and language itself, nowadays . . . thanks to a series of errors and illusions, as common as an optical illusion might be").[20] They are in fact endlessly preoccupied with language, forever trying to bypass it, or rid it of its impurities:

> For Terror depends first of all on language in this general sense: that the writer is condemned to only express any longer what a certain *state* of language leaves him free to express: restricted to the areas of feeling and thought in which language has not yet been overused. That's not all: *no writer is more preoccupied with words than the one who is determined at every turn to get rid of them, to get away from them, or even to reinvent them* [My emphasis].[21]

This, then is the crux of the dilemma facing terrorist writers, and it is described by Paulhan as a kind of blindness to the rhetorical dimension of their own enterprise. Paulhan's fondness for exposing these kinds of perceptual errors is already apparent in *Entretien sur des faits divers,* where he discusses a whole series of similar illusions, such as the illusion of totality (by which one deduces the whole from a part), or the illusion of a "forecast of the past" ("prévision du passé") (by which one establishes the motive, or cause, after the event or effect). Terrorists want their language to be transparent, like a window, but its inevitably refracting, distorting quality reveals it to be of necessity rhetorical. Only by virtue of a "double illusion" is literature possible for the two kinds of terror that Blanchot indicates. These illusions are necessary to save literature from extinction or paralysis, since on the one hand it would suppress language completely, and on the other, it would be constantly aware of how its "pure" language is inevitably corrupted by usage.

If, according to Paulhan, both terrorists and rhetoricians are justified in their conceptions of literature, and therefore both equally unjustified, *Les Fleurs de Tarbes* seems in danger of becoming an endless exchange of reproaches and rebuttals, and the reader is liable to become dizzy watching what Michel Beaujour has referred to as "the whirligig of rhetoric and terror" (le tourniquet de la Rhétorique et de la Terreur).[22] The problem is compounded in that the two sides in this exchange are in fact one and the same. What appears to some as verbalism appears to others as expressiveness. Victor Hugo, for example, is taken by post-Romantics as the most formulaic of writers, yet in his own time he was considered a revolutionary in his rejection of classical literary forms. Elsewhere, the division of thoughts and words is formulated as a distinction between an author and a reader who see things differently from either side of the divide, but this is in fact the central enigma of *Les Fleurs de Tarbes*; how can we tell whether an author intended his or her words to be read as commonplaces or as original expressions? Commonplaces thus become for Paulhan the locus of a deep-seated tension within language and literature, and far from being banal, they are, as Blanchot rightly points out, "monsters of ambiguity" (des monstres d'ambiguïté) (*Faux pas,* p. 94). How, then, does Paulhan attempt to resolve this tension?

Paulhan's rather ingenious solution to the paradox he has just described takes the form of a revalorization (or a "reinvention") of rhetoric. From the point of view of rhetoric, the author is freed from a constant preoccupation with language precisely by submitting to the authority of commonplaces. In order to have a renewed contact with the "virgin newness of things" (nouveauté vierge des choses) (*Fleurs,* p. 92), writers should mutually agree to recognize clichés *as* clichés, and thereby institute a common, communally agreed-upon, rhetoric as a means of resolving the perplexing ambiguity that characterizes commonplaces:

> Clichés will be allowed to become citizens of Literature again [pourront retrouver droit de cité dans les Lettres] the day they are at last deprived of their ambiguity, and their confusion. Now all it should require, since the confusion stems from a doubt as to their nature, is simply for us to *agree,* once and for all, to take them as clichés. In short, we just need to *make* commonplaces *common.* . . .[23]

In his essay, Blanchot likens this solution of a "reinvented" rhetoric to a revolution that is both Copernican (since thought, in order to rediscover its authenticity, is made to revolve around and be dependent on the constant gravitational pull of language), and Kantian (since it involves an apperceptive awareness of the linguistic illusions according to which we are able to write). This granting of a "droit de *cité*" (my emphasis) to clichés makes them acceptable "citizens" of the realm of literature in that they become publicly quotable, marked by a communally recognized citationality. Paulhan often sets apart such expressions within his text precisely by marking them with italics, and is aware of similar conventions in literature. ("We should also cite those conventions of writing, the italics, the quotation marks, and the parentheses, which proliferate among romantic writers once rhetoric is abolished.")[24]

The most alluring appeal of *Les Fleurs de Tarbes* is not simply its intricate argument about the nature of literature, but the manner in which this argument is narrated, and in particular the way in which it is framed by the allegory of that most communal of locations, the public garden of Tarbes. A notice ("écriteau") at the entrance to the gardens reads something like a terrorist slogan: "IT IS FORBIDDEN TO ENTER THE GARDENS [Le Jardin] CARRYING FLOWERS."[25] As the story goes, the sign was erected by the keeper of the gardens (clearly intended to be the "garden of literature") to prevent people from taking the flowers (here the flowers of rhetoric or literary commonplaces) and claiming they had brought them into the garden with them. But some visitors are determined to carry flowers and find various ways around this interdiction, which correspond to the different "alibis" that authors give when confronted with the accusation of theft; for example, they carry ever more exotic flowers (the claim to a perpetual originality), or they say that the flowers just fell into their hair from the trees (the denial of authorial responsibility). The keeper's ban fails to solve the problem, and as Paulhan explains, it is merely compounded, since the continuous ingenuity of the visitors makes it increasingly difficult to determine whether the flowers are their own or are stolen public property (in Paulhan's terms, are they commonplaces or original thoughts?). The keeper's solution is consistent with Paulhan's reinvented rhetoric, and the allegory is concluded accordingly when the sign at the entrance is changed to: "IT IS FORBIDDEN TO ENTER THE PUBLIC GARDENS WITHOUT FLOWERS IN YOUR HANDS."[26] The addition of "public" to "jardin" in the reworded sign underlines the common agreement to read commonplaces as commonplaces; it becomes a truly public park when the visitors, too burdened with their own flowers, will not even think of stealing the public ones. The allegory could thus be said adequately to frame the "apparent" version of *Les Fleurs de Tarbes*. It follows the argument from terror's denunciation of rhetoric, through rhetoric's exposure of terror's illusions, to the reinvention of rhetoric which recovers literature's authenticity within its commonplaces.

In his book *Agonies of the Intellectual*, Allan Stoekl situates Paulhan's text in relation to a Durkheimian concern with the place of the

sacred within Western society, and offers what is one of the most rigorous and perceptive readings to date of *Les Fleurs de Tarbes*, and of
what he sees as Blanchot's "revision" of Paulhan. Stoekl sees Paulhan's project as part of a French tradition, going back to Durkheim,
of the intellectual as an abstract rationalist. With Paulhan, the problem takes the following form: "Paulhan's strictly apolitical attempt
to rehabilitate rhetoric is nothing other than a late attempt at recon-
ciling abstract reason and sacred violence, language and that which ex-
ceeds it, in a new version of the intellectual, the Rhetorician." [27] Stoekl
thus correctly reads the tension between terror and rhetoric as a vicious
circle of two mutually purgative forms of linguistic violence, which
are then "projected" onto the political domain, as the mutual political purge of two different forms of collaboration (the argument of
Paulhan's polemical *Lettre aux Directeurs de la Résistance,* which I will
look at in more detail in the following chapter). For Stoekl the allegory
of the public park in *Les Fleurs de Tarbes* marks the moment when the
linguistic in Paulhan inevitably spills over into the social and political.
Returning to the earlier 1936 *NRF* version of Paulhan's essay, in a
section Paulhan omitted from the 1941 Gallimard edition, Stoekl as-
tutely points to Paulhan's choice of the metaphor of the sun as the
figure of the unknowable, that which cannot be seen directly, but
which is the condition of the very possibility of seeing. In terms of the
argument of Paulhan's book, this figure could be read as a "master
cliché" or a kind of "generating matrix" that commands and controls
the endless reversals and purgations of terror and rhetoric. In short,
the sun as master trope is itself a trope for a master Rhetorician, Paulhan himself:

> In this way, Paulhan would save the argument of *Les Fleurs
> de Tarbes* from the dilemma that he himself poses. Once
> again—as at the end of the "first volume" of *Les Fleurs
> de Tarbes*—Terror is subordinated to Rhetoric. The havoc
> it wreaks in the stable operation of the linguistic "machine"
> is exiled: now too it serves as a guarantee of Paulhan's pro-
> ject, which is nothing other than a stable knowledge of
> Letters. (p. 158)

This also allows Stoekl to see Paulhan's project as a political one,
whose ultimate (even if unavowed) aim is to *subordinate* the social
to the linguistic.

Does Paulhan, as a kind of master Rhetorician, in fact end up "resolving" the dilemma he poses himself? I would argue that the question hinges on a reading of the allegory of the public park, and on the "ending" of *Les Fleurs de Tarbes*. Is the 1936 version the hidden, neglected ending? Why, however, should we stop reading there? Other "endings" point rather to an author who is never satisfied with the illusion of intellectual victory, especially when it is based on a *rational* mastery of the problem he is dealing with. This can be seen in the allegory of the public park: the "solution" for which it is a figure is not the end of the book (not even of the "first volume" of *Les Fleurs de Tarbes),* which in fact closes with the famously enigmatic retraction: "There are thus glimmers of light, visible to whoever sees them, hidden from whoever looks at them; gestures which cannot be performed without a certain negligence. [. . .] Let's just say I said nothing." [28]

It seems at first to be just another example of the kind of modesty typical of Paulhan. It takes the form of a communal agreement ("Let's just say") that is phrased again as an optic metaphor. We can no more fully comprehend the solution than we can look squarely at the sun, and the negligence required could well be the passivity involved in just seeing, as opposed to the effort involved in looking. The ending seems to be an example of this kind of negligence. However, if we look at it more closely, or at any rate read it more attentively, it is a very troubling ending. How are we to read this disavowal? Is it intended to be taken literally, as an authentic expression of the author's feelings? But then how could the book be "nothing" since if it were, we would not even be able to read this final sentence? Or is it to be read rhetorically as something that is just said, a cliché, a careless throwaway remark? But then was the entire book composed in a equally negligent fashion? What are we "seeing" or "reading" when we see or read this "nothing?" In Paulhan's own terms, this final sentence is strictly unreadable. Earlier on in the book, he says that "commonplaces can be intelligent or stupid, I don't know which, and I don't see any way ever of knowing it with any rigor." [29]

This ending was in fact prepared earlier on in a moment of textual self-awareness, in a sub-section of Part III entitled "Le lecteur se voit mis en cause" (The reader is put into question). Within the text's many vacillations, it is at one level just another argument in favor of terror:

And who doesn't agree with Terrorists that the mind loses its dignity if it goes round and round a word like an animal that's tied up; if it remains stuck at this first stage when one is teaching oneself to speak; if it is more concerned with commas, rules and unities than with *that* which it has to say.[30]

Yet if, as Paulhan goes on to say, one were to pay attention less to the terrorist myth itself than to the way in which it has been uncovered or demystified, one will notice something rather odd: "If there is any baseness or cowardice in thinking *around* a word, and in thus submitting one's thought to language, you don't have to look very far to find who is at fault: we are the ones who are guilty." [31] The previous pages, according to Paulhan, were an exercise in precisely that which he had been denouncing and attempting to overcome: "We ourselves are at stake." [32]

This discovery upsets, not only the project of a communally agreed upon convention, whereby the ambiguity of clichés would be removed by marking them with quotation marks, but also the very possibility of reading (or writing) commonplaces: "it is no longer Bourget or Carco, whose thought must seem to us to be enslaved to words and phrases—but ourselves, and our thought *when we read Bourget's or Carco's commonplaces.*" [33] This is in fact none other than Paulhan's conclusion, that is, that terror is always already "read" by rhetoric ("We have pushed Terror as far as it will go, and discovered Rhetoric").[34] Yet it is no longer simply a possibly naïve theory about literature, but it puts the whole book into question. Is it "merely" a catalogue of citations? Do we now read these citations differently, having perhaps passed over them a little too negligently? What does it mean to read a citation? And what if the citation is *invented*, as are many, if not all, of the epigraphs to the chapters of *Les Fleurs de Tarbes*? The book is thus a performance of the very radical ambiguity that it talks about, an ambiguity that is not simply an equivocation about *what* the book is saying, but that suspends it between saying and doing, stating and performing, original and commonplace. As Blanchot says, "[Paulhan] factors in this equivocation, and does not attempt to dispel it." [35] How can we read the "nothing" at the end of the book, since no sooner are the means given to us (the common agreement which allows us to read) than they are taken away again?

The allegory of the public gardens is thus itself "framed" by the final retraction of the book. The frame of this book now requires an allegory that takes into account the failure of the apparent allegory. So that rather than the allegory being an allegory *of* the text, the text itself becomes an allegory of (the impossibility of) this allegory. In Paulhan's own terms, it is figured as being caught within the very illusion it believed it was catching out. The text is framed by what it was attempting to frame, so we can never tell whether we are inside or outside the frame, and we might well wonder if this could be said to be a "figure," since it involves the failure of figuration. The framing allegory of *Les Fleurs de Tarbes,* far from defining literature by clearly marking the boundaries that surround the garden, makes it impossible for us to tell whether we are in the garden or not, since it is impossible to know where the flowers Paulhan hands to us have come from.

In his essay "How Is Literature Possible?" Blanchot is highly attentive to this "nothing" and to this radical unreadability. For him, the "nothing" is the reappearance and reaffirmation of the terror that Paulhan's book had so painstakingly discredited. A "reinvented" terror, to be sure, but one that testifies to the persistence of the claim of literature to authenticity and originality despite the demonstrated impossibility of this claim (since it is always preempted by rhetoric). Indeed, for Blanchot it is no less than literature's "soul" (p. 97), and its very claim to existence. Blanchot's insistence on this "reinvention" of terror takes us back to the beginning of his essay. He had started out by saying that it is possible to read *Les Fleurs de Tarbes* as two books: a visible one, and one that is ironically hidden by it. The second, secret book only begins to work on the reader once the "first" book has been finished, and according to Blanchot:

> It is only through the uneasiness and anxiety we feel that we are authorized to communicate with the larger questions he poses, and he is prepared to show us these questions only by their *absence* [My emphasis].[36]

As we saw earlier on, Blanchot answers the essay's title question at one level—the level of the "apparent" book—by saying that literature is possible by virtue of the illusions which allow terror to assert itself despite its impossibility. At another level, the level that makes the reader dimly aware of the far deeper questions, literature is said to appear only through its absence. From the perspective of both terror and rhetoric, therefore, it is always already lost; we are left with a terror that can only ever be re-invented, and a rhetoric that never allows itself to be codified into any kind of literary convention. It is neither terror nor rhetoric, and both of them at the same time. Blanchot stresses that the duplicity of the two books cannot be overcome. The second book is only readable *after* the first book, thus confirming Paulhan's own observation in *Les Fleurs de Tarbes*: "The reader places this extreme presence and this obsession with words at the *origin* of the incriminated phrase or passage, whereas it is in fact produced for him—as happened to us—at the *end* of his efforts." [37] In responding to the "hidden" book of *Les Fleurs de Tarbes,* Blanchot truly implicates himself in the essential questions it raises, and begins to articulate concerns which will become major *topoi* in his later criticism. Allan Stoekl takes Blanchot's reading of *Les Fleurs de Tarbes* as a revision of Paulhan, insofar as the former reformulates Paulhan's essential paradox of literature as "writing on writing." As we saw in the previous chapter, this is precisely what the *récit* (and possibly all of Paulhan's writing) is in any case. Stoekl admits this possibility when he says in passing that Paulhan's text may well not be in need of any correction, but he does not pursue it.

The solution of the book *is* a necessary failure—"a sort of law of failure" as Paulhan calls it[38]—so that the "understanding" of this failure is not ultimately subsumed under the mastery of language, but through a kind of *parody of understanding.* This is how Paulhan describes it towards the end of the "Pages d'explication" (Some Explanations) where he makes the link between *Les Fleurs de Tarbes* and another key theoretical text (which Stoekl tellingly omits to read), *Clef de la poésie (Key to Poetry):* "do we need to look for even more rules in which the arbitrary predominates? This is the question adressed by *Clef de la Poésie.*" [39] Blanchot himself begins his essay on *Clef de la poésie,* "Le Mystère dans les Lettres," (a title borrowed from Mallarmé's famous essay of the same name) by returning to *Les Fleurs de Tarbes.* He calls the "nothing" at the end of the book a "strange, somewhat disorienting privilege," and clearly makes the link between the two texts by Paulhan.[40] The figure of the unknowable, factored into the equation, becomes that of "poetic mystery" (le mystère poétique).

POETIC JUSTICE

Clef de la poésie, published in 1944, does not offer us any kind of methodical system of interpretation such as a Poetics, but assigns itself a task both grander in its ambition and more specific in the precise object of its attention. It is worth reflecting for a while on this full title. Like other Paulhan titles—for example *Petite préface à toute critique (Short Preface to All Criticism),* and *Essai d'introduction au projet d'une métrique universelle (Attempt at an Introduction to the Project of a Universal Metrics)*—it is "modest" in exactly the way we saw "Manie" to be modest, that is, in an inherently excessive or transgressive fashion. The opening lines provide us with an assertive orientation, which is no less "modest" than the title, whose tensions are thus by no means resolved:

> I'm not looking to make the least discovery, I'm only looking for a way to judge all poetic doctrines. I'm not hoping to formulate some new poetic doctrine; I'm only looking for a procedure able to test all poetic doctrines. In short, my argument is neither critical nor—by all appearances—literary. It is strictly logical.[41]

Clef de la poésie, despite the uncertainties of its title, is thus a clearly programmatic attempt to apply the rigor of logical thinking to the phenomenon of poetry, to submit it to some kind of law. Paulhan proposes to deduce such a law from what is common to all poetry, its lowest common denominator as it were. This common, unifying element or trait is that which makes poetry the *least* common of enterprises, what Paulhan terms "poetic mystery" ("le mystère poétique"). Poetic mystery may be as vacuous a commonplace as one could find, but it is a necessary point of departure according to Paulhan. Since what makes poetic mystery mysterious—and poetic—is that it is undefinable, the project of *Clef de la poésie* is the difficult one of "finding a law whose legality is founded upon mystery [dont la légalité soit celle du mystère]" as Blanchot puts it in "Le Mystère dans les lettres."

This may not be as difficult as it appears at first sight; as Paulhan says in his *Essai d'introduction au projet d'une métrique universelle* when discussing Valéry's constant preoccupation with a self-reflexive moment in literature ("watch oneself watching oneself"): "The task is not difficult: It is strictly impossible."[42] How to account for this impossibility is precisely what is at stake. Any law that applies to poetry will need to be rigorous and uncompromising in its recognition of the absolutely indefinable nature of its essence. Such a project *appears* futile, but it is in terms of its appearances that poetic mystery allows itself to be approached.

The very least it demands, and perhaps also the very most, if it is to function with the constancy which is the minimal requirement of a law, is that the relationship between thought and language remain stable. How this is achieved, Paulhan argues, is by making the first (and only?) principle of the law of poetic mystery one of absolute reversibility of terms:

> I'm thinking now of a poetic law such that, expressing a particular relationship of sounds to meanings, and of ideas to words, it is able, without thereby losing its validity or its verisimilitude, to stand seeing its terms inverted; to stand being inverted.[43]

In submitting itself to its own poetic law ("it is able . . . to stand being inverted"), or in giving in, immediately, to poetry's demands, this law—which is still only, it should be remembered, a hypothesis—would be true to the inconceivability of poetic mystery:

> It is clear that such a law, whose formula would be double, would go further than verisimilitude [vraisemblance], to reach the truth. For want of rendering mystery directly—which is by definition impossible—it would in effect yield to this mystery: it would mime it, show it.[44]

So it is precisely because of the "vraisemblance" (verisimilitude) of its simulation of poetic mystery that this law avoids falling into the trap of actually rendering or translating poetic mystery. Since the most it could do would be to make manifest what *appears* as the truth of poetic mystery (its "vraisemblance"), in surrendering immediately to poetic mystery's inexpressibility, it is at least somehow truly involved in poetry's (apparent) truth.

The ambivalence of a law that is true only insofar as it appears to be true points to a generalized doubleness that is central to an understanding of this text. How this doubleness or bifurcation works at the level of a linguistic analysis is suggested at the very beginning of the essay when Paulhan describes the impetus for his text as "the keenest desire finally to distill some method or key, which would allow us to separate the true from the false."[45] Paulhan continues: "I propose here to forge that key" (Je me propose ici de forger cette clef). The French expression "forger cette clef" can be read on two levels. As a "method," it is an essentially Cartesian project, and corresponds to the intention to separate the true from the false, and to "reach the truth." But the verb "forger" could just as well be read as precisely an operation of making a double, or a counterfeit, of an original, something that would be "vraisemblable." In linguistic terms, the question of doubleness, and of the appearance of truth, is very much the question of figurative language. The "proper meaning" of poetic mystery would only be accessible, therefore, via the detour of a figure, and Paulhan's text, slightly reformulated, becomes an inquiry into the status of figurative language itself.

If poetic mystery can only be approached via its appearances, or indirectly by the detour of a figure, we can only hope to achieve an authentic simulacrum of it by circumscribing its apparent "elements": on the one hand "the letter and the sign, breath, sound, everything material and outside of us," and on the other, "ideas, wishes, feelings—everything known to us through intimate experience."[46] Taking the poets themselves as his "witnesses," Paulhan finds that they fall naturally into precisely the two opposing camps which he delineates above and that, more surprisingly, they in fact coexist very harmoniously:

> Now their explanations and doctrines offer a singular trait: each of them is ingenious, probable—and what's more, since they are poets, proven by the facts. But not any more than the opposite explanation also remains probable—and no less proven.[47]

A little later on, in transferring this double schema to a metaphysical, then to a *political* domain, Paulhan finds that positions are switched with equal ease, such that Paulhan is led to conclude: "One suspects that the key, once discovered, would be valid also for domains other than literature or poetry."[48] The apparent nonchalance with which each side betrays its position allows Paulhan to speculate, as was suggested before, that a form of betrayal is necessary in poetic mystery, and that it is even its most singular trait:

> We saw that there was a constant trait with poetry: it is the regular flaw [*défaut*] which each doctrine or reason betrays when dealing with it. . . . If I attempt less to explain this trait, or even to understand it, than to express it—to formulate it—it comes down to the following: that in poetry words and thoughts happen to be *indifferent.*[49]

This formulation is an absolutely crucial one in Paulhan's essay. It gathers together in its concision all of the preceding hypothetical speculation, and offers a first version of the law that the essay will elaborate. We might feel that such a perfect formulation leaves no room for mystery, which seems to be itself betrayed, and that the effacement of differences leaves us with nothing, or with the flatness of a platitude. However—and here we can understand how such a formulation is possible—it never claimed to be anything other than a platitude, or rather, it only ever claimed to simulate poetic mystery ("In which we express mystery for lack of being able to think it"[50]), it only claimed to be apparently true. It does not give us poetic mystery, which is not there to be given, but it allows it to insinuate itself as the invisible trait that only reveals itself in its appearances. It always appears as what it is not, and so the duplicity of its constant self-betrayal is the surest guarantee of its continuing effectiveness.

In a surprising move, Paulhan then goes on to pursue his argument by borrowing a system of expression from the field of mathematics, since he is concerned to satisfy both the scientific requirement of non-contradiction as well as (simultaneously) the poetic requirement of indifference. In fact only by satisfying this double requirement will it be truly a law of poetic mystery. The mathematical formula he elaborates is as follows: since the sets of oppositions which govern any expression are not made up of isolated elements, that is to say, there is always a more or less complex configuration of, for example, language and thought, sounds and meanings, Paulhan designates these sets by groups of symbols, calling them "functions." The necessarily double formula is thus:

From F(abc) it follows that F'(ABC)
From F(ABC) it follows that F'(abc)[51]

How this is to be understood is that "a b c are words for classical poets and rhetoricians, and A B C thoughts. But that for romantic poets and terrorists a b c are on the contrary ideas and A B C words" (*Clef,* p. 251). Filling in the double equation we get:

The function F(words) implies the function F' (ideas)
[just as]
The function F(ideas) implies the function F' (words)

The first half of the formula works like any scientific formula, and is even consistent with scientific precedent in assigning terms to something which is temporarily inconceivable. The second half, however, is of a different nature:

The second test, which interests me, is particular to a poetic law: it is a question of knowing whether this law remains valid *despite* the mystery and the transmutation of its elements: if it is likely to resist this mystery and (so to speak) soak up the obstacle.[52]

According to this double law, it makes absolutely no difference whether we go from cause to effect or from effect to cause, from thoughts to words or from words to thoughts. While the two directions are perfectly comprehensible in terms of scientific laws (the first is logical, the second is "simply" illogical), their simultaneous coexistence and interchangeability is not, and it thus fulfils the requirement of the law of poetic mystery.

Paulhan is careful to point out, however, that this is merely a "model law," a simulacrum, and that he is by no means sure that such a law actually exists. In fact, he admits that he could not care less whether it exists or not, and ends the essay with a triumphant declaration of success, and an invitation to the reader to test out the effectiveness of the law by applying it "to the commentaries, confidential remarks, themes and doctrines currently pertaining to poetry." [53]

Paulhan anticipates possible objections to his argument, and he does so by stating that the performance of the text has both "overtaken his argument" (dépassé mon propos), and in doing so has itself become an example of the law he is attempting to formulate: "I have proposed nothing which I have not undergone. . . . I was the very discovery that I was making." [54] The text of *Clef de la poésie* is poetic to the extent that it obeys exactly the law of poetic mystery which it articulates; it functions on two registers, each absolutely distinct from the other, yet both interchangable, self-betraying, and coexisting in a singular, indifferent relationship. *Clef de la poésie* is its own primary proof, precisely because it is a poetic "event" *as well as* a logical argument. But in declaring his text subject to its own law of poetic mystery, and to the illusions which always inform literary and critical endeavors, Paulhan seems to open and immediately close again an interpretive circle. We are justified in asking whether in doing so, he does not forever foreclose the possibility of considering a generically circumscribed poetics. Is he being unduly naïve in forbidding himself access to an external, objective perspective?

According to Blanchot, Paulhan is the least self-deluded of critics, precisely because of the rigor of his concentration on what appears simple and commonplace. Since literature always tends to produce the same division into rhetoric and terror, Paulhan's naïveté is, as Blanchot remarks, "the least unreflective possible." [55] In subjecting his own texts to the same rigorous critical scrutiny he exercises in reading other texts, he is demonstrating that he is subject to the same illusions as other writers, and that there is no guarantee that even such obstinate attention to the simple and the commonplace allows for any greater critical distance or demystification. What is so difficult to grasp (for Paulhan too) is why he should find the self-evident so perplexing. As Blanchot says of *Clef de la poésie:*

> The provocative nature of these remarks comes from their simplicity, and yet also from the impossibility of going beyond them. [56]

Language is, according to Paulhan, always two-faced. In his essay on *Clef de la poésie* Blanchot demonstrates how the metaphorical extension of this duplicity works. He shows how, for Paulhan, the side of the division which is made up of words, sounds, form, etc. is often said to correspond to the writer, and to the mouth, while the opposite side is made up of thoughts, meanings, ideas, an author, and an ear. This division of the acts of reading and writing into two opposing and mutually exclusive camps is as illusory as the irreducible separation of, say, words and thoughts, and Blanchot focuses on those rare moments of "short-circuiting" between the two. At such moments, Blanchot writes, both aspects appear simultaneously, "the whole of language, whose two sides we only make out otherwise when they are folded on top of one another, and hide one another."[57] Blanchot pushes the logic of this play of appearance and disappearance to a point where a comparison between Paulhan and Mallarmé becomes possible, and it allows for a clarification of the distinction between "ordinary" language and poetry in *Clef de la poésie*. If, for Paulhan, words exist in an indifferent relationship with things, for example, then they have, as Blanchot says, a triple existence. They exist in order to make the thing appear (while themselves disappearing), they reappear as deictic signs showing the thing which only exists by virtue of being called forth by the words, and they again disappear to maintain the illusion of the thing existing independently of words. From the opposite perspective, the same "short-circuiting" takes place, but inversely. In defining the project of Mallarmé's poetics as the evocation, not of things but of the *absence* of things,[58] Blanchot arrives at the following reformulation of Paulhan's law:

> . . . words vanish from the stage to usher in the thing, but as this thing is itself nothing more than an absence, what appears in this theatre is an absence of words and an absence of things, a simultaneous void, nothing supported by nothing.[59]

Thus, by very different routes, Paulhan and Mallarmé reach a strikingly similar conception of poetry, or of poetic mystery. Mallarmé's disappearing words and things leave us with an enigmatic emptiness that resembles the empty platitude of Paulhan's poetic law. Does this mean that poetry tends always towards the destruction of ordinary language? If so, we might feel doubly anxious: not only is poetry essentially empty, but once we reach this emptiness of poetry, there is no going back to "ordinary" language. This, however, is once more to presume that poetry is simply a particular form of language, and that it is accessible to cognition in the same way. Blanchot points out how absolutely different the dimensions of "poetry" and "ordinary language" are, and this radical incompatibility is itself irreducible to a logic of contradiction or paradox. The strange temporality involved is now in fact familiar to us as the characteristic movement of the

récit, and it also produces in Blanchot's essay a number of consequences which follow from this description of poetry. Poetry can only
appear as something *inapparent*; it renders language unworkable, yet
is the very condition of possibility of language; and poetic mystery is
absolutely hidden from sight, yet illuminates everything.

In showing his essay to have been a poetic as well as a logical
text, Paulhan does not simply reassert the supremacy of poetry over
science. If we at first took the rather barren mathematical formula to
be a subordination of poetry to the discourse of science, the affirmation of the text as a poetic event is what *makes* it a poetic event. In the
text's own terms, it becomes a matter of indifference whether the text
is a logical argument or a poetic event. In other words, we cannot tell
whether poetry is subordinated to the discourse of science, or whether
science is subordinated to poetry. Indeed, this very opposition could
be expressed in terms of the law of poetic mystery, giving the following double formula:

From F (poetry) it follows that F' (science)
From F (science) it follows that F' (poetry)

It is impossible to tell whether *Clef de la poésie,* which is the only evidence we have, the only place where the question can be decided, is
a poetic or scientific discourse. As Blanchot puts it, Paulhan's text is:

> . . . both a scientific and a nonscientific process, the dis-
> junction as it were between the two, and the mind's hesi-
> tation between the latter and the former. . . .[60]

The question "What is . . ." (*Clef de la poésie,* "poetic mystery," literature)?" is necessarily a question of science and one which simply
does not interest poetry. Neither is poetry "interested" in something
else, some more important question, since it is essentially disinterested, indifferent.

The "key" to poetry, which should have provided us with the
means of distinguishing between "the false and the true," tells us only
that when poetic mystery is at stake, it is impossible to tell the difference between true and false. Poetic mystery is both true and false, and
neither, all at once; it is both the essence of poetry and absolutely
inessential; both the impossibility of language (its ruin) and its possibility. We, as readers, are absolutely caught up in the text's impossi-

bility. We thought we were going to read a text about poetry. It seemed to have nothing to do with poetry. But then, what is poetry? The only answer the text offers is that there is poetry when it is impossible to tell whether there is poetry or not. But is *Clef de la poésie* poetry? It is impossible to tell, yet this impossibility is our surest guarantee that it is poetic. Once we decide that it is poetic, however, it is no longer poetic. If it is impossible to read such a text, how did we even get this far? It is impossible to measure how far we have come in our reading, since not only was it impossible to begin reading, but it is also impossible to stop.

Which brings us back to the problem of the "ending" of *Les Fleurs de Tarbes*. If Stoekl's reading depended on a determined end point, which would allow for a re-reading of the relationship between Paulhan and Blanchot, I have pursued this ending by continuing to read Paulhan's own commentaries of his texts, and have followed the thread of Blanchot's reading, both of which point to the significance of what I would see as very much a "key" text of Paulhan's, *Clef de la Poésie*. But this is not the end of the story, since Blanchot, as if to confirm the interminability of the process of Paulhan's writing (and of our reading of Paulhan), wrote a further, crucial text on Paulhan, "The Ease of Dying," which (elliptically, but maybe deliberately so) tells us much about the relationship between Paulhan and Blanchot.[61]

NON-COINCIDENCES

"The Ease of Dying" was originally written for the 1969 issue of the *Nouvelle Revue Française* commemorating Paulhan's death a year earlier, and was subsequently included in *L'Amitié* (1972). The significance of writing on the "occasion" of Paulhan's death is not lost on Blanchot, and he starts out the essay recounting the story of their friendship, in what is for Blanchot an unusually anecdotal style. As a story of friendship, however, it is presented in the barest of terms—as Blanchot says, it was a "relationship without anecdotes"— and its solemnity is accentuated by what he sees as its chance alignment with some of the watersheds of recent French history. Blanchot tells of their first encounter in May 1940, how their relations were severed in 1958 over the question of Algerian Independence, and how their planned reconciliation was thwarted by the events of May 1968.

As the essay develops, it calls to mind Blanchot's discussion of literature and revolution in "Literature and the Right to Death." Paulhan, as Blanchot notes, had a marked tendency to publish during periods of great historical change (the First and Second World Wars), when the whole of history was being put into question. The historical vacuum thereby opened up (what Blanchot calls "a time outside of time") increases the chances of a kind of anonymity which is a requirement of the impersonal or neutral "rapport" which Blanchot speaks of:

> . . . great historical changes are also destined, because of their burden of absolute visibility, and because they allow nothing but these changes themselves to be seen, to better free up the possibility of being understood or misunderstood intimately, and without having to spell things out, the private falling silent so that the public can speak, thus finding its voice.[62]

This confusion of public and private is affirmed by Blanchot because of its potential to allow for the emergence of a different kind of intimacy, that would be neither an anecdotal relationship, nor one "without anecdotes." The "relationship" between Paulhan and Blanchot only begins, it seems, after Paulhan's death. It is surely no coincidence that only once Paulhan has died is Blanchot able to write: "I often observed that his *récits* —which touched me in a way I can better remember now. . . ." ("Ease of Dying," p. 122). A few sentences earlier, quoting Paulhan's "prophetic" words in 1940, "We will remember these days," Blanchot effectively transfers their relationship to a time that is a "time outside of time," one that would escape the double bind of an anecdotal or a non-anecdotal rapport, and one in which personal friendship would be subordinated to the "rapport," or "non-rapport," of reading and writing. Indeed, what we know of their relationship is very little, and one could certainly not count Blanchot among Paulhan's vast circle of friends with whom he kept up long and unfailingly loyal correspondences.

Although "The Ease of Dying" is devoted to Paulhan's *récits,* and quotes mainly from Paulhan's early fictional texts, this is, as we saw, a way for Blanchot to talk about Paulhan *as a writer* in general. As he says: "It is through the movement of the *récit* (the discontinuity of the continuous *récit*) that we can perhaps best understand Jean Paulhan" ("Ease of Dying," p. 123). For Blanchot the figure of this radical discontinuity (or irreversibility) is death, while the *récit*'s continuity is guaranteed, conversely, by the play of reversals of Paulhan's texts, which Blanchot names "illness." Thus "death" and "illness" become figures of irreversibility and reversibility respectively. It might appear that "death" carries the greater theoretical burden of the two terms. But the title of the essay, "The Ease of Dying" warns of a dangerous trap; nothing could be easier than "dying," in the sense that thinking and writing can easily recuperate and accommodate its own discontinuity. Reversibility—"illness"—thus becomes in Paulhan's texts a form of endless narrative vigilance and a paradoxical guarantee of irreversibility, or "death." What the *récit* names, therefore, in "The Ease of Dying" is a "reading-writing" which responds to its own essential condition, that is, an experience of radical incommensurability or non-coincidence. It is, in other words, very close to the symmetrical impossibility of writing and reading which Blanchot discusses at the beginning of *L'Espace littéraire*. The only place, or space, or occasion, for literature is a kind of "non-place" [non-lieu]; this is the "place" that Blanchot, in "The Ease of Dying," accords to the *récit*: "The *récit* alone provides the space, while taking it away, for the experience which is contrary to itself. . . ." (The Ease of Dying, p. 137).

If writing is necessarily its own impossible occasion, how can we understand the "occasion" of the "encounter" between Paulhan and Blanchot? We could see it as one in which the logic of the *récit* is *already* at work. If the *récit* names an essential non-coincidence between a text and itself ("writing"), then Blanchot's critical response to Paulhan's *Fleurs de Tarbes* in 1941 is equally a form of reading that responds to the "unreadability" of Paulhan's text, its mysterious, inaccessible otherness. And the turn from political commentary to "reading-writing," occasioned in part by the reading of Paulhan's book, could be seen not as a forgetting of, or indifference to, the political circumstances of the time, but as the inauguration of a deeper questioning of the relationship between writing-reading, and history. "Literature and the Right to Death" points the way towards an engagement with political questions that will be implicit or explicit in Blanchot's writing henceforth, passing through precisely a critique of language's claims to immanence and transparency, and including a critique of forms of immanent (and potentially totalitarian) political ideology.

So have I fallen into the trap of a kind of immanent form of reading in proposing the relationship between Paulhan and Blanchot as a decisive and fully determined turning point in Blanchot's career? Yes and no. Shifting the focus to the *récit* allows us to see a logic of non-coincidence at work at the three levels of political writing (the non-coincidence of language and the world, or language as a fundamental negation of the world), literary act (writing is only truly writing if it responds to its own impossibility), and critical response (reading only occurs if it takes into account the fundamental unreadability of literature). By taking the *récit* as a medium of serious critical reflection, we avoid the reductive and ultimately stultifying division of writing into *either* politically aware *or* "literary" (i.e. implicitly "unpolitical").

Consequently we are "now" (in the "timeless" time of reading) in a better position to read Blanchot's opening remarks in "The Ease of Dying": ". . . his *récits* —which touched me in a way in a way I can better remember *now* —" (my emphasis). Consistent with the "after the fact" (après-coup) logic of the essay itself—or to quote from one of Paulhan's "causes célèbres," which Blanchot himself cites in "The Ease of Dying": "But how can we succeed in seeing at first sight things for the second time?" ("Ease of Dying," p. 137)—only "now" is Blanchot able to "read" Paulhan's *récits*. The essay itself replays the same logic of non-coincidence, both asking (again) the question of writing and its circumstances, and at the same time answering it in its very performance by narrating the impossibility of ever understanding the moment of their "encounter" as a "rapport."

This is not to deny, of course, that there *was* an empirical relationship between Blanchot and Paulhan during the war, with its own history and anecdotes, that remain to be told. Although Paulhan's wartime activities were far more visible than Blanchot's, the latter's writings (critical, literary and political) have tended to eclipse the former's, for reasons that have more to do with notoriety than with any genuine critical understanding. I hope to have gone some way toward correcting this imbalance, and would like in the following chapter to look more closely not only at just what Paulhan *was* doing during the war, but also (following perhaps a similar "après-coup" logic) at the polemic texts he wrote after the war.

4

Resistance,
Collaboration,
and the
Postwar Literary
Purge in France

*"I am only too aware of the awful
dangers presented to us by the racisms,
nationalisms, and all of the forms of love of
one's* patrie *which we have seen happen
successively. But perhaps we should not for
all that forget a certain part of this love: its
mysterious part, if I can call it that, precisely
that part which we are too inclined to
neglect these days.*

*Such a love is perhaps the only possible
line of defense against the dangers of
prejudice. . . ."* [1]

Modestie de l'Occident
(Modesty of the West), 1947

t has been argued that the discovery of Paul de Man's wartime writings has decisively altered the landscape of literary theory.[2] My intention in this chapter is not to enter the fray of the de Man affair and its aftermath, which has at this point in time been exhaustively commented upon,[3] but to attempt, somewhat obliquely, to read the phenomenon of literary theory grappling with its own identity, and its ethical and political exigencies, less as a feature of "today's" academic scene, than as a reformulation, a different version, of a question which had its own contingent urgency in postwar France. If current reassessments of the ideological ancestry of writers such as Maurice Blanchot and Paul de Man are being conducted in an atmosphere that is at once triumphantly vengeful and painfully traumatic (depending on which way one looks at it), then our understanding will surely benefit from looking more closely at the years in France when the literary community reacted for the first time in public to the writers who had collaborated with the Nazi occupiers during the Second World War.

Paulhan emerged (and is now re-emerging) as a figure of some significance at the time, but as someone whose intervention was very problematic and extremely controversial. Unlike Blanchot or de Man, Paulhan maintained no aura of secrecy about his past, and made no attempt to disown or disavow his literary affiliations. Instead, he fully embraced them, with all of the uncomfortable contradictions this implied. This has led to a consistent misinterpretation or simplification of Paulhan's position, most often in the form of an appropriation of his texts to other ends, or of discreet or elliptical references to them. Jacques Derrida, in his article responding to the wartime writings of Paul de Man, makes a passing reference to a text by Paulhan, *De la Paille et du grain [Some Wheat and Some Chaff]*. This text is evoked in the course of Derrida's commentary on de Man's article, "Sur les possibilités de la critique" (On the Possibilities of Criticism),[4] in which de Man discusses the notion of literature as a politically or morally independent domain, implicitly condemning the ideological agenda that is often present behind the appropriation of this "neutrality." Derrida remarks:

> The logic of this argument anticipates, up to a certain point, that of Jean Paulhan (whom de Man was rediscovering during the last years of his life, no doubt in reference to other themes, but it is still not insignificant). Writing after

the Liberation in *De la Paille et du grain,* this writer-resis-
tant disputed the right of his "friends" on the National
Committee of Writers to conduct, as writers, political tri-
als of other writers known to have collaborated with the
enemy. If there were grounds for such a trial, then it was
the province of other tribunals competent to judge political acts: there ought to be no literary "épuration" [purge],
no writers' tribunals to judge the politics or morals of other
writers *as writers.*[5]

Derrida does not elaborate any further on this allusion to Paulhan,
and one might see his reluctance to engage Paulhan's discourse as
being possibly strategic, since Derrida's name had been yoked together
with Paulhan's, and his own work implicated in what critics such as
Jeffrey Mehlman have seen as a wholesale "politics of collaboration"
among proponents of deconstruction.[6] Much of Mehlman's argument,
however, relies on rather randomly juxtaposed moments, and suggests at the very least the need to look more closely at Paulhan's texts
from this period.

In very broad and general terms, the Second World War was a
period of extraordinary and unprecedented upheaval and change for
the entire literary world as much as it was for the rest of French life,
even though literary production continued almost unaffected, and
even invigorated, during the war.[7] Very few writers emerged from the
war unchanged by their wartime experiences, and it had a profound
effect on the direction French literature was to take. As Herbert
Lottman puts it:

At no other time in French history had a transformation
seemed as radical. A new generation literally emerged from
the shadows: young men, young women, whose only cre-
dentials for admission into the society of letters were their
records of courage and commitment. An older generation
largely compromised by enemy occupation slipped into
purgatory.[8]

This "purgatory" one might also term a purgation, since the younger
generation of writers emerged very much at the expense of the older
generation. Read in this light, Paulhan was one of the writers who was
least transformed by circumstances, since he steadfastly maintained

the same views before, during and after the war, and demonstrated a remarkable consistency throughout his works. Such intransigence has often been interpreted as an indifference to the historical and political reality of the time, as taking refuge in literature. Paulhan himself by no means discouraged this view of his relationship to politics in general, and the prominence of the term "indifference" as a key theoretical notion is often read as confirming this view of his involvement, or lack of it.

Paulhan was by no means, however, as innocent about the French political scene as many commentators would have us believe. He was elected to the post of *conseiller municipal* of Châtenay-Malabry in 1936, when Léon Blum's Popular Front coalition government came to power, even though Paulhan was not affiliated with any party in particular. The 1930s were a period of great political ferment in which the furiously competing ideologies of Communism and Fascism held powerful attractions for many intellectuals (right-wing "revolutions" were conceived by writers such as Robert Brasillach and Thierry Maulnier, who were inspired largely by Maurrassian royalism, while writers such as André Gide, André Malraux and Paul Nizan placed enormous faith and hope in Soviet Communism). Paulhan himself was reputedly a Maurrassian, but it is important to stress the eclecticism of his associations, which cut across political divisions. He was at once close to writers who were to become some of the most outspoken of collaborators, such as Marcel Jouhandeau,[9] while also counting among his friends most of the writers who figured on the list of "unpublishable" authors drawn up by the German ambassador, Otto Abetz, a list that was directed chiefly against Jews, Communists, those engaged in Resistance activity, and supporters of de Gaulle. Paulhan's non-partisan approach to politics went very much against the grain of the times, when intense political pressures dictated an almost irresistible choice for or against Russian Communism, the Republicans in Spain, and the Fascist governments in Germany and Italy.

In discussing Paulhan's presence on the literary scene in the years leading up to the war, one ought also not forget the position of unrivaled power and prestige he had earned for himself as the director of the *Nouvelle Revue Française* since taking over from Jacques Rivière in 1925. Paulhan was perhaps best known at the time as the highly influential editor and promoter of other authors, than as the author of *Les Fleurs de Tarbes,* despite the unquestionable interest aroused by the preparation and publication of this book. His policy as director of the review very much reflected his own heterogeneity of taste, and he refused to allow the *NRF* to become a victim of political or ideological pressures. His position on this is most clearly expressed in an editorial written on the eve of the war, entitled appropriately enough "Il ne faut pas compter sur nous" (Don't Count on Us).[10] In this text Paulhan stresses the need, in a democratic society, to protect an author's right to disagree with the political and moral precepts of the State. His conception of democracy was an odd, seemingly naïve mixture of Maurrassian royalism and utopian socialism. As he describes it in "La démocratie fait appel au premier venu" (Democracy is an Appeal to Anyone and Everyone),[11] the truly democratic society is the one which makes a prince of "the man in the street," Paulhan's famous "premier venu" (lit. "the first person to come along"):

> If one wants to make a bridge, a castle, or a newspaper, one is happy to find an architect, an engineer, a journalist. But to make a nation, one has first of all to turn to the man who is neither a journalist nor an architect. To the man in the street, who could as well be a construction worker, or a fruit and vegetable seller, or nothing at all. Democracy is an appeal not to aristocrats, and especially not to intellectual aristocrats, but to *the first person to come along*.[12]

How seriously can we take Paulhan's definition of democracy here? It appears to be the exact opposite of a theoretically informed political conception, since its "appeal" is to the lowest common denominator. This is precisely the point; Paulhan's strategy is determined by the need to hold on to this position of naïvety as a kind of gauge, or constant point of reference, against which democracy can measure itself. It differs, for example, from Benda's secular humanism in its insistence on the need to include a disinterested, indifferent perspective at the very heart of a theory of democracy, which itself is to be understood deliberately in the vaguest of terms.

Following the Occupation, the German forces were eager to allow literary activity in France to continue uninterrupted, while retaining the authority of censorship, so as to present to the international community an appearance of successful collaboration. Standard histories of the period, which glorify the many acts of courage by Resistance writers, have tended to draw attention away from the more sober reality of actual events, which were that the majority of Parisian publishers continued to publish, and the majority of writers continued to write, all the while in full knowledge of the circumstances which allowed them to publish.[13] Paulhan thought for a while that he might be able to keep the *NRF* open as an independent literary revue, but it soon became apparent that no such freedom from Nazi censorship was possible, and he relinquished control of the journal.[14] The review was closed for a short while, but the German occupiers were eager to reopen it, provided it was run by someone who would be from their point of view ideologically malleable. The task was offered to Pierre Drieu la Rochelle, a fervent believer in the New Europe exalted by Nazi propaganda, and he accepted it gleefully, hardly believing the opportunity he was being given to occupy the seat of literary influence left vacant by his predecessor. Paulhan fought unsuccessfully to prevent it from continuing under the same name. It is still unclear how much influence Paulhan in fact continued to wield while Drieu la Rochelle directed the *NRF* from 1940 to 1943, but it is certain that he shared none of Drieu's convictions.[15] Even while officially out of work, Paulhan commanded great respect, both from Drieu and from the German officer responsible for overseeing the censorship of literature in Paris, Gerhard Heller.[16]

At the same time as he was apparently continuing to work with Nazi occupying forces, and with outright collaborators, he was also, in 1941, founding the first Resistance journal, *Les Lettres Françaises,* with Daniel Decourdemanche (known by his pseudonym of Jacques Decour), and was allowing Vildé and Levitsky, the editors of the underground journal, *Résistance,* to mimeograph their paper in his apartment. He was a pivotal contact for the editors of the then clandestine *Editions de Minuit,* Pierre Lescure and Jean Bruller (the latter better known by his pseudonym of Vercors), and for *Messages,* a literary revue banned by the Nazis. He was arrested once by the Germans, who had been informed of the mimeograph machine in his apartment (he had in fact dismantled it earlier and disposed of it in the Seine), and he spent a week in solitary confinement.[17] Vildé and Levitsky, however, were both shot in February 1942. On another occasion, when the Germans came to search his apartment, he managed to escape across the roof of his building. It was his friendship with Heller and the respect he earned from Drieu la Rochelle which protected him from further suspicion and betrayal, despite being vilified in collaborationist journals such as *Je suis partout.*[18] So while being closely associated with collaborators, he was just as loyal to Resistance writers, and was indeed one of the founding members of the underground National Committee of Writers (Comité National des Ecrivains, or C.N.E.), along with François Mauriac, Jean Guéhenno, Edith Thomas, Albert Camus, Jean-Paul Sartre, Simone de Beauvoir, Elsa Triolet and Louis Aragon. As the principal organization of resistance writers during the Occupation, they were immediately recognized as the authoritative body of opinion once the question of the *épuration* came to the fore in 1945. They took upon themselves the responsibility of conducting an intellectual purge of French literature along lines similar to the general purge of collaborators in France after the war. Their concern was to clear away all remaining traces of collaborationist ideology from the literary world, to wipe the slate clean, as it were.[19]

Their first public act immediately following the Liberation was to address a request to General de Gaulle to take "vigorous judicial action" against collaborationist writers.[20] They then drew up their own blacklist of about 150 French writers, alongside whom they refused to be published.[21] It was the manner in which the C.N.E. pursued these writers that led Paulhan to resign from the organization, and finally to criticize in no uncertain terms their procedures and their goals. At first willing to go along with the decisions of the group, he refused to vote for the blacklist, and at no time was he in favor of such a list. Jean Paulhan was not alone in distancing himself from the C.N.E. in 1946; he was joined by writers such as François Mauriac and Georges Duhamel, who like him were also discouraged by the increasingly powerful hold the Communists exercised on the group. De Gaulle responded to the C.N.E.'s appeal, and the most prominent writers on the blacklist—Charles Maurras, Marcel Jouhandeau, Lucien Rebatet and Robert Brasillach, the latter two colleagues at *Je suis partout*—were tried early in 1945. Brasillach was sentenced to death and executed in February 1946, despite a petition sent to de Gaulle for a stay of execution, and signed by 59 prominent writers, among them Paulhan, Albert Camus and François Mauriac. This petition became the focal point of a highly charged public debate about sanctions to be imposed on writers who had collaborated during the Occupation. For those writers who had refused any form of compromise whatsoever, such as Claude Morgan (who took over from Jacques Decour at *Les Lettres Françaises)* and Jean Bruller (who founded the Editions de Minuit with his clandestine novel *Le Silence de la mer),* and for those who had lost close friends during the war, or who had themselves returned from prison camps, there was no question that an absolutely merciless condemnation was called for.

It is hardly surprising, then, that Paulhan's attitude should have angered many writers, particularly those with whom he had been closely associated during the Resistance. Paulhan attracted the scorn of writers like Claude Morgan, one of the members of the C.N.E. most strongly in favor of the purge. Looking through headlines of the national newspapers in 1947 and 1948, one gets a keener sense of the scale of the controversy. It was followed by the popular press for several months, as if it were a titanic sporting contest ("The Benda-Paulhan duel," *Lettres françaises,* October 1947) or a sensational trial ("Jean Paulhan accuses Aragon and Benda of Pre-Collaboration," *France-Dimanche,* July 1947).[22] The C.N.E. referred, for example, to "the frivolousness of his opinions" (la légèreté de ses propos),[23] and Julien Benda asked: "Is it bad faith on Paulhan's part? Or feeble-mindedness? Is he a jester entertaining himself? Does he have psychological problems?" (*Paille,* p. 361). Even the commentators most favorably inclined to his point of view—leaving aside the question of its opportunistic appropriation by what Peter Novick has called "*revanchiste* anti-Resistance circles and Vichy apologists"[24]—indulgently accepted his argument while still regarding it with some suspicion. This is particularly true of historians attempting to understand Paulhan's position. Pierre Assouline, who devotes large sections of his book *L'Epuration des intellectuels (The Purge of Intellectuals)* to the importance of Paulhan's part in the debate about the purges, reduces his argument to a plea for tolerance and for the writer's "right to error."[25] Assouline defines the writer's responsibility as a constant awareness of the ideological context and subtext of his or her work, so that even while claiming to understand Paulhan's defense of collaborationist writers, he implicitly condemns Paulhan for refusing to acknowledge his political responsibility:

> What motivates Paulhan in his attitude, which is from the outset singularly decisive, is above all, it seems, a certain understanding of literature. The rest (a writer's duty, political commitment . . .) is just an epiphenomenon. If he maintains a critical mind with respect to people, and especially their works, he is quite prepared to grant extenuating circumstances to those who are guilty.[26]

How can one reconcile this view of Paulhan with the Paulhan of the Occupation and Resistance? While not wishing in any way to condone or justify his position, I would like to look beyond the heat of the polemic, and do what commentators have failed to do with astonishing consistency: that is to *read* what Paulhan actually wrote. His contemporaries were unable to take what he said seriously, and dismissed his texts as frivolous, and lacking the gravity, or the solemnity, which the occasion called for. Yet Paulhan claims he is being very serious, and our task will be, if not to separate out, at least to identify the serious and the playful in his texts. Whether one condemns Paulhan by focusing on his refusal to take his political responsibilities seriously, or whether one praises him for the ethical strength of his non-partisan stance, in both cases Paulhan's texts are reduced to a single argument, a determinate position which generates the fierce opposition we have seen. Since the political positions that made up the ideological spectrum were so clearly defined and deeply entrenched, it is hardly surprising that this failure to read Paulhan should have occurred so consistently. Moreover, the voice that commanded the greatest attention immediately after the war, that of Jean-Paul Sartre, spoke with irresistible eloquence and conviction about the need for ethical and political commitment by writers. The literary activity centered around Sartre's *Les Temps modernes*—which put the C.N.E.'s purge into effect by refusing to publish any of their blacklisted authors—lent weight to the general feeling that a postwar generation of writers was about to lead French literature into an optimistic new era, one which would have as its preliminary task to cleanse France's literary past of its moral turpitude. While Paulhan in fact played a decisive role in the revival of French letters, the compromised status of the *Nouvelle Revue Française*—which was not to reappear again until 1953—inevitably led many people to associate Paulhan with France's ignominious past, rather than with its revitalized future. The irony of seeing the war as a radical historical break could not have been lost on Paulhan, for whom the French Revolution represented a major paradigm of ambitious reinvention.

The question of the relationship between literature and political commitment was broached in the previous chapter, as it was the crucial question of the 1940s in France. The exchange between Sartre and Blanchot, revolving around the question "What is literature?" brought the debate into sharper focus. Even though this question took an apparently irreducible form, I argued that it was nonetheless radically divided between Sartre's rhetorical reading of it—he for one was sure he knew what literature was or ought to be—and Blanchot's literal reading, in which literature begins with its own self-interrogation. This rift in what appeared to be an irreducibly fundamental question points to precisely the kind of radical ambiguity which Paulhan never allows to settle, and which is at the heart of all of his texts. Whether it is the metalepses of the *récits,* or the indifferent relationship of poetry as analyzed in *Clef de la poésie,* or the interplay between Terror and Rhetoric in *Les Fleurs de Tarbes,* this doubleness is a constant and fundamental concern of Paulhan's writings. For anyone familiar with these texts, the coexistence of two Paulhans—the courageous Resistance writer and the outspoken defender of collaborators—will not be at all surprising. Rather than revealing a duplicitous inconsistency between the commitment during the Resistance and the equally tenacious support of the "enemies" of the Resistance, the affirmation of this doubleness is in fact a deep-seated and rigorously consistent position. Only by taking into account the theoretical rigor of this duplicity is it possible to understand how Paulhan articulates the conjunction between literary and historical, or political concerns.

In *De la Paille et du grain,* Paulhan frames his argument by considering the question of patriotism in a larger perspective. He takes the examples both of Rimbaud's relationship to France during the Franco-Prussian war in 1870–71, and that of Romain Rolland in 1914 on the eve of the First World War, and points out that these two writers would have been considered traitors in the context of the Second World War. Paulhan reminds Louis Aragon—who condemned Paulhan's choice of Rimbaud as a French writer who was no less "anti-French" than certain collaborators—that he had himself in 1934 written about Rimbaud's antipatriotic, defeatist attitude. Paulhan's tactical ploy is to force the discussion towards the question of patriotism, a ploy which on the face of it seems a very reactionary move, opening the way as it does for collaborators to argue that they were acting in the best interest of "France." The charges brought against the collaborators by the C.N.E. center on their betrayal of France. As Paulhan puts it:

> The one thing you hold against the writers on your blacklist is neither greed nor error, neither meanness nor a penchant for degradation, it is "the irreparable crime, the irreversible wrong, perpetrated against the nation."[27]

The crucial question, asked explicitly by Paulhan, is: "What is patriotism?"[28] For Paulhan it is essential to distinguish between being a partisan and being a patriot. True patriotism would transcend partisan differences, and according to this definition, the members of the C.N.E. would not qualify as patriots. As Paulhan points out to Julien Benda (one of the writers most critical of Paulhan):

> With what, then, Benda, do you reproach these collaborators, whose execution you are demanding? Is it that they betrayed their country? No, if you were prepared yourself to betray it. It is because they admired a régime which disgusts you. It's because they belonged to a party which is not yours. You are not a patriot, and if you happen, in a given situation, to find the *patrie* on your side, you can loyally say that it's not your fault. You are a partisan, which is a completely different thing.[29]

Paulhan felt that the retribution they called for was less an appeal for justice than a cry of vengeance, and that similar calls for vengeance had already given rise to a large number of summary executions immediately following the Liberation.[30]

What, then, is Paulhan's definition of patriotism? Paulhan divides the "patrie" into two inseparable components; "la France charnelle" (the land itself) and "la France spirituelle" (which he also calls "the cause of France" [*Paille*, p. 349]). Paulhan continues: "Now patriotism consists in no more separating this material France from this spiritual France than one would separate a man's face from his profile."[31] What saved France, according to Paulhan, was that it was fortunate enough to have had Pétain to preserve the sentimental or physical half of France, and de Gaulle to preserve the rational or spiritual half. From a strictly literal point of view, the Pétain government was legally elected to represent France in 1940, while de Gaulle's establishment of an expatriate Free France was a usurpation of power.[32] While under alternative circumstances the French would probably not have dreamed of electing Pétain, according to Paulhan it is a partisan and not a patriot who would claim that de Gaulle alone "represented" France. Moreover, if de Gaulle represented the spiritual "essence" of France, it was an essence that had migrated abroad. This critical empirical moment in French history (the history of "France") was for Paulhan no less indicative of a *linguistic* crisis. If language is inseparably composed of a physical and a spiritual half, what happens when the spirit, the essence of language, wanders off and becomes estranged from its physical half? What if, Paulhan wonders, the essence is always to some extent contaminated by the accidental (Pétain causing France to deviate from its "true" course)?

The main thrust of Paulhan's argument is that the C.N.E. had no right to judge on the basis of the patriotic loyalty of writers, since the committee was an interested party, and had a very strong partisan view of the question. As Paulhan says in *Lettre aux directeurs de la Résistance,* one would not think of forming a jury of thieves, or of victims of thieves, to judge a thief, or of technicians to judge a technician, so why form a jury of people with a vested interest in the question of collaboration to judge collaborators? He writes:

> As long as it is a question of somewhat extraordinary acts, such as making a watch, or drawing up a marriage contract, or building a courthouse, only one person can do it: the architect, the lawyer, the watchmaker. Yes, but as soon as it is a question of simply telling the time, or of being in love, or of dispensing the justice which goes on (or ought to go on) within the courthouse, well then we are all capable of it. And sometimes—in love, for example—the person who knows the least succeeds even better than the professional.[33]

Paulhan states quite simply that the actual meting out of justice should, in a democratic society, be the work of an independent jury, randomly selected from the general public. This conception of democracy, in which the common man, "le premier venu," "the man who has nothing to do with it" (l'homme qui n'a rien à y voir) (*Lettre,* p. 441), is both the lowest common denominator and the highest ideal to which it should aspire, and as such is consonant, as we have seen, with the view expressed in "La démocratie fait appel au premier venu." From 1938 ("La démocratie fait appel aux premiers venus") to 1953 (*Lettre aux directeurs de la Résistance*) Paulhan is absolutely consistent on this point. It also corresponds to his theory of linguistic doubleness studied in the previous chapters, and his writings on the question of the *épuration* can thus be read as an attempt to articulate linguistic with political considerations. As Thomas Ferenczi puts it: "Jean Paulhan's attitude with respect to language commands both his theoretical reflection on political discourse, and his political appreciation of events." [34] Only when we consider that, for Paulhan, the enigmatic doubleness of language is matched by an identical doubleness informing patriotism, can we truly begin to read these texts. Paulhan formulates this doubleness in *De la Paille et du grain* as a kind of radical *indifference*:

> Here I come to my point: as long as they have not decreed that there are opinions that are guilty, and worthy of death, the pacifists of 1914 have no right to display such aggression toward the pacifists of 1940. Nor those who were shot to death in 1915 (if I may say so) to look down on those who were shot in 1945. From the simple point of view of the *patrie* they are equivalent: it's six of one and half a dozen of the other ["c'est blanc bonnet et bonnet blanc," lit. "It's white bonnet and bonnet white"].[35]

This clarification condenses a range of important considerations, which will deepen an understanding of the two texts of Paulhan I have been looking at rather paraphrastically, in particular *De la Paille et du grain*. In fact it could be said to constitute the major turning point of a reading of this latter text, a pivotal moment which will either lead us further into the text, or back out of it to "history." As a rather neat summary of Paulhan's various sets of parallels, the phrase "c'est blanc bonnet et bonnet blanc" is precisely the kind of reversal that we have seen to be so typical of Paulhan's texts. Its exemplary status is all the more striking in that it is formulated as a cliché. We know that for Paulhan, there is far more to clichés than first meets the eye. The tension inherent in commonplace or proverbial expressions was described in the first chapter as a doubleness or a radical division that pitted their semantics against their syntax.

Indeed, it is precisely this vacillation which informs the way in which this particular saying in *De la Paille et du grain* is read; the semantic or referential reading of the cliché—from the point of view of patriotism it's all the same, it doesn't matter whether one is a Fascist or a Communist—leads directly to the extratextual, empirical context, and to a politically overdetermined condemnation (or praise) of Paulhan; a purely syntactical reading—the inversion of noun and adjective makes no difference to the meaning—would not be much more help, since it would seem to advocate the priority of language over

experience, or the indifference of literature to politics. Only by reading them as being equally valid can one begin to discover the resonances within the text. In other words, the semantic reading is only
valid *if* one reads it simultaneously with the syntactical reading, just
as the syntactical reading is only valid when read in conjunction with
the semantic one. Paulhan's text only really begins to come into focus
if the explicit political discussion is read as a version of the fundamental indifference informing the linguistic analysis, both in this text
and everywhere else in Paulhan. The inverse is equally the case. The
argument of political indifference only makes sense when read in terms
of linguistic indifference, just as the syntax of the commonplace expression (read as the trope of hyperbaton, or the inversion of the normal order of words[36]) only makes sense if it is given referential determination. Once given its full theoretical weight, this structural
ambivalence points to a deeper coherence in the apparently disparate
components of *De la Paille et du grain.*

For example, the theme of "whiteness" pervades the text. The
épuration is literally a cleansing of past crimes, and the French verbs
"blanchir" (to whiten, or whitewash) and "laver" (to clean) both have
these connotations. The members of the C.N.E. themselves were very
certain of their position on the moral spectrum, and indeed their ability to discriminate depended upon the establishment of just such a
spectrum. For Paulhan, however, the ethical "colors" are by no means
allotted once and for all. One might speculate, in this light, what it
would mean to speak of someone's "true colors." As a way of illus-
trating his argument, Paulhan borrows what were the standard political clichés of the history of France beginning in the early '30s and
going through to the post-war period. There are two parties, the Reds
and the Whites, who would have been clearly recognized as Communists (and, by association, the Revolutionaries of 1789 with their
"red caps") and, if not Fascists, then at least Capitalists ("these people who stuffed our heads full of their *patrie*! A *patrie* made up of
their small stocks, their portfolios, and their trust funds"). Paulhan's
argument about reversibility thus has its perfect political demonstration. The Communists, who before the war had sided with Hitler,
and supported the Hitler-Stalin pact, were now desperate after the
war to regain the moral high ground, and proclaim themselves "true"
patriots. "These Whites betrayed the *Patrie*! You were ready to betray
it yourself, if need be. Just admit the truth. You are executing them because they are white." [37]

A similar reversible movement is at work in the *Lettre aux directeurs de la Résistance (Letter to the Directors of the Resistance).* The possibility of a dual interpretation of Article 75 of the Penal Code is phrased as the difference between a literal and a figurative reading, that is, between following the law to the letter, and acting within the "spirit" of the law:

> It is only too true that the gap separating Law from Justice is almost the same as that separating the letter from the spirit: the letter, always ready to encroach upon the spirit, to restrict it and to diminish it—always ready to become a dead letter. But the spirit is alive and free, escaping the traps of automatism, born anew at every moment.[38]

Thus one can pass from the linguistic model (the division of a word into *letter* and *spirit*) to its "real life" application (Law and Justice), and back again, just as the two components of each pair continually vacillate back and forth. The necessity of accounting for the codified aspect of the law is in fact explicitly stated in terms of the grammar of a language: "There is a kind of grammar of ideas at work here, which is no less prompt or decisive than our grammar of words (that spontaneous grammar which rubs us up the wrong way, or which makes us burst out laughing when we see a badly constructed sentence, or a mispronounced word)." [39]

The central metaphor of *De la Paille et du grain* is of course the one that gives the text its title, the separating of the wheat from the chaff.[40] The C.N.E. would claim that the *épuration* was intended as precisely this kind of an operation, as an expulsion of what was no longer wanted, of what was responsible for the degeneration of France. This works on the level of language and literature insofar as it implies that there is a part of language that is dispensable, and a part that is essential. Just as in Paulhan's descriptions from *Les Fleurs de Tarbes,* it is initially terror (or the priority of thoughts over words) that is aligned with authenticity and essence, and rhetoric (or the priority of figures over thoughts) that is deemed inauthentic and inessential. The complicity of rhetoric and aesthetics is clearly marked, according to the stern moralism of the "purgers," since both are considered frivolous pursuits by comparison with the seriousness of their own task. The title *De la Paille et du grain (Of the Wheat and of the Chaff,* but also *Some Wheat and Some Chaff)* could indicate that the text is concerned with precisely this question of separating out the essential from the dispensable, but the *de la* and the *du* could also be read as partitives, which in fact dovetails even better with Paulhan's argument; language is always necessarily made up of *some* wheat and *some* chaff, of *some* rhetoric and *some* terror. And just as a true patriot is incapable of separating out the "physical" from the "spiritual" country, so the reader is incapable of deciding whether the literal or the figurative reading is what can be dispensed with. One might appeal to the determining instance of a context, but one can never tell whether the context determines, or is determined by, the linguistic dilemma. It is impossible to tell the difference: once again, it is "blanc bonnet" and "bonnet blanc." Yet one cannot overlook the fact that the indifference of "blanc bonnet/bonnet blanc," and all the other reversible pairs of terms that are in play in these two texts, are indeed different. How can one account for this difference within indifference? The answer may be found in the most consistently overlooked of all of the linguistic allegories of this text, the opening sections of *De la Paille et du grain.*

Their sub-titles may explain the neglect which has been the lot of these two introductory sections: "Un Secret de polichinelle, ou La littérature comme fête publique" (An Open Secret, or Litterature as a Public Celebration) and "Des Amateurs de bridge aux policiers bénévoles" (From Lovers of Bridge to Volunteer Policemen). The obviously playful tone and theme of these pages is in striking contrast to the main body of the text. Yet these sections are absolutely crucial to the argument of the rest of the text. The beginning is almost always overlooked as being marginal to the "central" argument (simply frivolous examples), as *chaff* to the *wheat* of the main text. Read in the light of Paulhan's other texts, this introduction is anything but a petulant display of impatience with the rather ponderous attitude of the *C.N.E.*

The innately joyous quality of literature and language is the apparent theme of the opening section of *De la Paille et du grain.* It begins: "What a pleasure to read, in the closing pages of Eugène Marsin: 'This horse has two *joquets* [= jockeys].' *Joquet,* like *croquet,* and like *jacquet,* is a nice little French word." [41] Words that began as foreign words, such as *joquet,* are particularly pleasing, since despite being imported, they respect the homogeneity of the French language, and Paulhan finds them as amusing as the slightly baroque words that emerge within the language itself. He admires the capacity of the language to thus welcome foreign words, but questions the acceptability of words that make little effort to integrate themselves into the language, such as *hapéfiou* ["happy few"] ("when they could say *la fine fleur,* like everyone else" [*Paille,* p. 315]). Like the potted history of the Reds and the Whites which comes later on, the narrative that begins the text recounts a fundamental shift in attitudes from the pre-war period to the post-war period, an attitude which symptomatically involves precisely the loss of an aesthetic enjoyment of the language.

The "fête publique" of language is then described as a fancy-dress party ("un bal masqué"), of which the golden rule is that foreign words have to be disguised in order to be admitted along with native participants such as "flâneur" (a person who likes to stroll), "tourte" (a kind of pie), "spatule" (spatula) and "ornithorynque" (duck-billed platypus). Thus *Sauerkraut* is playfully transformed into *choucroute,* where *chou* means *Kraut,* and *croute* is made to stand for *Sauer.* In the context of the decline of aesthetic enjoyment that seems to be a sign of the times, the question, according to Paulhan, is "knowing whether the French language is still capable of holding its own, and of putting on, as it pleases ["d'habiller à sa guise"] the exotic words its welcomes." [42]

The mystery of language and literature ("an open mystery" [un secret de polichinelle]) — and not the somber gravity of modern philosophy or science — is what, according to Paulhan, ought to determine our relationship to language. As Paulhan goes on to say:

> It can be summed up, if you prefer, in a single piece of advice: "Welcome your words as you would your thoughts." (To which I would want to add: treat foreign words as if they meant nothing.) And I'm not saying that this is a straightforward maxim. No. In fact if we look at it closely it's even absurd. It remains to be seen, looking at things—and literature in particular—from an honest point of view, whether we ought not to begin by tolerating a certain absurdity, welcoming it, making room for it. [43]

It seems that Paulhan is simply advocating a kind of linguistic chauvinism, and a kind of anti-intellectual patriotism that would be nationalistic in the worst possible sense, given the context in which it is written. If we look at his argument more closely, while it is unashamedly patriotic (and it now becomes clearer why the opening pages defiantly assert the necessity of a mystery of patriotism that is no less enigmatic than the mystery of language and literature), it is also a plea for the recognition of other nationalities or nationalisms, with their own linguistic structures and internal tensions which may or may not correspond to those of another language. The fact of differences between languages, and the strange effect that is created when they are brought into conflict with one another, is similar, Paulhan argues, to the difference within language itself. One need only translate a language other than one's own for this to become clear:

> And I know there's more than one man who, in his heart of hearts, believes that, through some mystery, words reveal the nature of things to us: the unfortunate thing is that it is an opinion which is likely to vanish fairly quickly—precisely when one learns a language other than one's own.[44]

What then becomes difficult to determine is whether there are linguistic differences between nations *because* there is a mysterious difference within all languages, or whether the reverse is true. To put it another way, it is impossible to decide whether translation is the cause or the effect of differences between languages.

The text addresses this question through two further allegories of translation. The first uses the recent refinements of the bidding system in the game of contract bridge to look at the advantages and disadvantages of a language (the "language" of bridge) that strives to become a perfect system of communication. The discussion is at the same time a critique of the ambitions of artificial international languages such as esperanto. While the tendency towards perfection of the bidding increases the efficiency of the game of contract bridge, it is in danger of becoming so automatic that one might as well play with one's cards on the table. Its desire for absolute refinement is its surest guarantee of failure, since it is still a *language,* and therefore always open to absolute misunderstanding: "You talk of nuances, of intimate thoughts, of delicate feelings, and he hears vowels and consonants, sentences, words. It is at the precise moment that your language seems to you to be perfect, that it appears detestable to the other person" (*Paille*, p. 327). The second allegory comes in a section appended to *De la Paille et du grain,* which is in part a eulogy of Garry Davis, an American pacifist who renounced all national allegiance, and spent several weeks on the steps of the United Nations building claiming he was ready to fight in a war, provided it was for a World State. This idea must clearly have caught Paulhan's imagination. Davis' great merit, according to Paulhan, was to force the United Nations to follow through the consequences of its desire for an International State. Garry Davis' action revealed the inherent absurdity of the United Nation's claim. The mistake of organizations such as the U.N., and of contract bridge specialists and esperantists, according to Paulhan, is to want a language that is unfailingly and universally comprehensible. Without the constitutive failure within language, of which Paulhan's texts offer us numerous examples, there could be no difference between languages, or even worse, no language whatsoever. Yet what do these allegories of translation between and within languages have to do with the *épuration?*

The kind of purge of French literature proposed by members of the C.N.E. is analogous to the desire for a perfect language. In fact the wish to cleanse the literary world of its "impurities," while practically amounting to a "fascist sentence" (*Paille,* p. 329), is exactly the kind of program that Paulhan had already identified twenty years earlier as terror. Paulhan again refers to the members of the C.N.E. as "white writers" ("écrivains blancs"), ironically contrasting their self-righteous moral purity with the blacklisted collaborationist writers, who had been "carefully blackened by you" ("noircis par vos soins"). Just as members of the U.N. would like to efface all differences between languages in the hope of establishing a kind of universal communication, so the C.N.E. would like to efface the writers whose political differences are taken as antipatriotic, and whose immoral acts have sullied the face of French literature.

On a purely empirical level, it would be hard to disagree with the C.N.E.'s point of view. No-one would argue about the immorality of the acts and deeds, for example, of Robert Brasillach, with their very real and tragic consequences. But if the manner in which this condemnation is carried out implies a wholesale rejection of "immoral" literature, then the political consequences may be damaging and far-reaching. As Paulhan argues, there have always been immoral writers in France ("We have always been proud, and not without reason, of Frenchmen who gave France something of a rough time" [p. 330]),[45] who have been guilty of far greater antipatriotism than the writers on the C.N.E.'s blacklist. The tolerance of antipatriots is, according to Paulhan, a sign of a healthy democracy, and a healthy *patrie* ("Anti-patriots are a *patrie*'s luxury" [p. 329]).[46] Just as there is no perfect language (in fact, it is constitutively imperfect), so there is no perfect *patrie*. The mystery of language (how can language continue to function in its essentially imperfect state?) is identical to the mystery of patriotism (how can a *patrie* be reinforced by the existence and tolerance of antipatriots?). It requires keeping this mystery in play, since its expulsion endangers the very existence both of language and of the "patrie." Paulhan is determined to safeguard the mystery of differences between languages (and nations) since this mystery is also a guarantee of the existence of the difference within languages (and nations). Yet how can one tell the difference between the mystery between languages and the mystery within languages? Is it the same difference (that is, is it indifferent)? Is it simply "blanc bonnet et bonnet blanc?" How can we read the difference within language (between *mot* and *idée*, syntax and semantics, *blanc bonnet* and *bonnet blanc*), when this difference makes no difference, when it exemplifies the mystery of the reversibility of *indifference?* Perhaps the only way to read it is as the very mark of difference itself. As we saw in our discussion of Paulhan's studies of Malagasy proverbs, it is precisely those untranslatable elements of the proverb that could be said to constitute a claim to national linguistic identity, the difference within language that marks the difference between languages.

The C.N.E.'s proposed purge was seen by Paulhan as having potentially very serious consequences, both for the *patrie,* and for literature itself. One can easily understand that Paulhan's vocabulary (indifference, duplicity, betrayal and mystery) could be misappropriated and judged offensive ethically and politically. In reading Paulhan's texts not just in terms of what they literally are saying, but also in terms of their rhetorical strategies, it becomes clearer that Paulhan does not claim that "mystery" or "duplicity" are located outside of political, ideological, or ethical considerations. Instead, he claims the "mystery" to be the safeguard of the continued existence of a *patrie,* and of literature:

> . . . provided one remains a little naïve, one never stops
> setting this mystery in motion and being surprised by it,
> or throwing words into the air, and seeing them trans-
> formed into ideas. And even quarter words, an accent, a
> simple letter.[47]

This by no means asserts the primacy of literature (the place where language can freely exercise its right to disturb and to unsettle) over ideology, since for Paulhan literature is just as ridden with ideology as is politics. The reception of Paulhan's texts has, ironically, been motivated by the very illusions about the nature of literature and ideology that they call into question. The most common assumption about these writings is that they are indifferent to the political and ethical questions of the moment. A careful reading of these essays, and a reading that first and foremost places them in the context of Paulhan's sustained and rigorous analysis of the articulation between literature and ideology, makes such claims seem at the very least short-sighted. According to Paulhan, the C.N.E.'s call for a literary *épuration* was characteristic of such short-sightedness, and represented the immense danger of falling back into the very political errors they claimed to be opposing.

To return to the original context of this chapter, it is ironic that "deconstruction" seems to have undergone something of a similar purge, based on the erroneous view that it "forgets" history. We could do well, when reflecting on the ethical and ideological imperatives of contemporary literary theory, to heed the warnings of *De la Paille et du grain,* which alert us at the very least to the necessity of careful reading. While readable at one level as a banal insistence on the necessity of learning the lessons of history, at another level Paulhan's text subtly articulates the ideological mechanisms which lead to a constant repetition of historical errors. It also suggests a highly original understanding of the movement of history itself, which is posited, not as a dialectical resolution of conflict or ambivalence, but as a radicalizing of this ambivalence (or indifference), which Paulhan makes into the very condition of possibility of difference.

Domestic Spaces, Aesthetic Traces

> [*Art critics*] *fall silent . . . in order to make us understand that painters also—painters before anyone else—have given up beginning, detailing, situating, that they throw us into a space rather than showing it to us, participate instead of describing, and so critics in their own way fall silent. . . . In short, there appears to have been, between painters and critics, a somewhat clumsy contagion of this silence.*
>
> *But the ways of writing are not those of the arts, and I don't entirely regret having tried to break this silence.*[1]
>
> Jean Paulhan, *La Peinture cubiste*

Cubes, Cubes, and More Cubes

One of the most surprising friendships of occupied Paris was the one between Jean Paulhan and Gerhard Heller, the German officer responsible for overseeing French literary production, and its censorship, during the Second World War. Heller later published the memoirs of his years in Paris, *Un Allemand à Paris, 1940–1944.* His account depicts the author as a "protector" of French literary culture, a reluctant Nazi sympathetic to the aspirations of French writers, who intervened personally on many occasions to allow authors to be published who ought to have been on Otto Abetz's blacklist (such as Elsa Triolet), and to prevent writers being arrested (among them Paulhan). Paulhan figures prominently in his memoirs, being the subject of an entire chapter entitled "Paulhan My Master" (Mon maître Paulhan), and an important presence in the following chapter, "The Discovery of Modern Art" (La Découverte de l'art moderne), which focuses on Heller's introduction to the world of Cubist art. Heller describes, for example, his first visit with Paulhan to Picasso's apartment, and his ensuing education in Cubist aesthetics by Paulhan. The "lessons" Paulhan gave to Heller were in fact early drafts of what were to become *Braque le patron [Braque the Boss],* first published in the journal *Poésie 43,* in 1943, and *Fautrier l'enragé,* a text written originally for the catalogue of an exhibition of Fautrier's paintings.[2]

This anecdotal beginning to the chapter serves to emphasize, on the level of literary and art history, just how closely Paulhan was involved with the artists of his generation. He was in fact one of the most vocal champions of modern art in all its forms, and in particular of Cubism. He was often called upon to write the catalogue for exhibitions, and his articles would regularly appear in the art sections of national newspapers. He was very much what the French call "l'ami des peintres" (the artists' friend), and counted among his close acquaintances Georges Braque, Pablo Picasso, Juan Gris, Jean Dubuffet, and Jean Fautrier.

At a less flattering level, it serves to highlight a common perception of Paulhan, namely that his interest in art and aesthetics *during the Occupation,* was further confirmation of his willful ignorance of the historical and political circumstances of the time, to such an extent that he engaged in a kind of aesthetic collaboration with an important German in Nazi-occupied Paris. How could he allow himself the luxury of being "distracted" by such frivolous pursuits, when more serious and pressing matters should have absorbed his attention? The accusation parallels the claim, as we saw in the previous chapter, that Paulhan's preoccupation with literature was a way of avoiding political commitment, a problem which has its very precise and concise paradigm in the two opposing conceptions of literature and language, rhetoric and terror. Indeed, it is no coincidence that Paulhan's writings on rhetoric, and his writings on Art, begin to appear around the same time (during the Occupation), and in relation to very parallel concerns.[3] Paulhan's essays on Cubist art, and modern art in general, are in fact inextricably linked to his other writings in ways that may not seem clear at first. For while these essays thematize, and dramatize in a manner very typical of Paulhan, the relationship between writing and painting (or rather, in more theoretical terms, between rhetoric and aesthetics), in so doing they seem to suggest to Paulhan a new angle on the questions already explored in his other texts.

In *Les Fleurs de Tarbes,* Paulhan talked of terror's suspicion of rhetoric's "beauty machine" (machine à beauté), in which aesthetic considerations were regarded as inessential, superfluous, in the same way that "flowers of rhetoric" were seen as the dispensable parts of language, when compared to the more serious and indispensable literal meanings. The questions about the status of literature raised in *Les Fleurs de Tarbes* might be posed in terms of aesthetics: what do we *see* when we are confronted with a given sentence: just words, or thoughts? Any reduction of language's irreducible duplicity is based on an immediacy of perception, which a second look—and the beginnings of a reading—would undermine. The undecidability would then be, at one further remove, whether or not we can think of literature as a primarily aesthetic experience.

Rhetoric and aesthetics are thus part of a single problematic for Paulhan, in that he is trying to understand the relationship between the two. A reader previously unacquainted with Paulhan's art essays could be forgiven, however, for wondering about their purpose. How can their tone of discovery and celebration be justified a full thirty or forty years after Picasso and Braque first burst upon the art world, and long after Picasso had returned to a more representational mode of painting? Indeed, at first glance, Paulhan adds little to a general understanding of Cubism, and his essays (such as *La Peinture cubiste* and *Braque le patron*) seem to be straightforward narratives of the early history of Cubism. Even the polemical tone—the insistent defense of Cubism against an imagined skeptical public—appears quite out of place taken out of the context of the urgency of Cubism's first few years. Moreover, as commentators have shown, Paulhan's factual information is not always accurate, since he has a tendency to confuse Cubism with *all* modern art, or to group together several distinct modern artistic movements in a single argument.

But just how original is Paulhan's attempt to bring together literary concerns with a Cubist aesthetic? Paulhan was by no means the first writer to link the two artistic domains (in fact, he again appears to be about thirty years late in doing so). Writers, art critics and poets championed the movement from the moment Braque and Picasso took the Parisian art world by storm in 1907 and 1908 with their first pieces of Cubist art. Apollinaire, André Salmon, Max Jacob, and Pierre Reverdy, for example, were close friends of the Cubist artists, and they formed a close-knit community whose influences on one another were apparent in the new literary and artistic forms that were generated. Apollinaire's writings on the Cubist painters of the circle were collected in a volume entitled *Les Peintres cubistes* [*The Cubist Painters*] which, as well as introducing many of these artists to the public, also contained Apollinaire's analysis of the phenomenon of Cubism (the original title of the book, which became its subtitle, was *Méditations esthétiques* [*Aesthetic Meditations*]). Apollinaire's subsequent innovative poetic style owed a great deal to the aesthetics of cubism; the emphasis on the everyday, the break with long-established formal conventions, the random juxtaposition of incongruous elements, and the temporal and spatial discontinuities of the poems' narratives. His emphasis on the visual in his poetry, while not in itself particularly original (in fact, in "Zone" [*Alcools,* 1913] he openly proclaims his debt to Christian, iconographic imagery), ushered in radical new ways of conceiving of the relationship between text and image in modern poetry. It culminated in the writing, between 1913 and 1916, of his *Calligrammes,* which he described as "lyrical ideograms." These were poems arranged typographically so as to produce a picture of the object which the poem is "about." Subtle and witty plays on words allowed for a diversity and instability of interpretation, but the most important achievement of these poems (and the richest effect of the interpenetration between poetry and cubist painting) was to foreground the visual, sensorial qualities of poetic language.

Apollinaire might be called the first of a generation of Cubist poets, and even though Reverdy, for one, refused to accept this label, the latter's journal *Nord-Sud* became one of the chief vehicles for the promotion of a Cubist aesthetic. In his own poetry, Reverdy stressed the autonomy of the poetic object, in the same way that the Cubist works of Braque and Picasso foregrounded their own materiality as paintings. Max Jacob, in the famous preface to his collection of poems *Le Cornet à dés* (*The Dice Cup,* 1917), also talks of the poem as a *constructed* object, and his poems attempt to depict within a single poetic moment events that would normally be separated in space and time. An important moment for Cubist art was the invention of *papiers collés,* the incorporation of ready-made images and printed text into collages. As Christine Poggi writes:

> Writing entered the field of Cubist painting as part of a means of drawing attention to the conventional and arbitrary character of pictorial codes. Splintered and loosened from a verbal context, the words and letters in Cubist paintings and collages exemplify the same multivalences as the fragmentary pictorial forms, and in the variety of their typography take on a visual character in their own right.[4]

The possibilities this opened up for a radically new conception of the interplay between literature and painting was quickly taken up and pursued by the Italian futurists, particularly Marinetti, who devised a new poetic form known as *parole in libertà.* In these, the dislocation and compression of conventional linguistic forms was a way of charging words and images with a new kind of energy.

So what do Paulhan's texts—curiously out of place and time— have to add to this dialogue between literature and art? On the face of it, very little, since they have none of the formal innovativeness or the exhilarating energy of the poems of, for example, Apollinaire or Marinetti. What is it then about Cubism and Modern Art that held such a continuing fascination for Paulhan? Why only begin to write on Cubist art in the 1940s, a good thirty years after all of the fuss had died down? I would like to suggest that Paulhan's essays are best read not simply in terms of their statements *about* art, but as dramatizations, or even artistic performances, which engage in the very aesthetic experiences they set out to describe. I would like to take two examples of this—from *La Peinture cubiste* and from *Fautrier l'enragé*—to show how the interlocking discourses of rhetoric and aesthetics push Paulhan's thinking and writing in a new direction, one that will significantly inform his subsequent writings.

As one might expect, it is the momentous and radical departure from traditional artistic conventions and practices which for Paulhan is perhaps the strongest appeal of Cubist art. The analogy with the literary revolution that produced the shift from Classicism to Romanticism at the beginning of the 19th century is not lost on Paulhan, and he makes the comparison explicit early on in *La Peinture cubiste* when he says: "People like to symbolize revolutions by the assault on some palace. Modern painting, too, breaks free from stage scenery, architecture and perspective, and storms its own Bastille a good century later on." [5]

Paulhan's account of the origins of Cubism are, for the most part, fairly routine and unexceptional in terms of art history, although they are narrated with his usual playfulness. He seizes on the opportunity to point out the humor of the term "cubism" itself: while it is a term that was quickly adopted (if somewhat ironically by the artists themselves), evoking as it does the geometric appearance of much early Cubist art, it also suggests the very framing of the world which one finds in classical treatises on perspective in art, and which the Cubists so strongly rejected: ". . . the rough sketches and the studies they present to young painters resemble the cages of a menagerie, which enclose not tigers and panthers, but cubes seen close up and far away, from the front and from the side, cubes and more cubes." [6] Rather than Cubism, then, it is "academic art" (la peinture académique) which is "cubist" in the usual, restricted sense. By jolting us out of a conventional understanding of the term early on in his essay, Paulhan signals to the reader that this is not just one more dreary historical survey of Cubism, but that something about the artistic significance of Cubism itself for him goes beyond an interest in its formal innovations. As Paulhan says, Cubism involves an aesthetic experience which ultimately undoes the fundamental principles of a classical definition of aesthetics itself:

> By what name should we call a concern—a revelation—
> which deals not with the beauty (the ugliness, or character)
> of a house, a crate, or a flower, nor even with the details
> of the petals, the wood, the stones which they are made
> of, and other natural elements—no, but which goes be-
> yond them (or, if you prefer, transcends them)? [7]

This transcendence is, however, firmly anchored in the concrete world of things themselves. Indeed, this ritual destruction of the past ("Throw the niceties and fine nuances, the flowers and iridescences onto the fire!" [8]) is seen by Paulhan as an experience akin to Roquentin's in Sartre's *La Nausée*: "It's like an initiation. It's like a conversion. It seems as if [you] touch, if only for a split second, the rock bottom of things, beyond appearances, ideas, illusions." [9]

The experience is described in various ways, which bear witness to Paulhan's firm sense of the sea change twentieth century philosophy was undergoing, as a kind of rediscovery of the immediacy of the world ("It would seem, then, that with modern paintings the sense of touch takes precedence over the sense of sight, tactile space over visual space").[10] This is referred to a little later on in explicitly phenomenological terms:

> From Bergson to Husserl, from Alexander to Heidegger, a new form of realism has as its task to take us back to things themselves, untouched by interpretation, and refuses to consider the slightest reflection, the most fleeting perception, without taking into account our presence in the world [. . .] it [. . .] emphasizes the pre–given, the un–reflective, in short *that* which exists before we become aware of it—and one would also have to say that the cubist space precedes any thoughts which we might formulate about it.[11]

It is not surprising that the claim of Cubist painting to enter into a more physical and immediate relationship with the world should find a number of philosophical correlatives, from Heidegger's return to a pre-Classical or pre-Hellenic philosophy, to Husserl's return to "things themselves." If this renewed contact with the world is achieved through a celebration of, and participation in, the activity of creation itself, it is at the same time coextensive with its disintegration ("The whole universe is breaking apart" [12]), and in the latter half of his essay Paulhan discusses the various Cubist techniques which demonstrate this disintegration, such as fragmentation, the use of multiple perspective, "papiers collés" and collage.

About halfway through the essay, Paulhan more fully articulates the association between Cubism and terror (Cubism being to art what terror is to literature), and the link with the literary and linguistic resonances of the terrorist revolution. At this point Paulhan elaborates the other half of his equation. Although painting is an essentially visual medium, it is no less saturated with conventions and codes than language and literature are:

> Painters talk space, as an Englishman talks English, or a Chinaman Chinese. It is a language which has its words

and its familiar expressions, its lines and its combinations of lines, its colors and its juxtapositions of colors; which even has its clichés: the circle, the sphere, the section in gold; its onomatopeias in trompe-l'oeil; which has its grammar, and even, as we have seen, its rhetoric, its rules, and its unities—and, as with the other rhetoric, these rules can suddenly seem artificial and purely conventional.[13]

The rhetoric of painting is detailed in order to foreground all the more forcefully painting's terror, the Cubist revolution. In Paulhan's analysis, figurative language is devalorized to the same extent as Classical art, since both are revealed as unimaginative and habit-ridden: "So words become inert from over-use, and lose the sharpness of their meaning. Usage degrades, as does repetition." [14] The task of Cubist painting is thus likened to that of giving fresh life to worn-out commonplaces, of resuscitating dead metaphors. This seems to conform to the trajectory of many of Paulhan's writings, and one might expect a subsequent twist, in which terror and rhetoric exchange positions, with Cubism's claims to originality, immediacy, realism, and so forth, being exposed, as they ultimately are as subject to convention as traditional art is. What is uncommon, and difficult to reconcile with texts such as *Les Fleurs de Tarbes,* is that the writings on Cubist painting appear to contain no moment of reversal. Rhetoric— or the commonplaces of Classical art —is condemned outright, while Paulhan's enthusiasm for Cubist art seems categorical. Are we dealing with an uncritical espousal of modernity (terror) in art, or does the aesthetic experience specific to Cubism allow us somehow to move beyond the play of reversals that is typical of Paulhan's texts?

As an essay that seems to go against the grain of Paulhan's other writings, *La Peinture cubiste* (and Paulhan's praise of modern art in general) may surprisingly offer the most appropriate allegory of Paulhan's *oeuvre* as a whole. The construction of Paulhan's texts—especially in the endless working and reworking of a book such as *Les Fleurs de Tarbes*—owes more to a "papiers collés" technique than to any teleological or architechtonic principle, with Paulhan always recycling his own material just as the Cubists used ready-made material in the construction of their collages and "papiers collés." [15] *La Peinture cubiste* provides a number of descriptions which could equally be applied to the mobility of Paulhan's texts, and the sheer diversity of their subject matter, as for example when he refers to Cubism as "the assembly of heterogeneous elements." [16] The Cubist disruption of the conventional techniques for rendering perspective, particularly in the deliberate confusion of background and foreground, could also be seen as analogous to Paulhan's compositional style, and the constantly shifting ground of his texts. Paulhan uses the example of the change of perspective produced by the technique of anamorphosis—here the optical illusion created by a simple bird's-eye view of a drawing of a pyramid—to underline this incessant play of proximity and distance: "it is easy to see the pyramid animated by a back-and-forth movement, now coming so close as to almost touch your eye, but now receding quickly into the distance." [17] In *Traité des figures* the same movement is defined in explicitly rhetorical terms. This book continually moves back and forth between figures of language and figures of thought, or between worn-out metaphors whose "edge has been dulled, and whose liveliness has been deadened," and metaphors whose "force is intensified." [18] And in *Les Fleurs de Tarbes*, similarly, "a metaphor keeps on appearing and disappearing; it never stops." [19] The phenomenality of this incessant motion is underlined later on in the essay when the equivocality of rhetoric is said to "make language vacillate before our eyes." [20] *La Peinture cubiste* might be said to give, therefore, an aestheticized version, or an allegory, of the fragmentation, heterogeneity and constant mobility of Paulhan's texts. This allegory relies on the primacy of the visible or sensible, to the detriment or even exclusion of the invisible or intelligible; it implies that the instability and disruptive potential of language can in the last instance be phenomenalized, in the strongest sense of the term. If the illusion of the pyramid is a visual realization of this instability, as a geometric figure it seems insufficient evidence to carry the burden of proof of the demonstration. We will need to look elsewhere in *La Peinture cubiste* for a fuller exposition of this analogy, and the place where Paulhan's claims are put to their own test.

The third chapter of *La Peinture cubiste* gives us just such an allegory. It is the story of a "little adventure in the middle of the night"; appropriately enough, Paulhan later extracted it from this context and pasted it into several other contexts.[21] It performs a similar function to the story of the garden of Tarbes in *Les Fleurs de Tarbes* in that it is a kind of *mise-en-abîme* that serves, if not to frame the text in which it is inscribed, then at least to act as a constant point of reference. Like the allegory of the garden of Tarbes, it gives narrative coherence to the book, yet one of the paradoxical effects of the experience it narrates is the violent breaking apart of narrative. In its place is the experience of a startling revelation. As in "Manie," the location is the narrator's home, and it begins with a domestic scene that is no less ordinary than the one in "Manie." The narrator returns home late at night after spending the evening with friends. It is almost two o'clock in the morning, and his wife, Germaine, is asleep. He swears he has not been drinking. Their bed is in the opposite corner to the entrance of their small apartment, and so as not to awaken his wife, he decides to turn on the bedside lamp, just long enough to remind himself of the location of the objects in his path. He sets off quickly, but soon slows down. As he makes his way across the apartment, he is struck by the impression that his sense of space has undergone a radical transformation:

> In fact it had nothing in common, for example, with the space you see from a window, with its vaguely starry space. . . . No, it was even the exact opposite. There were none of those distant places, or nearby places. Here everything was right next to me.[22]

The journey suddenly becomes fraught with unpredictability, and is undertaken with a mixture of exhilaration and anxiety.

When he finally reaches his bed, and is about to fall asleep, he is struck by another impression: "That I had crossed the space of a modern painting. I had, to be precise, stepped into one of Braque's or Picasso's canvasses (and had just stepped out of it)."[23] The narrator experiences at first hand the world of a Cubist painting. In stepping in and out of the frame of a painting, he does not so much see things in a new light, as it were, but rather "experiences" Cubism's complete overturning of classical perspective. Accordingly, it occurs as a sudden break with his habitual perception of the world, and it is replaced by a sense of seeing everything for the first time:

> I had seen all of my obstacles perfectly well, I had never seen them so well, I had almost seen them too well, in this blinding light—as if they had never before been there; as is they had just been created; as if they had just created themselves![24]

The narration itself seems to be caught for a while in this Cubist prism, as the sentences follow one another with slight differences, in much the same way as different aspects of an object are shown from various angles in a Cubist painting, and this section is contrasted with a more classical narrative, which nostalgically recounts the history of some of the objects which have been so brutally transformed. It begins with a speculation as to how these objects would have appeared had the narrator turned on the light and kept it on, that is, in the continuous light that allows for the establishment of habitual perception. This part of the narrative is marked generally by a return of sequentiality (as opposed to the simultaneity of the experience), and by a momentary shift back to a more traditional aesthetic terminology ("Ah! but it is a fine transparent clock" [25]). And then, as if chastising himself for a lapse in concentration, he ends this passage with "But let's not be distracted." [26]

Although the narrator finds it an extraordinarily joyful experience, it is also profoundly troubling, since he claims he has literally become one of the objects in the space he is crossing:

> It was the opposite of a dream, it was completely unlike a thought: not one of those fluid spaces which gradually gain in depth; no, it was perfectly opaque and solid; and I was no less solid nor less opaque than it was. I was of exactly the same substance. Caught in the same jelly.[27]

This loss or, to be more precise, disintegration or dissolution of the self is, according to Paulhan, entirely consistent with the Cubist experience. The narrator's description of his journey across his bedroom is marked not only by a kind of eruption of his body outside its normal boundaries ("as if I had grown eyes in the back of my neck, antennae in my back" [28]), but also by a coming to life of the inanimate objects in the room; the closet door "yawns," the stool is "ready to jump around in every direction," the typewriter is "very aggressive," and the screen is "compassionate (although unsure of itself)." [29] Once the essay begins to bring into play the question of figuration, we can see at least the suggestion of a "Rhetoricial" critique of Cubism. If one of the manifestations of the desubjectivized experience of Cubism is the fragmentation of the unity of the human body, then Cubist paintings attest to the aesthetic gain from this disfiguration of the human, and affirm it as an adequate artistic recompense. This aesthetic return is readable in rhetorical terms as a movement of reversal and recovery.

The affirmation of this reversibility points to the need to explore the deeper complicity between rhetoric and aesthetics in Paulhan's Cubist account of Cubism. Cubist art proposes itself as a violent overthrow of established aesthetic precepts, yet it is introduced within Paulhan's text precisely as a means of recuperating the enigmatic episode the narrator has just lived through:

> In short, the space in which I was advancing was for me perplexing, and would have remained so, if I had not, as I said, by chance, just as I was falling asleep, remembered modern painting.[30]

Significantly enough, it is only once he is *out* of the picture that he can recall, that he can recognize what he has gone through. The text thus not only implies that aesthetics (and rhetoric, or the play of disfiguration and refiguration) is ultimately a reversible, and reassuringly human and domestic means of recuperation, but that there is also a measure of reciprocity *between* rhetoric and aesthetics. Cubism, for all its disruptive energy, reveals itself to be as codified and as predictable as the very forms of artistic expression it attempts to go beyond. So that, even when Paulhan describes space—the essential realm of aesthetic experience—as something that "unfolded across time, it came to me in successive waves . . . it was made up, if I may say so, of a series of sketches," [31] there is at least a corresponding discontinuity between space and time.

The measurement of time within the text in fact considerably complicates the notion of figuration. The narrator says early on that "time at least remained faithful," but a few lines later that "even time was disordered" (se déréglait).[32] The narrator's advance across the room is measured by four clocks, which all chime two o'clock at different times. The narrator has the sense when he reaches his bed that he had "advanced backwards," which he reformulates later as a kind of rejuvenation: "What joy to have at one's disposal both the experience of old age, but also the inventiveness of childhood." [33] The sense of time advancing (while not advancing) is appropriate for the alleged simultaneity of the whole experience, as if, as well as being a painting, it were a snapshot (in French, a "cliché"). It is described in terms of sudden and violent "blows" and "knocks." This is reinforced by the momentary return to a classical narrative, with its traditional perspective, where the signs of wear and of time passing are in evidence.

This is most precisely figured by the story of the "fine, transparent clock," but also by the "old country wardrobe . . . which has aged well right up until me," and the reflection at the end of this short passage: "The number of dead on our walls, at our windows! The number of mummies, who were once active, lively, disturbing characters, and who then faded like leaves." [34]

The notion of a sudden spasm of time corresponds to the linguistic version of the Cubist experience. In order to restore the freshness and purity of a metaphor, and give it back its original catachrestic force, one would have to efface time, or the effects of time. This is exactly the terrorist project of *Les Fleurs de Tarbes,* which is based on the presumption that, of the two indivisible parts of language—words and thoughts—, words are the only element that can be used and thus become used, or worn-out. Paulhan notes at one point in *Les Fleurs de Tarbes* that there are two semantic laws: "One has to do with the *wearing away of meaning.* It says that the word is worn out before the idea, and easily lets its expressive value be changed, if not lost altogether, while the idea is in and of itself lively, and striking. . . . Far from a word surviving an idea, it is the idea which survives the word." [35] However, the concept of "wearing away" *(usure)* is itself extremely problematic. As Derrida remarks in "White Mythology":

> How can we make this *sensible* except by metaphor? which is here the word *usure.* In effect, there is no access to the usure of a linguistic phenomenon without giving it some figurative representation. What could be the *properly named usure* of a word, a statement, a meaning, a text? [36]

Derrida is playing on the double sense of *usure,* as both a movement of loss, of wearing away over time, and at the same time as the accumulative gain over time of "usury." Although "usury" seems to be a kind of master-trope, it cannot escape the effects of figuration. In Paulhan's text, time presents itself as a kind of "meta-signified," as that which survives all words. The question is not just how to figure time (as chimes, numbers, an old man, a pendulum, etc.), but how to figure that which outlives all figuration. In the allegory of the Cubist experience, the difficulty becomes one of figuring the effacement of time.

What would be the corresponding linguistic version of this attempt to attain a transcendent aesthetic experience be? The answer in

Paulhan's text is "une enseigne." [37] The term is quoted as a supposedly derogatory description by Claudel of a Cubist painting ("painters of fairground signs"). In a passage worth quoting in full, Paulhan turns this notion of a "sign" to remarkable advantage in his essay:

> And what does a sign mean? It doesn't claim that it is good for your health to smoke, or that a calf with two heads is an instructive spectacle. No, it doesn't even suggest that the tobacco in question tastes good, nor that the calf is particularly graceful. *A sign has nothing to do with morality or aesthetics.* It simply says: here you can find tobacco, you can see a calf with two heads. All it says, simply, is "there is" (and even "THERE IS"). It says so brutally, without in the least trying to show what a civet or a calf really looks like. It's not at all like a trompe-l'oeil. No-one would mistake it for the animal itself. . . . [My emphasis] [38]

The linguistic concept of a "sign," and particularly the relationship between its signifier and its signified, was obviously of central importance to the Cubist project, although different Cubist artists exploited it in different ways. Braque and Gris, for example, were more technically disciplined than Picasso, and were concerned to produce a formal compositional harmony in their paintings, within the context of the wider aesthetic disruptions their art implied. Picasso, on the other hand, was intent on deliberately resisting the conventional iconic values of painting by drawing attention to its abitrary nature, in much the same way that Saussure, around this time, was proposing a linguistic theory based on an understanding of the arbitrary nature of the sign. According to Christine Poggi:

> By deploying sets of binary opposites—recessed versus projecting forms, transparent versus opaque planes, straight versus curved edges—Picasso called attention to the relational value of the formal signifier in the *Guitar*. This pairing allowed him to treat his formal elements as empty signifiers that would be granted meaning by the context. (*In Defiance of Painting*, p. 49)

In this sense, a "trompe-l'oeil" would be the extreme form of the kind of mimetic relationship Cubism was attempting to undo, since it is

motivated purely by an illusion of referentiality. The corresponding linguistic version of a "trompe-l'oeil" would be onomatopoeia. In a footnote to the description of the "rhetoric of painting" quoted earlier,
Paulhan underlines the resemblance between a "trompe-l'oeil" in
painting, and the figure of onomatopoeia, a word which "pretends
to be a real sound." For the Italian futurist poets, onomatopoeia became an important technique, although they were never, as Poggi explains, able to fully resolve the ambivalence about its mimetic function:
"Marinetti himself seems to have wanted it both ways: to motivate
poetic signs through the principle of self-illustration and onomatopoeia
and to claim that these signs were self-sufficient bits of reality, and
therefore non-referential." Paulhan's use of the term "enseigne" is
linguistic to the extent that it is deictic, that is, it simply points to the
here and now of a tobacconist's or a two-headed calf. But it functions
as a "sign" deprived of its referent, that is, a kind of pure referentiality. An onomatopoeia voided of any illusion of mimesis—like a trompe-
l'oeil stripped not only of any "verisimilitude" but of any "similitude"
at all—would be nothing but a collection of entirely meaningless letters. With no (hypothetical) proper meaning, nor any figurative meaning, the materiality of the letters reduces language to a random repetition of traces without spatial or temporal determination.

Paulhan continues the passage: "and what does a civet have to
do with tobacco? No-one knows. A play on words no doubt: some
Monsieur Civet, who put a tax on cigarettes." The "play on words"
(a civet is either a cat, or the perfume made from its scent, but it is just
as likely that it is a proper name), is easily understandable as long as
we impose a semantic determination on it, but once it is deprived of
this, it becomes a kind of indeterminate trace, like the letters and bits
of words that begin to appear in Braque's and Picasso's paintings
when they invent *papiers collés*. If the "enseigne" can account for
the presence of the "tobacco," what can account for the here and
now, the "there is" of the material traces? These traces, or traits, or
bits of language are outside of any system of determinability, be it semantic, rhetorical, spatial, temporal or aesthetic, and yet they are said
to carry the very burden of proof of the Cubist experience, they are said
to be "quite enough, like the bit of wardrobe, to convince us." [39]

What would a language be that is an "enseigne," and can we actually find an example of this in *La Peinture cubiste*? The allegory of
the Cubist experience that the narrator recounts in his "little adventure in the middle of the night" seems to bear the mark or signature

of Paulhan in its typical fragmented *récit* form. As we noted earlier, however, the narrator insists on denying the experience any personal value, and Paulhan stresses Braque's refusal to sign his paintings: "A *papier collé* is usually unsigned. But more than that, it seems very much that it does not lend itself to being signed. . . ."[40] The signature is particularly appropriate here, since it indeed functions as a kind of "enseigne." It has to be absolutely unique and personal, and its signification is inseparable from the immediacy of its every occurence. In terms of the literary originality that terror advocates, the signature is essential as the very mark of individual departure from the accepted tradition. How, then, does one sign a work that has nothing to do with personal experience, but everything to do with originality, such as a "papiers collés" painting? The same question would hold for Paulhan's *oeuvre,* which is put together very much like a Cubist painting, and whose "originality" lies paradoxically in its tireless attention to the enigma of commonplace expressions, that is, examples of language to which one would not attach a signature. A signature only "signifies" to the extent that it marks both its difference from other signatures, as well as the simple materiality of its occurence. Yet as Derrida has argued, signatures—like performatives—only function because of the very iterability that legitimates them. A signature can always be counterfeited, and with it "the possibility of extractional and of citational grafting which belongs to the structure of every mark." [41] We can see a very similar "dissemination" at work in Paulhan's own (self-)citational grafting, his collage technique of composition, which we might refer to metaphorically as the "signature" of Paulhan's texts.

In emphasizing the materiality of Cubist paintings, their *presence* as constructed objects and as unmotivated visual signs, Paulhan also suggests that they are nonetheless able to motivate their referents. In a text entitled "Peinture sacrée" (Sacred painting), intended to be a conclusion to *La Peinture cubiste,* and which Paulhan hoped to publish in 1956 (but which in fact has only just appeared in two recent editions [42]), the process whereby fragmented, random, apparently insignificant details of Cubist works assume the full aesthetic burden of the painting, *precisely because* of their unaccountable presence, comes to preoccupy more and more Paulhan's thinking. As he says:

> In short, there was on the canvas a flaw, a defect, an anti-pictorial element. There was a precise object, more or less clearly presented. But because of the effect created by the

painter, it is the anti-pictorial element which would become the occasion of the painting, the flaw which made the object possible. . . .[43]

This focus on the materiality of Modern Art can be seen even more clearly in Paulhan's short, but important essay on Jean Fautrier, a relatively neglected artist whose paintings enjoyed a rather erratic popularity in France, from the 1920s to the 1940s (which was when Paulhan first began to write about him).

PAINTING BY LETTERS

The reception of Paulhan's essay, "Fautrier l'enragé" (literally, "Fautrier the Furious"), has an important bearing on the way it evolved over the twenty years Paulhan wrote and rewrote it, from its original appearance in the catalogue of the exhibition of Fautrier's paintings in 1943 at the Galerie René Drouin, to the version in the 1962 Gallimard edition. Although Paulhan and Fautrier were close friends by 1943 (and were to remain so), after reading the first version of Paulhan's essay, Fautrier responded angrily with a letter to Paulhan in which he addressed one of the central themes of the essay: virtuosity.[44]

Paulhan's text is in part an evocation of Fautrier's unique artistic style. He combined a heterogeneous mixture of media with a particular violence (or "fury" [fureur]) in the actual act of painting, whence the title of the essay. As in *Braque le patron,* and in a manner which reminds one of Baudelaire's famous description of Constantin Guys in *Le Peintre de la vie moderne,* Paulhan describes the artist at work, and tries to capture the fleeting nature of the creative moment itself, and the specific quality of "fury" in Fautrier's paintings:

> . . . he seems now to be acquiescing to the desires of the oil and of the coating, to some need in his paste.
>
> It's a strange paste, one that is uncomfortably difficult to detail. What makes so many vapours and shimmers, perhaps the subtlest but also the most violent that one has ever seen in a painting, are thick flattened lumps, a colorwash of make-up, smudges of oil and pastel, all over

cardings of thick chalk. Then you discover that Fautrier has created his own materials, from watercolor and fresco, from tempera and gouache; in which crushed pastel is mixed with oils, and ink with gasoline. This is all made into a putty, ground, smoothed out by hand, and hastily applied, without corrections (in the manner of fresco painters), on thick paper, which is glued onto the canvas with a coating.[45]

Paulhan's description itself seems to be caught up in Fautrier's artistic style, the crowded, incongruous catalogue of artistic terms reflecting the unusual mixture of materials Fautrier uses to make his "paste" (which is "uncomfortably difficult to detail"), and its quick shifts of focus mimicking the rapidity of application of these apparently incompatible media. One can almost feel the thick consistency of the materials in the density of the consonant-rich nouns ("épais grumeaux aplatis," "badigeon de fard," "sabrage de craie grasse"); the contrasting lightness of the subtle effects Fautrier creates in the airier "tant de vapeurs et de poudroiements, les plus subtils peut-être . . ."; and the indiscriminate (yet very discriminating) cocktail of watercolors, oils, pastels, inks and so on, in the incongruities of the whole passage itself. Yet are we not, by taking Paulhan's text as a kind of literary calque of Fautrier's paintings, falling into precisely the same cratylistic trap, the assumed natural resemblance of onomatopoeia or the trompe-l'oeil, which painters such as Fautrier so vigorously resist? Can we in fact read Paulhan's text in the same way that we would respond to a Fautrier painting? This touches on the very question which frames his description of Fautrier.

Paulhan's point of departure concerns the critical reception of Fautrier's work, and what he sees as two contrasting reactions to it. In 1927, Fautrier's first period of public recognition, critics talked of the "virtuosity" of his paintings, while his more polished works of the 1940s would often be referred to as more "beautiful" than his earlier ones. Paulhan's essay carefully teases apart the implications of these two terms "virtuosity" and "beauty." Both are, in a sense, disparaging, and indicate an unspoken criticism. Virtuosity, with its primarily musical connotations, suggests an astonishing speed in the creative act, a technical brilliance, but its very focus on technique leaves it open to the suspicion of a lack of "genuine" artistic expression. As Paulhan puts it, "we notice a little too much the artist's paintbrush" (on voit un peu trop le pinceau de l'artiste). If it were a truly "virtuoso" performance, he goes on to remark, it would be able to disguise skillfully the impression of its "empty" virtuosity, "for this mastery would have nothing more urgent to do than to wipe away this trace, and make itself invisible." [46] But it would then run the risk of being seen as a "beautiful" painting, which carries with it its own implicitly negative connotations of a rather commonplace charm and seductiveness. "For *beautiful* nowadays, oddly, makes one think of silk trees and rivers of spun glass. . . ." [47] Beauty and virtuosity are two sides of the same coin, and have their correlates in literary criticism; with virtuosity, it is the technique which is visible, but not the content, or the end result, whereas with beauty one only sees the end result, but not the skill that went into its production.

Fautrier's letter to Jean Paulhan is based, oddly but perhaps appropriately, on a misunderstanding of Paulhan's intention. Fautrier accused Paulhan of not insisting enough on the *force* of his paintings, of saying—in an excessively convoluted and rhetorically elegant manner—that Fautrier was essentially a "virtuoso" painter. In short, Fautrier was reading Paulhan's text as an example of (literary) virtuosity. Paulhan was not in fact claiming that Fautrier was guilty of virtuosity, but was saying that *because* his paintings were open equally to both reproaches, he escaped them both, in that he was a master of both at the same time, combining the "fury" of modern painting with the technique of Classical art. In a sense, it is Fautrier (at least the Fautrier described by Paulhan in his essay) who could be seen as an imitator of Paulhan, the "terrorist" rhetorician.

In any case, Paulhan went one step further in his final version of *Fautrier l'enragé* (although not until the 1962 version, since he was secure in his knowledge that his original essay was in no need of correction as it stood).[48] He added a final chapter which stressed what we might call the "terrorist" side of Fautrier, praising the artist's ability to make us see habitual objects with a new and surprising freshness. As with the subsequent addition to *La Peinture cubiste,* there is a focus on the fragmentary, the apparently insignificant detail, and the unexpected aesthetic gain generated by the material leftovers of the world. We can see this best perhaps in a passage that also recalls, both "Manie," and the "adventure in the middle of the night" of *La Peinture cubiste*:

It's like when one wakes up in the middle of the night, or even in the morning just as one is getting up. What does one see, as one emerges from a dream (which is generally somewhat conventional, even academic, and in which houses have roofs and windows; and the characters have arms and legs), what does one see, if not a zigzag, a flash, a spark; something like a line of twigs, bits of squares and lozenges (fixed to the baseboards of the wall), a cloud traversed by luminous rays. What are these, but debris and waste ["des débris, des déchets"]! One usually closes one's eyes from the disappointment one feels. (Not to mention the desire to go back to sleep.) And yet, this is what is true. It's this waste which carries the whole rest of the world. It's this debris which is present.[49]

So Fautrier and Paulhan again seem to mirror each other. Just as for Fautrier it is the "debris and waste" which "carry the whole rest of the world," so for Paulhan it is not words, but bits of words, the materiality of the letters set free from the semantic motivation of their context, which are given the full weight of the rest of the text. The reading of Paulhan's text as "imitating" Fautrier's paintings proves to be correct, to the extent that it is *both* a display of technical virtuosity, an argument of typical rhetorical sophistication, *and* a text which foregrounds its own very material conditions, especially in its artisanlike feel for the texture of its language which, beyond the argument, carries the burden of the demonstration.

Whether or not we can refer to this as the "aesthetics" of Paulhan's texts is now open to question, since it is an aesthetic which relies on a kind of anti-aestheticism. At any rate, it forces us to rethink the terms in which we posed the question at the beginning of the chapter of Paulhan's turn to rhetoric and aesthetics "away" from politics. One should not be misled by Paulhan's turn around that same time to an increasingly "mystical" vocabulary (the sacred, mystery, rapture, Eastern religions), for, as he makes clear in *La Peinture sacrée,* these are merely analogies for the profoundly secular experience he is attempting to circumscribe and inscribe. He is, as he says, "mimicking" the sacred ("we have less analyzed the sacred than we have acted it out"), just as in *Clef de la poésie* he was only able to mimic "poetic mystery." We can see the same lingering over the traces and marks, the leftover bits of language, at key moments in Paulhan's other texts. In

De la Paille et du grain we saw the description of the mystery of a "patrie" (and of literature) being founded on, and sustained by, the unaccountable material excess of language:

> And providing one remains a little naïve, one never stops setting this mystery in motion, and being surprised by it: throwing words into the airs, to see them being transformed into ideas. And even quarter words, an accent, a simple letter.[50]

While Paulhan appears here to be advocating a convergence of literature and aesthetics, our reading of *La Peinture cubiste* demonstrates that the critical thrust of his texts goes beyond this identification. The conjunction of aesthetics and literature is only achieved by stripping language of its semantic (or ideological) determination, and by leaving the responsibility for the demonstration with the material traces, or leftovers, of language ("quarter words, an accent, a simple letter"), the sheer inscription of black on white. Although not spelled out by Paulhan, the complicity uniting ideology and a traditional understanding of aesthetics is clear. Both rely upon totalization by a process of illusion or disillusion, a purification that is always an assertion of uniformity, whether there is a semantic plenitude or a semantic emptiness. Both achieve this by way of a kind of theoretical purification of language, which ultimately reveals both aesthetics and ideology to be the victims of a deeper illusion that cannot be accounted for either in aesthetic or ideological terms, and that one might venture to call, mimicking Derrida's essay of the same title, a "white mythology."[51] In terms of Derrida's argument, one might say that, since ideology derives essentially from the assumed totality of semantics, of image or metaphor, it fails to leave a space for the non-semantic effects of language (syntax, the play of the letter, the supplementary logic of the *pharmakon*, etc.).

In *La Peinture cubiste* the discourse of traditional aesthetics occurs as a moment of recuperation in Paulhan's "adventure in the middle of the night," and one can see it having a similar function in "Manie," that is, in the figure of the furniture spray that attempts to wipe away the marks on the coffee table. The parallels with *La Peinture cubiste* are striking. If in "Manie" the allusion to aesthetics appears as the author is waking up, in *La Peinture cubiste* is does so just as he is falling asleep. The sleeping figures in "Manie" are reawakened, but put to sleep again by the anesthetic effect of the "rapidex," while in *La Peinture cubiste* the narrator's conception of aesthetics is radically disrupted, but the disruption is accommodated by referring to it *as* an aesthetic experience. *La Peinture cubiste,* perhaps Paulhan's most sustained and rigorous attempt to assert the priority of aesthetics over literature, ends up reaffirming the "mystery" of language and literature, as the irreducibility and unreadability of an "enseigne." In both texts, Paulhan dramatizes aesthetic considerations within a very domestic setting in order to suggest a kind of complacent alliance between traditional aesthetics and systems of thought based on a particular conception of language. Rhetoric (as the promise of a semantic wholeness) and aesthetics (as a form of totalizing ideology) work together to contain, or domesticate the world, but Paulhan undermines these claims by affirming an anti-aesthetics originating with the detritus which traditional aesthetics discarded, but on which it is shown to depend.

What, then, can we conclude about the relationship of Paulhan's writings to the artists and their works, which Paulhan both describes and mimics? I proposed earlier that the Cubist aesthetic might provide the best allegory of Paulhan's *oeuvre,* whose principle of construction is not so much architectural or dialectical, as it is one of continuous "self-grafting," a kind of self-citational "papiers collés" technique. The expository content of the texts gradually fades into the background as the formal, material aspects come to the fore, almost by force of repetition. This produces a very "painterly" kind of writing, that one might describe, less in terms of (self-)intertextuality, than of "inter-texture," a kind of surface sensuousness of language, with its rhythms and tones, the different shades and nuances which are brought out as the different parts are juxtaposed, and the very materiality of the letters and bits of letters themselves. This can be seen beyond the obvious context of Paulhan's texts "on" modern art. In the closing pages of *Clef de la poésie,* for example, we could see the argument as determined not only by an insistent etymological (or paronomastic?) link between "trait," "trace," "traitor" (traître), "betrayal" (trahison), and the important related term, "distraction," but also by the insistent stuttering of the "tr-" itself. The ending would thus be both under- *and* over-determined, in that there is not really enough evidence to suggest that a mere play of letters could motivate the argument, but that at the same time these letters could possibly carry the entire burden of the text. As such they are both figures *and* traces of Paulhan's text.

This doubleness (both exposition and mimicry, originality and repetition, figure and trace, reading and seeing) marks all of Paulhan's text(ure)s, and might ultimately be their most singular *trait*. It underlines the importance of Paulhan's writings on art, which belong neither to the various forms of Cubist literary experiments from the early part of the century, nor to the domain of art history or theory, but in a sense straddle all of these. Their originality lies in their insistent repetition, and their theoretical force in the playfulness of their artistic performance. This dynamic is one which we have seen at work in other theoretical contexts, but nowhere does it achieve the same exuberant textual *presence* as in the essays on modern art.

CONCLUSION

I f Paulhan's place within a certain epoch of French intellectual history is assured, what relevance do his texts have to the more sophisticated, self-critical contemporary theoretical landscape? By stressing the importance of the "duplicity" of Paulhan's writing in this study, my intention has not been to reduce them to a series of textual figures of doubleness which proliferate across his texts, such as ambivalence, metalepsis, reversibility, indifference, and so forth. These figures, with their appearance of reassuringly domesticating tropes, are in fact founded—as a closer reading of their language has revealed—upon a radical gap or rift, which is also their condition of possibility. In the *récits*, this disruptiveness takes the form of a "strangeness" (étrangeté); with the essay on proverbs it is a crucial though unlocatable gap between two versions of the proverb, and the two halves of the essay; in *Clef de la poésie* it is simply termed "poetic mystery"; and in the essays on Modern Art it becomes the excess of the non-semantic effects of language (syntax, materiality, signatures, the play of the letter, etc.) over the semantic. These absolutely irreversible elements, within the play of reversals, become the key to an understanding of Paulhan's texts, and yet only by virtue of denying access to this key. Furthermore, the texts themselves are caught up in, and subjected to, the theoretical disruptiveness which they attempt to describe and circumscribe, producing a radically unsettled and unsettling textual space, which the term *récit* seems barely adequate to account for. These strange textual performances straddle literature and literary theory, belonging to neither, but to both at the same time. In other words, "duplicity" can be understood *both* as a linguistic term (derived from Paulhan's models of language) *and* as an ethical term (the apparent "betrayal" of Paulhan the *résistant,* for example, when he takes the side of the collaborators). Paulhan's duplicity is not, as has commonly been interpreted, a playing off of one side against the other, in a game suggesting the cynicism of a double agent. Nor is it a kind of relativistic refusal to take a stand. Rather, it is the simultaneous affirmation of two opposing positions. Even this, though, does not adequately account for Paulhan's textual dynamics, since the "positions" are not really firmly established at all, but are continually disappearing and reappearing.

Lest this begin to seem as if it sends Paulhan spinning out of the orbit whose trajectory I have traced in this study, I would like to resituate his texts briefly within the context of a very contemporary theoretical discussion, one which finds distinct echoes in the texts of Walter Benjamin and the recent work by Homi K. Bhabha. This is not done in order to "reinvent" Paulhan (yet again!) as a "precursor of postmodernism," but I would like to take his thinking about the question of translation (as well as his performances *of* translation) as an example of the insistent critical thrust of his writing, when it seems on the face of it to be moving in the opposite direction, towards a literary and political conservatism. One would certainly not expect the names of Bhabha and Paulhan to share any very obvious common ground; the former resolutely post-colonial, impressively wide-ranging in his critical perspective, and alive to the subtle forces at work within the least visible of political discourses; the latter more and more ambivalent in his criticism of colonialism, and only rarely straying outside a francocentric frame of reference. Why, then, the association?

In "DissemiNation," one of the key texts of *The Location of Culture*, Bhabha argues for the need to rethink the category of nations, and narratives of the nation, by focussing on the ambivalent, emerging discourses being written from the "margins" of nationhood.[1] According to him, it is precisely the ambivalence of such agencies of national "narrative address" which are the most culturally productive, generating new forms of national identification that interrupt and disrupt the homogeneity of the national space and time in which they appear. Bhabha articulates his theory in terms of a series of spatial and temporal figures of doubling, and of repetition, but of repetition with a difference. In terms of collective national identification this is described as a tension between on the one hand "signifying the people as an a priori historical presence, a pedagogical object," and on the other "the people constructed in the performance of narrative, its enunciatory 'present' marked in the repetition and pulsation of the national sign."[2] It is the "time" of this disjunction that Bhabha is interested in articulating, and setting in opposition to the homogeneous time of "pedagogical" histories of the nation. This involves thinking about the concept of "cultural difference" not in terms of the opposition between two fully constituted nationalities, but as the gap, within a given national space, between two radically different forms of narrative; the pedagogical and the performative. Among the many writers he invokes is Benjamin, whose famous text "The Task of the Translator"—with its famous description of the "foreignness of language"—is seen to relocate the question of cultural difference as a question of translation:

> Benjamin's argument can be elaborated for a theory of cultural difference. It is only by engaging with what he calls the "purer linguistic air"—the sign as anterior to any *site* of meaning—that the reality-effect of content can be overpowered, which then makes all cultural languages "foreign" to themselves.[3]

That Bhabha should locate the productively disruptive energy of new forms of national affirmation (what he calls "hybrid sites of meaning"[4]) at the point of tension between "pedagogical" narratives and "performative" narratives makes not only for a startling comparison with Paulhan's own textual dynamic, but also opens the way within Paulhan's texts for a more active cultural or political intervention than has been attributed to them until now, and the potential of which I have explored in the preceding chapters. That this should also occur by way of a reflection on translation in Bhabha's text suggests an even more far-reaching affinity between the two writers.

As I mentioned in the chapter on Paulhan's Malagasy texts, his career might be said to have its point of departure in translation. He translated a collection of *hain-teny,* and as he himself would recognize at several points, the difficulty he experienced in speaking Malagasy proverbs is in fact a common problem of translation. Clichés in a foreign language always appear to us as more imaginative than the corresponding terms in our own language, and yet such commonplace or proverbial expressions are also those parts of language that are *most* language- or culture-specific. In translating proverbs, Paulhan noted, we necessarily run up against a more widespread linguistic tension, and one which Paulhan transfers, in *De la Paille et du grain,* to a discussion of the vexed question of patriotism in France during the Occupation.

A concluding example from one of Paulhan's narratives—one of the *récits, Le Pont traversé*—throws into sharp relief the problematic nature of translation as Paulhan articulates it. It comes near the end of the *récit,* in a dream that takes place in a strange country inhabited by people called the Nifis. The narrator of the dream seems to be in the same position as Paulhan was in Madagascar with respect to Malagasy proverbs. He describes two men talking together in their Nifi language:

> One of the men complained: he had a headache. His neighbor arose and, lying down by his side, pressed his forehead with this hands: "Harder," said the other one. These words reminded me of my surprise.
>
> Almost immediately I learned why. To the right of the sick man were some card players. One of them berated his partner: "I didn't tell you to put down the lowest one, did I? Those are just simple nifi words." They spoke a foreign language.
>
> Those words would doubtless have given me pause; I must have grasped their meaning before, in the very in-

stant when it was about to be translated into sentences—
and as if diverting part of it for myself.[5]

Although their language is unknown to the narrator, he is able to translate the *nifi* words through some mysterious process. He somehow catches the meaning precisely in the interval of its transformation from thoughts into words, but not without distorting it. It is as if he steals a bit of it away (diverts it from its proper course), and it never fully reaches its destination. The implication is that understanding is always at the expense of an incomplete translation; language never quite reaches its mark, but always falls short, or falls apart in some way. Paulhan ends up saying something very close to Benjamin in "The Task of the Translator," since both see translation as exposing a radical fissure or disjunction at the heart of all language. What this ultimately involves is undoing the myth that one's relationship to one's native language is unproblematical, and somehow more natural than one's relationship to a foreign language. This was, as we saw, one of Paulhan's insights on Madagascar, and it is an insight of some prescience, if we consider it in the light of Clifford Geertz's observation that understanding other cultures is "more like grasping a proverb, catching an illusion, seeing a joke than it is like achieving communion." [6]

It is entirely appropriate with Paulhan to end up talking about proverbs and jokes. For the question of the "seriousness" of Paulhan's texts is once more informed by the logic of duplicity. What does it mean to "take Paulhan seriously," when his entire enterprise involves a certain ironization of "serious" academic discourse? To overlook the wit and playfulness of his texts is not just to miss half the fun; it is to reduce them to a series of theoretical statements of rather limited interest. To take them lightly is to take them too seriously; to take them seriously, to understand the importance of Paulhan's defiantly non-solemn interventions in French intellectual history, one has to give equal weight to their lightness, the ways in which they playfully, performatively intervene in their own serious theoretical expositions. This is indeed the great challenge in reading them, and why their "easiness" is so hard to take, since it is at the same time a challenge to look anew at the twentieth century, in the prismatic light cast upon it by what Blanchot so precisely termed the "uncertain gravity" of Paulhan's texts.

Unless indicated otherwise, all translations are my own. French originals will generally be given in the endnotes, with reference to the *Oeuvres complètes* editon.

INTRODUCTION.
FIGURES OF DUPLICITY

1. "Je lis Derrida. Oui, c'est un esprit gentil et fin: très attachant." *Jean Paulhan-Francis Ponge: Correspondance 1923–1968, vol.* 2 (Paris: Galli-mard, 1986), p. 347. This was in the last letter Paulhan wrote to Ponge before Paulhan's death in October 1968.

2. "Jean Paulhan et la linguistique moderne," in *NRF* May 1969, no. 197, p. 811.

3. "Ce qui me frappe, m'amuse et même me charme dans cette volonté de naturel de l'égotiste, c'est qu'elle exige et comporte nécessairement une *convention.*" *Un Rhétoriqueur à l'état sauvage,* in O.C., vol. 3, 1967 (text dated 1928–1945), p. 204.

4. ". . . sitôt que l'on traite du langage ou de l'expression . . . cette expression . . . peut à tout moment présenter l'une ou l'autre face opposée. [. . .] Chaque réflexion de Valéry peut ici se renverser." Op. cit., p. 213.

5. "The Rhetoric of Blindness: Jacques Derrida's Reading of Rousseau," in *Blindness and Insight: Essays in the Rhetoric of Contemporary Criticism,* 2nd ed. (Minneapolis: University of Minnesota Press, 1983), p. 103.

6. The last graduate class de Man gave at Yale, on 21 September 1983, was in fact on Paulhan, in his "Theories of Rhetoric from the 18th to the 20th Century" seminar. The subsequent remarks are based in part on my own lecture notes from this class.

7. In his article "The Usual Terror, The Usual Suspects" (*Colloquium Helveticum: Cahiers Suisses de littérature comparée.* 1990. Vols. 11–12, pp. 21–38), Peter Hughes mentions a letter by de Man to Hans-Jost Frey in which de Man states his preference for Paulhan over Adorno. Hughes claims, in making the connection between de Man and Paulhan, that de Man in his articles in the pro-Fascist *Le Soir* was imbued with the ideology of political or cultural "terrorism," in Paulhan's sense of the term. He goes on to argue that de Man's work was caught within a Paulhanian dynamic; starting out as a "terrorist" critique of Montherlant's style as "empty," because it lacked substance, this set the stage, according to Hughes, for a "rhetorical" return of language which was to haunt the latter part of his career. My own reading of the connections between the two writers would approach with a great deal of wariness any attempt to read the work of either writer in terms of a chronological evolution (or to use the theory of the one to account for the writing of the other).

8. "Semiology and Rhetoric," in *Allegories of Reading* (New Haven: Yale University Press, 1979), p. 15.

9. See, for example, de Man's preface to *The Rhetoric of Romanticism* (New York: Columbia University Press, 1984), where he writes: "Such massive evidence of the failure to make the various individual readings coalesce is a somewhat melancholy spectacle. . . . Laid out diachronically in a roughly chronological sequence, they do not evolve in a manner that easily allows for dialectical progression or, ultimately, for historical totalization. Rather, it seems that they always start again from scratch and that their conclusions fail to add up to anything" (p. xviii); this is echoed in a passage such as the following, from Paulhan's last major theoretical text, *Le Don des langues*:

"Si l'on doit admettre avec les Hindous (et leurs disciples innombrables) que notre attention risque de déformer les idées et jusqu'aux faits auxquels elle s'applique, d'autant plus gravement qu'elle s'attache à ces faits avec plus d'assiduité et les considère avec plus de soin, eh bien! c'est un danger que nous n'avons pas cessé de courir. Il est possible qu'il soit venu vicier plus d'une de nos pages. Ici, je vois un moyen, sinon d'éviter, du moins d'atténuer le risque. [. . .] il s'agirait d'user d'une méthode à bonds et à saccades et de recommencer chaque fois notre enquête, comme si rien ne s'était encore passé." ("If one must admit, along with the Hindus . . . that our attention might deform the ideas, and even the facts, to which we apply it, all the more seriously so in that it is attached to these facts with greater diligence and considers them with greater care, well! this is a danger we have never stopped facing. It is possible that it has contaminated more than one of our pages. I see here a means, if not of avoiding it, at least of attenuating it . . . it would involve using a method of jerks and leaps, and of beginning our investigation anew each time, as if nothing had happened") (*Oeuvres complètes,* vol. 3, 1967), p. 395.

10. "Writing and Deference: The Politics of Literary Adulation," in *Representations* 15, Spring 1986, p. 5.

11. "More on Writing and Deference," in *Representations* 18, Spring 1987, 158–62.

12. "Response to 'More on Writing and Deference,'" in *Representations* 18, Spring 1987, p. 163

13. "Blanchot at *Combat,*" in *Legacies of Anti-Semitism in France* (Minneapolis: University of Minnesota Press, 1983), p. 12.

14. "Blanchot at *Combat,*" p. 22.

15. For a more extended reading of Mehlhman's various accounts of Paulhan, see my "Domesticated Reading: Paulhan, Derrida and the Logic of Ancestry,"in *French Connections,* ed. J. Wolfreys et. al. (Albany: State University of New York Press, 1998).

16. "La Pharmacie de Platon," in *La Dissémination* (Paris: Seuil, 1972), pp. 69–196.

17. "La Loi du genre," in *Parages* (Paris: Editions Galilée, 1986), p. 254. English translation by Avital Ronnell, in *Glyph 7* (Baltimore: Johns Hopkins University Press, 1980), pp. 202–32.

18. "The Ease of Dying," in *Progress in Love on the Slow Side,* p. 131.

19. In *La Part du feu,* p. 293. "Literature and the Right to Death," trans. Lydia Davis, in P. Adams Sitney, ed., *The Gaze of Orpheus and Other Literary Essays* (Tarrytown, N.Y.: Station Hill Press, 1981).

20. *L'Espace littéraire* (Paris: Gallimard, 1955), p. 13.

21. "Le va-et-vient du sacré chez les pragmatiques: Jean Paulhan," in *Le Signe et le poème* (Paris: Gallimard, 1975), p. 196. "He has constructed a literary genre which is his alone. . . . An anti-theoretical theoretical writing, which is precisely a writing, in that it accomplishes what it says. It *realizes* its main contradiction."

22. Reprinted in Jean Paulhan, *Chroniques de Jean Guérin 1953–1964,* ed. Jean-Philippe Segonds (Paris: Editions des cendres, 1991), pp. 80–97.

23. "Myth Today," in *Mythologies,* trans. Annette Lavers (London: Paladin, 1973). "And it is again this duplicity of the signifier which determines the characters of the signification" (p. 124).

1. Allegories of Ethnography

1. "J'aurais volontiers défini les Malgaches par leur subtilité d'esprit, la liberté de leurs moeurs, leur morale faite de prévenances et de politesses, si je n'avais craint de céder ainsi à un idéal assez européen, et peut-être à la part de cet idéal qui s'était déjà fait accepter des Malgaches." The original unpublished text of this lecture is in the Jean Paulhan archives at the Institut Mémoire de l'Edition Contemporaine, Paris. Translation is my own.

2. "Toutes les colonies se ressemblent." *Cahiers Jean Paulhan* 2 (Paris: Gallimard, 1982), p. 39, letter to Frédéric Paulhan (his father) in June 1908.

3. "Et c'est tous ces gens-là qui vivent des Malgaches. Quelle bourgeoisie pourrie!" *Cahiers Jean Paulhan* 2, p. 41, letter to Jeanne Paulhan (his mother) on 31 March 1909.

4. The "Hova" were the "middle-class" of Malagasy society, the Andevo being the slave class, and the Andriana the nobles.

5. One section of the thesis, "La Sémantique du proverbe," is now published in the *Cahiers Jean Paulhan* 2 (Paris: Gallimard, 1982), pp. 266–311.

6. James Clifford, "On Ethnographic Surrealism," in *The Predicament of Culture: Twentieth Century Ethnography, Literature and Art* (Cambridge, Mass.: Harvard University Press, 1988), p. 121.

7. For a more detailed account of the supposed influences of African painting and sculpture on Cubism, see Clifford, *Predicament,* and John Golding, *Cubism: A History and an Analysis 1907–1914* (London: Faber and Faber, 1959:1988), pp. 44–53. Golding points also to what he terms the "conceptual" quality of Cubist art, that is, its shift from an aesthetics of representation to one of subjective interpretation, as a feature which closely allies Cubist and African aesthetics.

8. Clifford, op. cit., p. 147.

9. See, for example, V. Y. Mudimbe, *The Invention of Africa: Gnosis, Philosophy and the Order of Knowledge* (Bloomington: Indiana University Press, 1988), and Paulin Hountondji, *African Philosophy, Myth and Reality*, trans. Henri Evans and Jonathan Rée (Bloomington: Indiana University Press, 1983).

10. "La Mentalité primitive," in *Oeuvres complètes*, vol. 2, pp. 141–53.

11. "D'un Langage sacré," in *Cahiers Jean Paulhan 2*, p. 329.

12. "Elle recompose de son point de vue l'image des sociétés qu'elle observe." "Les indifférences et l'indifférence: Paulhan écrivain ethnologue," in *Jean Paulhan le souterrain*, p. 28.

13. Christopher L. Miller, *Theories of Africans: Francophone Literature and Anthropology in Africa* (Chicago: University of Chicago Press, 1990).

14. The term "ethnophilosophy" is Paulin Hountondji's, from his *African Philosophy*, e.g., p. 34.

15. Cf. *Les Hain-tenys*, in *Oeuvres complètes*, vol. 2 (Paris: Cercle du livre précieux, 1968), p. 90: "There are other, less decisive hain-tenys, which might, depending on the situation, fall under the heading of consent, advice, pride . . . or rather, refusal, mockery, abandonment. But such distinctions would remain incomplete and false if one had to see in the theme a subject which was fixed once and for all. . . . A configuration of meanings is made and undone [*se fait et se défait*] at every moment through hundreds of exchanges."

16. "La valeur d'un hain-teny dépend de sa teneur en proverbes." *Les hain-tenys, Oeuvres complètes*, vol. 2, p. 82.

17. In *Oeuvres complètes*, vol. 2. Subsequent references to this essay will follow the quotation directly in parentheses.

18. *Le repas et l'amour chez les merinas* (Paris: Fata Morgana, 1970). Manuscript dated 1912–1913. Even in this socio-cultural study, the proverb comes very much to the fore. Paulhan's observations about the social importance of what we might call etiquette with respect to meals place proverbs at the juncture of the socially acceptable and the forbidden, between the inside and the outside. The proverb thus functions politically as a kind of moral safeguard, whose role in binding the fabric of Malagasy society Paulhan correctly points out. For an interesting extension of this question into the realm of psychoanalysis, see Roland Chemama, "L'Expérience du proverbe et le discours psychanalytique," *Ornicar?*, nos. 17–18, 1979, where the proverb is seen as a kind of key that opens up the analysis, acting as a bridge between the "repressed" and the "spoken."

19. Geoffrey Bennington, in his *Sententiousness and the Novel* (Cambridge: Cambridge University Press, 1985), provides a rigorous and exhaustive account of the valences of sententious discourse, specifically in its

relation to 18th-century novels. Bennington is acutely aware of the problems involved in any project of categorizing or anthologizing sententious statements, but identifies their principal effect as one of "laying down the law." Much of Bennington's discussion of the resistance of *sentences* to being taken out of context, of the problematical nature of their "truth" or "verifiability," and of the necessity of accounting for what he calls "the effects of fiction and simulacrum," is extremely pertinent to the rest of this chapter.

20. ". . . l'étrangeté des mots qu'il (= le proverbe) contenait . . . étrangère à notre conversation [. . .] Elle venait tantôt bouleverser le ton d'une discussion trop longue, la précipitait, l'accouchait; ou bien elle coupait court à une querelle naissante; dans la famille hova chez qui je demeurais, telle était la fin de toute dispute: il fallait un proverbe, mais il suffisait d'un proverbe pour la terminer."

21. "Elle en tenait lieu, si je peux dire, à moins de frais, et sans qu'il fût besoin de sortir du langage."

22. RAJAONA. – Pour aller au marché, prenons donc un filanjana [Footnote in text: "Un filanjana est une sorte de chaise à porteurs."]

MOI. – Il n'y a qu'une heure de route, allons plutôt à pied.
Le filanjana est bon pour les vieillards.
RAJAONA. – Le respect s'achète. Si tu vas à pied au marché,
l'on se moquera de toi.

Le respect s'achète est un proverbe. Je ne m'en aperçois pas, nul mot d'ailleurs ne m'en prévenait. Mais le tenant pour la simple suite de la phrase précedente, je réplique:

– J'aime mieux n'en faire qu'à mon aise, et que l'on me
respecte un peu moins. D'ailleurs est-il sûr que. . . .

23. ". . . le sens n'était pas exactement où je le plaçais."

24. "Une réflexion aussi détaillée est étrangère à la phrase réelle qu'a prononcée Rajaona."

25. "Ralay n'a pas voulu dire qu'une première hâte risquait d'en entraîner une seconde: plutôt, il a cité un fait qui enferme à la fois l'une et l'autre hâte, sans qu'on puisse les distinguer. Comme s'il avait dit: "Et la *hâte-à-se-marier-et-à-divorcer-aussitôt*, qu'en faites-vous, n'y songez-vous pas?"

26. "Je recours aux métaphores les plus inattendues: elles semblent aux Malgaches—comme, après tout, à moi-même—dites par simple jeu: l'intérêt de ce jeu, d'ailleurs, leur échappe."

27. "Je me voyais particulièrement dérouté par la difficulté que je trouvais à exposer à mes camarades malgaches la cause de mon embarras. Leurs réponses, encore que pleines de bonne volonté, offraient une maladresse symmétrique de la mienne."

28. "Paroles que tout cela. . . . Qu'est-ce que tu nous racontes. . . . Laisse-nous tranquilles avec tes proverbes!"

29. "Tout enfin se passait comme si ce proverbe mal employé et contraint d'avouer sa nature de proverbe venait en aide à l'opinion qu'il attaquait, plutôt qu'à celle qu'il devait soutenir. Son auteur devait sur-le-champ inventer quelque argument, quelque autre proverbe; encore se débarrassait-il difficilement du ridicule qui lui venait de sa première maladresse."

30. "Je passe quelques mois. Mon langage à son tour commence à contenir des proverbes. Certes, il arrive le plus souvent que je les cite innocemment dans quelque récit, "pour le plaisir," pourtant je parviens aussi parfois à les faire intervenir dans une discussion où ils viennent appuyer ma cause."

31. ". . . que font la plupart des voyageurs."

32. "Plus je me presse et m'oblige ici à la sincérité, et plus il me semble que lorsque je prononce un proverbe, *rien* ne se passe: j'entends rien qui soit de l'ordre du langage, rien que l'on puisse exprimer en le rapportant à cette sorte singulière de phrase, que l'on nomme proverbe."

33. ". . . je parle dans le vide," "on ne m'entend pas."

34. ". . . ce sont les termes mêmes, suivant lesquels je formais et me présentais cette inquiétude, qui me sont retirés."

35. Compare the corresponding moment, at least thematically, in the essay on *Hain-tenys,* p. 95, where there is a similar reversal, and p. 96, where there is a similar alignment of theme and text.

36. "Une phrase que je place habilement."

37. "Il n'est pas fort aisé d'imaginer par le détail comment se peut produire le retournement, dont on vient de voir l'origine, puis les effets. L'ironie, l'humour peuvent en donner une idée approchée."

38. The *Petit Robert* defines irony as it is used originally by Socrates in Plato's *Dialogues:* "Ironie < lat. *ironia,* from the Greek *eirôneia,* 'the act of questioning by feigning ignorance.'"

39. I am using "allegory" and "unreadability" in the sense that de Man uses them in his *Allegories of Reading,* in particular in the following passage from the chapter "Promises": "To the extent that it [Rousseau's *Social Contract*] never ceases to advocate the necessity for political legislation and to elaborate the principles on which such a legislation could be based, it resorts to the principle of authority that it undermines. We know this structure to be characteristic of what we have called allegories of unreadability," *Allegories of Reading* (New Haven, Conn.: Yale University Press, 1979), p. 275.

40. *Allegories of Reading,* p. 275.

41. The English translation (by Betsy Wing) of Caillois's lectures is in Denis Hollier (ed.), *The College of Sociology 1937–39* (Minneapolis: University of Minnesota Press, 1988).

42. "Vient le moment où une refonte est nécessaire. Il faut qu'un acte positif assure à l'ordre une stabilité nouvelle. On a besoin qu'un simulacre de création remette à neuf la nature et la société. C'est à quoi pourvoit la fête." *L'homme et le sacré* (Paris: Gallimard, 3ème édition, 1963) p. 119. Translations are my own.

43. ". . . ces sacrilèges sont tenus pour aussi rituels et saints que les interdictions mêmes qu'ils violent. Ils relèvent comme elles du *sacré.*" Ibid., p. 505.

44. "L'oncle maternel tombe sous la sagaie du neveu."

45. "Sur le fond, sommes-nous d'accord? Je veux dire que le terroriste ou le réfractaire tend—le voulût-il ou non—vers un pouvoir qu'il lui faudra assumer un jour. . . . Que ce pouvoir [. . .] s'exprime par cette rhétorique précisément que le terroriste repoussait par faiblesse . . . ?" *Cahiers Jean Paulhan 6: Correspondance Paulhan-Caillois 1934–1967* (Paris: Gallimard, 1991), pp. 55–56.

46. "En effet, à réfléchir, il contient un retournement comparable, au moins formellement, à celui des *Fleurs de Tarbes*: c'est la même dialectique, appliquée par vous au langage, par moi à l'existence sociale." Ibid., p. 59.

47. ". . . sa nature foncièrement équivoque." *L'Homme et le sacré*, p. 42.

48. "Un désordre général n'est plus de mise: tout au plus en tolère-t-on le simulacre." *L'Homme et le sacré*, p. 10.

49. For an excellent analysis of the difference between *la fête* and *la guerre* as opposite figures of a tension within Caillois's writing in general (dissymmetry/asymmetry, entropy/negentropy, positive retroaction/negative retroaction), see Annamaria Laserra, "Paroxysmes," in *Roger Caillois, la pensée aventurée,* ed. L. Jenny (Paris: Editions Belin, 1992), pp. 249–70.

50. Although it goes beyond the scope of this chapter, Caillois's understanding of historical evolution within the context of ethnography was put to a severe test in his famous polemic with Lévi-Strauss in 1955. In an article entitled "Illusion à rebours" (*Nouvelle Revue Française* n.s. 24 [December 1954]:1010–24; 25 [January 1955]:58–70), Caillois denounced Lévi-Strauss's *Race et histoire* for its methodological inconsistencies. His critique centred on the apparent double-bind of a science of ethnography that submits its own civilization to the open borders of cultural relativism. How can the ethnographer at the same time deflate the myth of the superiority of Western civilisation, and occupy a position within Western culture that has produced a theory of the complexity of structural anthropology that is able to determine what constitutes progress for another given civilisation? Lévi-Strauss in his

reply ("Diogène couché," *Temps modernes* 110: 1187–1220) accuses Caillois of being a defender of the values and aims of Western cultural imperialism. This hardly corresponds to the Caillois of *L'Homme et le sacré,* and much of the venomous tone of the exchange seems to have been generated by an incomplete knowledge of each other's writings. While it may be true, as Lévi-Strauss claims, that Caillois's essay is to some extent an attempt to come to terms with his own past involvement with ethnography, his own attraction to the primitive via the sacred, and his need to clarify the theories he espoused during the years of the College of Sociology, it is also rather disingenuous of Lévi-Strauss to deny any complicity in the influence of ethnography on Surrealism.

What of the sacred in this intellectual collision? What becomes of the sacred in the "devalued" world of structural anthropology? It is perhaps the *dispassionate* nature of Lévi-Strauss's work, at least in theory, that is most unacceptable to Caillois, since it deprives sacred rites and ceremonies of their essential energy and fascination. Moreover, in Caillois's universally extended "diagonal sciences" (*"sciences diagonales"*), anthropology in general takes its place as one more form of anthropocentrism to be contested.

51. In the discussion following his presentation "Les différences et l'indifférence: Paulhan écrivain ethnologue?" Augé remarks, for example: "Paulhan is sometimes very close to defining systems of taboo as a language, but his concern to see in Merina society the opposite of ours led him, I fear, to look for a sort of opposite message in it" (*Jean Paulhan le souterrain,* p. 32), and: "But as far as the relationship between the language of love and that of food is concerned, it seems to me that they were presented as homologous, while being properly speaking compared and contrasted to one another" (*Jean Paulhan le souterrain,* p. 35).

52. "L'étrangeté des choses à Madagascar répond à celle des hommes," *Oeuvres complètes,* vol. 1, p. 192 for original French. English is from *Aytré Who Gets Out of the Habit [Aytré qui perd l'habitude],* in *Progress in Love on the Slow Side,* p. 92.

53. "Aytré ne se suffisait plus. Je reconnais des signes faits pour moi; ils ne veulent pas dire: cheveux, rayons, enquête—mais cette autre chose qui s'ajoute maintenant à tout ce qui m'arrive, et même à mes souvenirs, pour les défaire." *Oeuvres complètes* I, p. 197.

2. Underwriting the Personal

1. "Danger de la modestie: être trop séduit par qui vous admire." (Ou si ce n'était qu'une ruse pour appeler cette admiration?)

«M'aimez-vous, demande Maast.
— Oui.
— Mais m'aimez-vous davantage? Songez que je suis
modeste, et peu sûr de moi, et peu demandeur. Et qu'enfin
nous ne nous aimerons que si vous y mettez du vôtre un peu
plus que je ne peux y mettre du mien.»

"La modestie, mauvaise ruse." From *La Vie est pleine de chose redoutables: Textes autobiographiques,* ed. Claire Paulhan (Paris: Seghers, 1989), p. 245.

2. "... j'ai toujours évité, dans la mesure de mes forces, d'ajouter une vue personnelle de plus à toutes celles qui courent déjà dans le monde."

3. See, for example, Silvio Yeschua, "Jean Paulhan et les *hain-teny*: de l'étude savante au récit initiatique," in *Cahier Jean Paulhan 2,* p. 355: "It is a real initiation which is recounted and proposed to us. Paulhan had gone through it on Madagascar between the ages of twenty-four and twenty-six; but he would need more than twenty years to fully grasp what had happened to him, and to be in a position to narrate it adequately. The story (*récit*) of his initiation (an initiation into poetry, literature, art in general). . . ."

4. The French *récit* does not really correspond to any of the comparable literary genres in the Anglophone tradition. It is sometimes a short story, sometimes a tale, but also simply a narrative account, which is often personal. As we shall see, this very indeterminacy is richly exploited by Paulhan as well as by Blanchot when he writes about Paulhan in theoretical terms.

5. See, for example *Les incertitudes du langage* (Paris: Gallimard, 1970), p. 95, when talking about "The Crossed Bridge," Paulhan claims: "Oui, ce sont des rêves qui se suivent d'une nuit à l'autre [. . .] Bien entendu, dans mon petit livre je constatais en même temps—ou du moins, je tâchais de suggérer—les événements réels dont le rêve était l'autre face: une histoire d'amour pas très heureux." ("They are dreams which follow on from each other from one night to the next [. . .] Of course, in my little book, I also recorded—or at least I tried to suggest—the actual events of which the dream was the other side: a not very happy love story.") And the following extract from the interview with François Leuillier in 1966 (in André Dhôtel ed., *Jean Paulhan* [Lyon: La Manufacture, Collection Qui suis-je?, 1986], pp. 51–61): "Q: *C'était vraiment le conte de votre vie?* JP: Oui, je n'ai pas beaucoup d'imagination. A peu près tous les contes que j'ai écrits sont très sincères, ce sont les choses comme elle se sont passées. Et surtout, avec ce moment d'extase ou d'éblouissement par lequel nous passons tous, et qui me semble être ce qui donne du prix ou de la valeur à tout le reste." (Q: Are they really tales about your life? JP: Yes, I don't have a lot of imagination. Almost all of the tales I wrote are very sincere, they present things just as they happened. Especially the moments of ecstasy and bedazzlement which we go through, and which seem to me what makes everything else worthwhile") (p. 56).

6. See the discussion following the presentation by Silvio Yeschua, "Jean Paulhan et la 'rhétorique' du secret" at the Colloque de Cérisy, reprinted in *Jean Paulhan le souterrain* (Paris: 10/18, 1976), p. 91.

7. See the recently published two volume collection of texts written by Paulhan under the pseudonym of Jean Guérin, *Chroniques de Jean Guérin 1927–1940,* and *1953–1964,* ed. Jean-Philippe Segonds (Paris: Editions des Cendres, 1991).

8. Jan Baetens has written on Paulhan along these lines (*Poétique* 78, April 1989, pp. 173–84), in a "micro-reading" of the opening sentences of "Le Guerrier appliqué," which pays particular attention to the name Maast. Baetens claims that "the passage from Jean Paulhan to Jacques Maast would be a means of blocking, without prohibiting it, the autobiographical reading of his *récit*" (p. 174).

9. *La Vie est pleine de choses redoutables,* ed. Claire Paulhan (Paris: Seghers, 1989).

10. *Progress in Love on the Slow Side,* trans. Christine Moneera Laennec and Michael Syrotinski (Lincoln: University of Nebraska Press, 1994). ". . . je ferai mon récit aussi nu que possible," p. 58.

11. "Je n'ai pas cessé de suivre ma pensée, depuis le commencement de cette maladie. Il est surprenant qu'elle soit restée pareille à elle-même, quand mon corps changeait tellement" (*Progrès,* p. 151).

12. "Je n'ai cessé de suivre ma pensée, mais il est venu un temps où j'ai voulu profiter d'elle. Je ne sais comment s'est fait le passage: c'était peut-être l'effet d'une familiarité dont il est facile de tirer parti. Ou bien encore. . . . Mais je ne puis guère parler de ces choses qui ne sont pas seulement de moi" (*Progrès,* pp. 152–53).

13. ". . . peut-être parce que sur ces lettres de Simone, l'on ne pouvait se tromper—au lieu que la fleur et le noeud, pensait-elle, étaient des signes" (*Progrès,* p. 169).

14. ". . . il me semble qu'elle prend dès maintenant à son compte, en échange, ma lenteur, tant d'idées gaspillées, dont j'éprouve aujourd'hui le défaut—et ma première maladresse à me défendre contre la facilité que l'on prend à mourir" (*Progrès,* p. 169).

15. "Mon désespoir n'est pas devenu plus grand; mais il m'a semblé qu'il passait dans mon corps . . . j'ai eu des contractions violentes, et des étourdissements si fréquents que je ne pouvais plus demeurer debout. . . . Mes idées se perdaient . . . je distinguais des vagues dans le papier bleu des vitres" (*Progrès,* p. 163).

16. "Mais il est arrivé autre chose: tout s'est passé comme si j'avais voulu préparer Juliette au moment où elle lirait les deux lettres" (*Progrès,* p. 168).

17. (Jacques) "Tous ces événements me fatiguent à écrire." (*Progrès*, p. 152)

(Juliette) "Je croyais voir ces mots écrits sur le mur, ou sur les couvertures. Je les appelais, je m'en emparais, je me pénétrais d'eux—mais au plus pendant une demi-heure, ensuite j'étais épuisée." (*Progrès*, p. 161)

(Jacques) "J'ai souvenir que l'effort pour écrire me parut anormal ou désagréable." (*Progrès*, p. 156)

(Jacques) ". . . les inscriptions utiles, qui certainement ont touché de plus près à cette guérison sévère, et sans joie elles-mêmes l'ont faite à leur image." (*Progrès*, p. 156)

18. Denis Hollier, "Afterword" to Roger Caillois, *The Necessity of the Mind*, trans. Michael Syrotinski (Venice, Calif.: Lapis Press, 1990). The following passage is particularly relevant here: "One day we will doubtless understand that autobiography was the great literary genre of Surrealism. In saying this I am not thinking of retired Surrealists who finished by reaching the age of writing their memoirs. On the contrary, the Surrealist autobiographical essays are all youthful works, works of an insolent immaturity, Surrealist above all—one might say—through their prematurity, the authors having rarely reached the age required for the practice of this type of exercise, the age when one has a life to recount" (*Progress*, p. 160).

19. "The Ease of Dying," in *Progress in Love on the Slow Side*, p. 123. Originally published in the *NRF* 197 (May 1969), (*La Facilité de mourir*, p. 744) ("Je suis près de penser . . . que Jean Paulhan n'a jamais écrit que des récits ou toujours sous forme de récit").

20. In this respect Paulhan's writing can be read as an instance of what Nancy K. Miller in *Getting Personal: Feminist Occasions and Other Autobiographical Acts* (New York and London: Routledge, 1991) has termed "personal criticism": "Personal criticism, as I mean the term in this book, entails an explicitly autobiographical performance within the act of criticism. Indeed, getting personal in criticism typically involves a deliberate move toward self-figuration . . ." (p. 1). Towards the end of the title essay of the book, Miller's definition of personal criticism seems to describe very well Paulhan's *récits*: ". . . by turning the autobiographical voice into spectacle, personal writing theorizes the stakes of its own performance: a personal materialism. Personal writing opens an inquiry on the cost of writing—critical writing or theory—and its effects" (p. 24). Miller's book argues principally for a feminist interaction between theory and autobiography, but she does not exclude the possibility of men writers producing the kind of writing she is laying claim to.

21. "La Facilité de mourir," p. 750. Christine Laennec and I have translated this, all too inadequately, as "the theoretical process."

22. "Que l'on place au début de ces récits quelque défaut du même genre: un défaut en amour, précisément" (*Progrès en amour assez lents,* p. 58).

23. "Que faire, dans la vie, d'un défaut? Il faut attendre qu'il devienne une qualité" (*Progrès,* p. 83).

24. "D'un mot, j'étais satisfait que tout entre Jeanne et moi se fût passé spontanément, sans paroles ou peu s'en faut" (*Progrès,* p. 47).

25. "Il me paraissait plus franc de laisser ainsi (me disais-je) chaque chose à sa place: aux actes ce qui est du désir, et aux paroles ce qui est—mon Dieu—de l'âme" (*Progrès,* p. 58).

26. "Je suis fière d'avoir pu vous inspirer de l'amour. . . . Un mot comme *inspirer,* il est évident qu'il pouvait nous séparer encore mieux que le reste" (*Progrès,* p. 60).

27.   Comme je lui disais la première nuit, avec une modestie peut-être maladroite:

   "C'est moi que tu préfères, n'est-ce pas?"

   Elle me répondit avec irritation:

   "Que veux-tu dire? Penses-tu que j'en ai trente-six?"

   Comme je me taisais, elle alla un peu plus loin, et ajouta:

   "Sache bien que je ne me suis donnée à personne avant toi. N'en doute pas."

   Et ces différences intérieures de son langage achevaient de m'embarrasser. (*Progrès,* p. 73)

28. Pourquoi me demandes-tu cela? Penses-tu que je t'aie menti jamais? Sache que mes paroles sont toutes sincères et non point menteuses.

   Tout doit aussitôt s'arrêter, et je ne sais plus ce que je voulais dire. Pourquoi parle-t-elle livre? (*Progrès,* p. 74)

29. "Malgré cette maladresse encore j'aime cette recherche de belles phrases, et cet effort de Simone" (*Progrès,* p. 76).

30. "Combien cette aisance à mentir s'ajoutait ici à cette finesse, que je pense nouvelle, et inventée pour moi" (*Progrès,* p. 79).

31. See especially *How to Do Things with Words,* ed. J. O. Urmson and Marina Sbisà (Cambridge, Mass.: Harvard University Press, 1975), and "Performative Utterances," in *Philosophical Papers,* ed. J. O. Urmson and G. L. Warnock (Oxford: Oxford Paperbacks, 1970).

32. "Favorable, de toute évidence, cette réputation, à ma surprise. Favorable, mais inquiétante, et je commençai de souhaiter qu'un ordre militaire vînt au plus tôt m'arracher à ce jardin de délices" (*Progrès,* p. 83).

33. "Maintenant que je vois en arrière ces aventures, qui se sont confondues, je m'étonne qu'elles soient aussi simples. Leur plus grande qualité est, sans doute, qu'elles me soient arrivées à moi; c'est aussi le plus difficile à expliquer: j'y tâcherai pourtant, je ferai mon récit aussi nu que possible" (*Progrès*, p. 54).

34. ". . . je n'ai pas ordinairement la pensée, ni la voix, qui me permettraient de raconter, comme Duffy: J'ai fait . . . J'étais à . . ." (*Progrès*, p. 66).

35. See *Figures III* (Paris: Editions du Seuil, 1972), pp. 211–12. Giving "what one does not have to give" is precisely how Lacan defines love in "La Signification du phallus" (*Ecrits*, p. 691). Also very helpful in this context is Shoshana Felman's *Le Scandale du corps parlant* (Paris: Editions du Seuil, 1980), which explores the relationship of love as an act and love as a speech act by juxtaposing Austin and Lacan, and reading them together with the Don Juan myth.

36.   D'ailleurs, je ne suis pas rapide et j'ai besoin que les aventures m'arrivent plus lentement qu'à un autre.

Le reste, il le faudrait écrire d'une façon différente, avec des mots différents et plutôt autre chose que des mots.

Mais voilà bien où j'ai tort. Il le faut au contraire écrire exactement de la même façon—et faire semblant que n'existe point le passage dont j'ai parlé, mais que tout se suit et se tresse sur le même plan. (La sincérité est ici un renoncement et une manière de s'abandonner. Comme il arrive pour l'homme qui se blesse, et se répète d'abord pour assurer son courage: "Tu ne sens rien, tu n'as rien." Ainsi se ment-il pour se tirer en avant. Dès qu'il veut simplement rechercher "ce qu'il y a," il retombe.)

Je le dirai donc, de la même façon. Cependant, que l'on imagine, parfois, sous ce récit, cet effort. (*Progrès*, p. 70)

37. "Pour moi, si j'arrive plus tard aux choses, je sais du moins comment j'y arrive" (*Progrès*, p. 73); "Tout m'arrive comme si j'avais trouvé une vie *déjà* trop avancée" (*Progrès*, p. 46).

38. "Que faire, dans la vie, d'un défaut? Il faut attendre qu'il devienne une qualité. Patiemment, s'il se peut" (*Progrès*, p. 83).

39. ". . . chercher le mouvement de la recherche" ("La Facilité de mourir," p. 746).

40. "Mais ce secret, n'est-ce pas précisément le «fait» mystérieux du renversement . . . ?" ("Facilité," p. 750).

41. The radio interviews with Robert Mallet were published as *Les Incertitudes du langage* (Paris: Gallimard Idées, 1970).

42. Many of these are gathered together in André Dhôtel, ed., *Jean Paulhan: Qui suis-je?* (Lyon: La Manufacture, 1986).

43. These scrapbooks are labelled "Dossiers de Presse," and are kept in the Paulhan Archives at the Institut Mémoires de l'Edition Contemporaine in Paris.

44. *Les Causes célèbres, Oeuvres complètes,* vol. 1.

45. *Oeuvres complètes,* vol. 1, p. 235. English translation by Christine Laennec and Michael Syrotinski:

> Après vingt ans de mariage, nous avons pris tout d'un coup une nouvelle habitude: à l'instant de nous endormir, nous nous pressons l'un contre l'autre. Tantôt elle me tourne le dos, et j'avance mes genoux sous les siens repliés. D'une main je la serre à l'épaule, de l'autre à la hanche. Ou bien elle dort allongée sur le dos: alors je l'entoure du bras gauche au faux du corps, tandis que mon bras droit se glisse sous son cou. Ainsi passent les nuits.
>
> C'est aujourd'hui le mardi vingt-deux août. En me levant, j'ai eu la surprise de trouver l'imposte de la croisée à demi arrachée par la tempête. A la place du morceau de bois, on voit un arbre, si proche qu'on a envie de lui dire son nom. J'ai reconnu notre chêne. J'ai réveillé Manie pour lui montrer l'arbre. Elle s'est étonnée comme moi. Avant le déjeuner, elle a voulu essayer le rapidex, que nous avons acheté hier. C'est un vernis qui permettra d'effacer les taches que j'ai faites à la table (prétend Manie) en y posant des plats trop chauds.
>
> Le résultat n'a pas été concluant. Pourtant les taches me semblent plus agréables à regarder.
>
> Peu de nouvelles dans le journal: l'on aurait observé des craquements dans l'édifice économique du pays. Oui. A l'enterrement d'un certain Dessaulle, jadis condamné pour polygamie, assistaient les cinq femmes du défunt. Il serait possible de parvenir à l'aisance en élevant des animaux—petits, je suppose, mais qui sait?—dont l'annonce ne dit pas le nom.
>
> Avant d'aller au travail, je me suis demandé si ma vie était délicieuse. Délicieuse, non; plutôt considérable. Un mot encore.
>
> J'ai plusieurs raisons de l'appeler Manie. D'abord, son nom est Germaine, dont j'ai fait Maine. Puis, il est vrai que l'amour est une manie, je ne songe pas à elle avec raison.

Sans compter qu'il est prudent de donner aux choses, et aux personnes, leur nom le plus modeste.

46. "On s'est moqué du prédicateur qui disait: 'Pour la modestie, je ne crains personne.' Mais il faut dégager le paradoxe, que cache la raillerie: c'est qu'il est contradictoire d'être modeste, et de *savoir* qu'on est modeste. . . . Se voir orgueilleux est le fait de la modestie, se voir modeste, de l'orgueil" (*Oeuvres complètes,* vol. 2, p. 174).

47. "Comme si notre monde se trouvait accolé à quelque autre monde, invisible à l'ordinaire, mais dont l'intervention, en des périodes décisives, pût seule le sauver de l'effondrement" ("Le Clair et l'obscur," in *Oeuvres complètes,* vol. 3, pp. 365–66).

48. "Si tout est récit, tout serait alors rêve chez Jean Paulhan jusqu'au réveil par l'obscurité, de même que l'écriture est de rêve, un rêve si exact, si prompt à se révéler, à dire le mot de l'énigme, qu'il ne cesse pas de réintroduire l'énigme dans le rêve et, à partir de là, de se *révéler* énigmatique" ("Facilité," p. 744–45).

49. "Juliette a imaginé que cette première page tachée de boue, du *Pont traversé,* j'y tenais pour quelque raison. «Je la trouve sale, je la trouve laide, je la trouve souvenir pour toi. . . . » Elle l'a prise et l'a déchirée en deux" (*La Vie est pleine de choses redoutables,* p. 191). Claire Paulhan notes: "This first page of *The Crossed Bridge* begins with the explanation of the dream Jean Paulhan had after a separation: this explanation, addressed to someone who is unnamed, is probably intended for Germaine Pascal."

50. "A peine eus-je pris la décision de te rechercher, que je me répondis par une abondance de rêves" (*Pont traversé,* p. 87).

51. "Il est étrange que l'on prenne, étant seul, tant de précautions et d'images pour se parler" (*Pont traversé,* p. 91).

52. ". . . ceux-ci s'arrêtaient lorsqu'ils étaient près de se résoudre en un sentiment pur [. . .] Je conservais le sentiment par quoi l'on se paraît à soi-même fondre" (*Pont traversé,* p. 92).

53. "J'avais inventé, à partir de mon rêve, une autre assurance, et ce pont entre nous deux traversé.(99) [. . .] L'on devinera, sur ce récit, plus de choses que je ne puis en citer (et qu'il n'est utile)" (*Pont traversé,* p. 99).

54. "L'on admet que nous apercevons clairement les choses réelles et les rêvées de façon confuse. Cette opinion tient à la seule confiance d'avoir les premières à notre disposition—en sorte qu'il est aisé, aussitôt qu'il nous plaît, de les faire nettes. Mais qui néglige cet aspect pratique, les objets vrais le surprennent par leur confusion" (*Pont traversé,* p. 96).

55. "L'on eût donc repoussé le mot s'il n'avait paru que son défaut même accusait plus nettement la sorte de confusion où l'on a reconnu le trait particulier des événements plus haut rapportés, et telle que les idées ou sentiments

naturellement faits pour rapprocher, à leur tout devenaient une raison d'éloignement" (*Pont traversé*, p. 100).

56. "Elle chantonne, et pour tromper le temps rêve qu'elle voit des moutons passer une barrière. . . . Lalie rêve encore: après le moutons, le troupeau des vaches et leurs chiens noirs, puis les renards, les écureuils, les grenouilles. Quelque chose a bougé dans l'herbe. Cette fois, c'est la longue chaîne des dames-de-puits" (*Lalie*, p. 18).

57. "J'attends, et les premiers moments sont légers; j'ai du plaisir à voir un champ de luzerne sur lequel des papillons blancs tous pareils sont si nombreux qu'ils semblent tenir les uns aux autres par de fils comme un grand tissu qui, à des milliers de places, s'élève et à des milliers d'autres s'abaisse" (*Progrès,* p. 77).

58. "Si notre inconscient est aussi malin que le suppose Freud, comment ne s'occuperait-il pas à changer de langue: par exemple, à inventer de nouveaux signes, à changer le sens des anciens? C'est une entreprise de cet ordre que j'avais pensé saisir sur le fait" (Jean Paulhan, *Les Incertitudes du langage,* pp.96–97).

59. "Enfin, nos rêves devenaient la moins secrète de nos vies" (*La Vie est pleine de choses redoutables,* p. 314).

60. "Freud: Réserve sur un point," in *Oeuvres complètes IV,* p. 419.

61. "Il est étrange que je désire une femme, non pas tant à proportion qu'elle me plaît, mais le contraire, et que je la puisse un peu mépriser" (*Progrès,* p. 41).

62. "Eh oui, c'est très différent: l'érotisme, c'est l'amour après réflexion. C'est l'amour sans plus rien de surprenant. Moi, je serais plutôt pour la surprise, pour les surprises. C'est un parti pris touchant l'amour. Je préfère l'amour dont on ne peut pas parler" (*La Vie est pleine de choses redoutables,* p. 311).

3. BLANCHOT READING PAULHAN

1. Jeffrey Mehlman, "Blanchot at *Combat,*" in *Legacies of Anti-Semitism in France* (Minneapolis: University of Minnesota Press, 1983). Maurice Blanchot, "How is Literature Possible?" trans. Michael Syrotinski, in *A Blanchot Reader,* ed. Michael Holland (Oxford: Blackwell, 1995).

2. "Writing and Deference: The Politics of Literary Adulation," in *Representations,* Summer 1986.

3. *Agonies of the Intellectual* (Lincoln: University of Nebraska Press, 1992).

4. *Modern French Philosophy* (Cambridge: Cambridge University Press, 1980), p. 14.

5. *Qu'est-ce que la littérature?* (Paris: Gallimard, 1948), pp.130–40.

6. "Literature and the Right to Death," in *The Gaze of Orpheus and Other Literary Essays,* trans. Lydia Davis (Tarrytown, N.Y.: Station Hill Press, 1981).

7. ". . . cette question enfantine: «Qu'est-ce que la littérature?»—enfantine, mais que toute une vie se passe à esquiver." *Les Fleurs de Tarbes,* in *Oeuvres Complètes,* vol. 3, p. 19. Subsequently abbreviated to *Fleurs.*

8. In *Faux pas* (Paris: Gallimard, 1943), p. 92. Subsequently referred to as *Faux pas,* with page numbers immediately following quotation in the text.

9. "Le néant poétique prend, pour Mallarmé, la forme d'un choix concret et précis qui n'a cessé de le préoccuper: 'A savoir s'il y a lieu d'écrire.' *La Musique et les lettres,* p. 645. La question ne nous a pas quittés. Cinquante ans plus tard, Maurice Blanchot intitule un article sur *Les Fleurs de Tarbes* "Comment la littérature est-elle possible?"; ces deux noms—celui de Paulhan et celui de Blanchot—unis de la sorte, résument toute une époque historique et une situation présente." "Poetic Nothingness: On a Hermetic Sonnet by Mallarmé," translated by Richard Howard, in *Paul de Man: Critical Writings 1953–1978,* ed. Lindsay Waters (Minneapolis: University of Minnesota Press, 1989), p. 18. Originally published in French as "Le néant poétique: Commentaire d'un sonnet hermétique de Mallarmé," in *Le monde nouveau* 88, April 1955.

10. The essay was first published as a series of three review articles in the *Journal des débats*: "La Terreur dans les lettres" (21 October 1941), "Comment la littérature est-elle possible?" (25 November 1941), and "Comment la littérature est-elle possible?" (2 December 1941); and then as a separate pamphlet by José Corti in 1942, before being included in his first collection of literary articles, *Faux pas* (Paris: Gallimard, 1943).

11. ". . . j'ai écrit quelque chose qui s'appelle les *Fleurs de Tarbes.* Sur le langage. Je te l'enverrai." Letter dated May 1925, in *Correspondance Jean Paulhan-Francis Ponge 1923–1968,* édition critique annotée par Claire Boaretto, vol. 1, p. 51.

12. Cf., for example, "Défaut de langage," in *Anthologie de la nouvelle prose française,* Editions du Sagittaire, 1926; "Sur un défaut de la pensée critique," in *Commerce* 16, Summer 1928; "Commentaire sur Bruno Latini," in *Mesures* 15, January 1937; "Lettre aux Nouveaux Cahiers sur le pouvoir des mots," in *Les Nouveaux Cahiers* 22, pp. 23–24, 25; "Le secret de la critique," in *Mesures* 15 July 1938; and "Éléments," in *Mesures* 15, October 1938.

13. This should not be confused with the text by the same name which Paulhan published towards the end of his life.

14. ". . . le reproche le plus grave sans doute qui ait cours de notre temps: c'est que l'auteur de lieux communs cède à la puissance des mots, au verbalisme, à l'emprise du langage, et le reste" (*Fleurs,* p. 30).

15. "Non que la possession mystique du savant—ni plus haut la révolution—me soient le moins du monde méprisable. Loin de là. Je me défie seulement d'une révolte, d'une dépossession qui viennent si bien à point nous tirer d'embarras" (*Fleurs,* p. 25).

16. "L'on appelle *Terreurs* ces passages dans l'histoire des nations (qui succèdent souvent à quelque famine), où il semble soudain qu'il faille à la conduite de l'Etat, non pas l'astuce de la méthode, ni même la science et la technique—de tout cela l'on n'a plus que faire—mais bien plutôt une extrême pureté de l'âme, et la fraîcheur de l'innocence commune. D'où vient que les citoyens se voient pris eux-mêmes en considération, plutôt que leurs oeuvres: la chaise est oubliée pour le menuisier, le remède pour le médecin. Cependant l'habileté, l'intelligence ou le savoir-faire deviennent suspects, comme s'ils dissimulaient quelque défaut de convictions. Le représentant Lebon décrète, en août 1793, que le tribunal révolutionnaire d'Arras jugera d'abord les prévenus 'distingués par leur talent.' Quand Hugo, Stendhal ou Gourmont parlent de massacres ou d'égorgements, c'est aussi à une sorte de talent qu'ils songent: celui qui se trahit aux fleurs de rhétorique. Comme si le méchant auteur—profitant de l'effet obtenu *déjà* par de tels arrangements de mots, telles astuces littéraires—se contentait de monter, de pièces et de morceaux, une machine à beauté, où la beauté n'est pas moins déplaisante que la machine" (*Fleurs,* p. 32–33).

17. "Ainsi les linguistes et métaphysiciens ont-ils soutenu tantôt (avec les Rhétoriqueurs) que la pensée procédait des mots, tantôt (avec les Romantiques et Terroristes) les mots de la pensée" ("Trois pages d'explication," in *Oeuvres complètes,* vol. 3, p. 140).

18. Commentators of *Les Fleurs de Tarbes* consistently fall into the trap of taking its historical allusions, and its broad period divisions literally. See, for example, Yves Lévy, "Jean Paulhan, Du jardin fleuri aux catacombes," in *Preuves* 153, November 1963; Ramon Fernandez, "Les Fleurs de Tarbes," in *La Nouvelle Revue Française* 333, 1 November 1941; and Michel Beaujour, "Jean Paulhan et la Terreur," in *Jean Paulhan le souterrain,* pp. 118–50. Yves Lévy's article, for example, is a trenchant criticism of Paulhan's alleged "forgetting" of the long history of the questions which Lévy claims he nonetheless puts within a historical (contemporary) context. Paulhan is reproached for his anti-literary, philosophical "coldness." Lévy fails to acknowledge, however, that the possibility of "illuminating" the history of rhetoric, or of bringing it out of the subterranean obscurity into which it has fallen, is precisely the

question of Paulhan's book. As the book proceeds, the question becomes one of just how a theory of reading would accommodate this reanimated rhetoric, or deal with the transformations that might occur once it was under way. As Paulhan puts it in a reply to Lévy (*Preuves* 155, January 1964): "The subject of our study shifted noticeably . . . everything we found escapes our categories" (p. 94), which is a critical turn that Lévy completely overlooks.

19. "Par conséquent, un seul objet pour l'art, mettre au jour le monde du dedans en le gardant intact des illusions grossières et générales dont un langage imparfait l'offusquerait"; "en veillant à chasser du langage tout ce qui pourrait le faire ressembler à une langue usuelle" (*Faux pas*, p. 95).

20. ". . . nous ne prenons aujourd'hui contact avec les lettres et le langage même . . . qu'à la faveur d'un enchaînement d'erreurs et d'illusions, aussi grossières que le peut être une illusion d'optique" (*Fleurs*, p. 67).

21. "Car la Terreur dépend d'abord du langage en ce sens général: c'est que l'écrivain s'y voit condamné à ne plus dire que ce qu'un certain *état* de la parole le laisse libre d'exprimer: restreint à l'espace de sentiment et de pensée, où le langage n'a pas encore trop servi. Ce serait peu: il n'est pas d'écrivain mieux occupé des mots que celui qui se propose à tout instant de les pourchasser, d'être absent d'eux ou bien de les réinventer" (*Fleurs*, pp.135–36).

22. "Jean Paulhan et la Terreur," p. 131.

23. "Les clichés pourront retrouver droit de cité dans les Lettres, du jour où il seront enfin privés de leur ambiguïté, de leur confusion. Or, il devrait y suffire, puisque la confusion vient d'un doute sur leur nature, de simplement *convenir*, une fois pour toutes, qu'on les tiendra pour clichés. En bref, il y suffit de *faire communs* les lieux communs . . ." (*Fleurs*, p. 80).

24. "Il faudrait citer encore, dans l'écriture, les italiques, les guillemets, les parenthèses que l'on voit abonder, sitôt la rhétorique abolie, dans les écrivains romantiques" (*Fleurs*, p. 81, n. 1).

25. "IL EST DÉFENDU D'ENTRER DANS LE JARDIN AVEC DES FLEURS À LA MAIN" (*Fleurs*, p. 24).

26. "IL EST DÉFENDU D'ENTRER DANS LE JARDIN PUBLIC SANS FLEURS À LA MAIN" (*Fleurs*, p. 165).

27. "Paulhan and Blanchot: On Rhetoric, Terror, and the Gaze of Orpheus," in *Agonies of the Intellectual* (Lincoln: University of Nebraska Press, 1992), p. 146.

28. "Il est ainsi des lueurs, sensibles à qui les voit, cachées à qui les regarde; des gestes qui ne s'accomplissent pas sans quelque négligence (comme la vue de certaines étoiles ou l'allongement *entier* du bras). Mettons enfin que je n'ai rien dit" (*Fleurs*, p. 94).

29. "... les lieux communs peuvent être intelligents ou sots, je n'en sais rien et je ne vois aucun moyen de le jamais savoir avec rigueur" (*Fleurs,* pp. 138–39).

30. "Et qui n'accorde aux Terroristes que l'esprit manque à sa dignité, s'il tournaille autour d'un mot comme une bête à l'attache; s'il demeure à ce premier stade, où l'on s'apprend à parler; s'il est plus soucieux de virgules, de règles et d'unités, que de *cela* qu'il lui faut dire" (*Fleurs,* p. 62).

31. "S'il y a quelque bassesse ou lâcheté, à penser *autour* d'un mot, et soumettre ainsi sa réflexion au langage, il ne faut pas aller chercher très loin le coupable: nous venons de l'être" (*Fleurs,* p. 62).

32. "Nous sommes nous-mêmes en jeu" (*Fleurs,* p. 63).

33. "... ce n'est plus Bourget ni Carco, dont la pensée nous doit paraître esclave de mots et de phrases—mais nous-mêmes, et notre pensée *quand nous lisons les lieux communs* de Bourget et de Carco" (*Fleurs,* p. 63).

34. "Nous avons poussé à bout la Terreur et découvert la Rhétorique" (*Fleurs,* p. 85).

35. "[Paulhan] fait entrer dans ses calculs cette équivoque et ne cherche pas à la dissiper" (*Faux pas,* p. 100).

36. "C'est par le malaise qu'on éprouve, et l'anxiété, qu'on est seulement autorisé à entrer en rapport avec les grands problèmes qu'il étudie et dont il n'accepte de montrer que l'*absence*" (*Faux Pas,* p. 92).

37. "Voici un trait curieux de la projection. C'est à *l'origine* de la phrase ou du passage incriminé que le lecteur place cette extrême présence et ce souci de mots qui se produit en réalité pour lui—comme il nous est arrivé—à la *fin* de son effort" (*Fleurs,* p. 65).

38. "Une sorte de loi d'échec." In the 1936 version of *Les Fleurs de Tarbes,* reprinted in *Les Fleurs de Tarbes* (Paris: Gallimard Folio, 1990), ed. Jean-Claude Zylberstein, p. 248.

39. "Et faut-il encore rechercher des règles où règne l'arbitraire? C'est à quoi répondait la *Clef de la poésie*" (*Fleurs,* Folio, p. 262).

40. "... étrange privilège, un peu déconcertant." *La Part du feu,* p. 65. Subsequently abbreviated to "Mystère," with page references following quotations in parentheses.

41. "... je ne cherche pas à faire la moindre découverte, je ne cherche qu'un moyen de juger toute découverte poétique. Je ne souhaite pas former en poésie quelque nouvelle doctrine; je ne cherche qu'un procédé, propre à mettre toute doctrine à l'épreuve. Bref, mon propos n'est ni critique, ni—de toute évidence—littéraire. Il est strictement logique." *Clef de la poésie, Oeuvres complètes,* vol. 2, p. 241. Subsequently abbreviated to *Clef,* with page references given after French original in footnote.

42. "La tâche n'est pas difficile: Elle est strictement impossible." *Essai d'introduction au projet d'une métrique universelle* (Paris: Le Nouveau Commerce, 1984), p. 13.

43. "J'imagine à présent une loi poétique telle qu'exprimant un rapport particulier de sons à sens et d'idées à mots, elle supporte sans y perdre ses preuves, ni sa vraisemblance, de voir ses termes invertis: d'être inversée" (*Clef,* p. 241).

44. "Il est évident qu'une telle loi, dont la formule serait double, passerait la vraisemblance pour atteindre à la vérité. A défaut de rendre directement le mystère—ce qui est par définition même impossible—elle se plierait en effet à ce mystère: elle le mimerait et le manifesterait" (*Clef,* p. 242).

45. ". . . le plus vif désir de dégager enfin quelque méthode ou clef, qui permette d'y séparer le vrai du faux" (*Clef,* p. 242).

46. "Or ces éléments du moins me sont familiers. Je les distingue, je puis les nommer. C'est, d'une part, la lettre et le signe, le souffle, le son, toutes choses à nous extérieures, matérielles et comme offertes à nos sens: à la vue, à l'ouïe, au tact. D'autre part, les significations qui leur sont associées: idées, vouloirs, sentiments—toutes choses qui nous sont connues d'expérience intime, échappant au sens comme à la mesure. Bref, la poésie est en elle-même aussi diverse—et de la même diversité—que les objets qu'elle nous montre" (*Clef,* p. 245).

47. "Or leurs explications et doctrines offrent un trait singulier: chacune d'elles est ingénieuse, probable—au surplus, puisqu'ils sont aussi poètes, prouvée par les faits. Mais non pas tant que l'explication opposée ne demeure, elle aussi, probable—et non moins prouvée" (*Clef,* p. 246).

48. "On soupçonne que la clef, une fois découverte, vaudrait pour bien d'autres domaines que la littérature ou la poésie" (*Clef,* p. 247).

49. "On a vu qu'il était à la poésie un trait constant: c'est le défaut régulier que trahit à son endroit chaque doctrine ou raison. . . . Si je tente moins d'-expliquer ce trait, ou seulement de le comprendre, que de l'exprimer—de le formuler—il vient ceci: c'est qu'il arrive aux mots et à la pensée d'être en poésie *indifférents*" (*Clef,* p. 249).

50. "Où l'on exprime le mystère à défaut de le penser" (*Clef,* p. 248).

51. De F(abc) il suit F'(ABC)
De F(ABC) il suit F'(abc) (*Clef,* p. 251)

52. "Mais la seconde épreuve, qui m'intéresse, est particulière à la loi poétique: il s'agit de savoir si cette loi demeure valable *malgré* le mystère et la transmutation de ses éléments: si elle est propre à résister à ce mystère et (pour ainsi dire) à boire l'obstacle" (*Clef,* p. 252).

53. ". . . aux commentaires, aux confidences, aux thèmes et doctrines qui ont cours sur la poésie" (*Clef,* p. 254).

54. "Je ne me suis rien proposé que je n'aie souffert [. . .] j'ai été la découverte même que je faisais" (*Clef,* p. 256).

55. ". . . la moins irréfléchie qui soit" ("Mystère," p. 50).

56. "Le caractère provoquant de ces remarques vient de leur simplicité et toutefois de l'impossibilité de les dépasser" ("Mystère," p. 51).

57. ". . . par un déploiement rapide d'éventail qui jette brusquement en notre présence, dans un étalement saisissable, la figure entière du langage dont autrement nous ne distinguons les deux côtés que repliés l'un sur l'autre et se cachant l'un par l'autre" ("Mystère," p. 53).

58. Cf., for example, "Crise de vers," "Quant au livre," and "La musique et les lettres." Probably the most well-known passage—which Blanchot cites elliptically in "La Littérature et le droit à la mort"—is from "Crise de vers":

> A quoi bon la merveille de transposer un fait de nature
> en sa presque disparition vibratoire selon le jeu de la parole,
> cependant; si ce n'est pour qu'en émane, sans la gêne d'un
> proche ou concret rappel, la notion pure.
>
> Je dis: une fleur! et, hors de l'oubli où ma voix relègue
> aucun contour, en tant que quelque chose d'autre que les
> calices sus, musicalement se lève, idée même et suave, l'absente de tous bouquets. (Mallarmé, *Oeuvres Complètes*
> [Paris: Bibliothèque de la Pleiade, 1945] p. 368)

59. ". . . les mots s'évanouissent de la scène pour faire entrer la chose, mais comme cette chose n'est elle-même plus qu'une absence, ce qui se montre sur le théâtre, c'est une absence de mots et une absence de choses, un vide simultané, rien soutenu par rien" ("Mystère," p. 55).

60. ". . . à la fois démarche de science et démarche de non-savoir, comme la disjonction des deux et l'hésitation de l'esprit entre celle-ci et celle-là . . " ("La Facilité de mourir," p. 131).

61. Mehlman, in his coda to "Blanchot at *Combat,*" quotes several passages that are presented as the final touch of his argument, but which it would not be an exaggeration to say are ripped (I would say, quite scandalously) out of the context of Blanchot's essay.

62. "The Ease of Dying," trans. Michael Syrotinski and Christine Laennec, in *Progress in Love on the Slow Side* (Lincoln: University of Nebraska Press, 1994), p. 122.

4. RESISTANCE, COLLABORATION, AND THE POSTWAR LITERARY PURGE IN FRANCE

1. "Je sais trop les redoutables dangers qu'offrent de nos jours les racismes, les nationalismes et toutes les formes, que l'on a vu successivement se produire, de l'amour de la patrie. Mais peut-être ne faudrait-il pas oublier pour autant certaine part de cet amour: sa part, si je peux dire, mystérieuse, celle justement que l'on est trop porté à négliger de nos jours.

"C'est qu'un tel amour est peut-être la seule barrière qui se puisse opposer au danger des opinions. . . ." The unpublished manuscript of this text is in the Paulhan archives at the IMEC in Paris.

2. The references for what I note here as a very general and widespread impression would probably run to several pages, so I quote representatively, and somewhat at random, from Peter Brooks's recent article "Aesthetics and Ideology: What Happened to Poetics": "At the moment when the media discovered 'desconstruction' and accused professors of turning from the evaluative to the normative function of criticism, another kind of swerve was in fact taking place, one which would turn even many of the deconstructionists into practitioners of ideological and cultural critique. [. . .] The posthumous drawings and quarterings of Paul de Man provide an allegory of the situation and its treatment. History is waiting behind the arras, ready to smite if you have appeared to turn from it" (*Critical Inquiry* 20, no. 3, Spring 1994, pp. 509–10).

3. See in particular Werner Hamacher, Neil Hertz, and Thomas Keenan, ed., *Responses: On Paul de Man's Wartime Writings* (Lincoln: University of Nebraska Press, 1989).

4. Paul de Man, *Wartime Journalism 1933–1943* (Lincoln: University of Nebraska Press, 1988), pp. 168–69.

5. "Like the Sound of the Sea Deep Within a Shell: Paul de Man's War," in *Responses*, p. 138.

6. "Writing and Deference: The Politics of Literary Adulation," in *Representations*, Summer 1986.

7. See Herbert Lottman, *The Left Bank* (Boston: Houghton Miffin, 1982). During the Occupation the number of books published in fact increased significantly. Lottman asks the pertinent question of who the authors of these books were, and what their contents were, but it is nonetheless true

that only a small number of writers did not publish at all with "official" publishers during the war.

8. *The Left Bank,* p. 231.

9. Paulhan's friendship with Jouhandeau in fact went back a long way, and was to continue for the rest of his life. Jouhandeau's antisemitism was already entirely unambiguous in 1936, when he wrote a provocative article for *Action Française* entitled "Comment je suis devenu antisémite" (How I became an anti-semite). From their correspondance we can tell that this was a point of fundamental disagreement between them. It continued to be so, despite Paulhan's general disappointment with the Popular Front's political platform once they had been elected, and even during his outspoken defence of Jouhandeau, among others, after the war was over.

10. December 1938, in *Oeuvres complètes,* vol. 5, pp. 271–73.

11. In *Oeuvres complètes,* vol. 5, pp. 277–81.

12. "La Démocratie," p. 278.

13. See Lottmann, *The Left Bank,* p. 162, and Pierre Assouline, *L'Epuration des intellectuels,* pp. 292 and 296 ff. Editors of almost all the publishing houses in Paris agreed collectively in May 1940 (before the Armistice, that is), as the "Syndicat des éditeurs français" (French Publishers' Union), to the conditions of collaboration laid down by Otto Abetz.

14. See Pierre Assouline, *L'Epuration des intellectuels,* p. 330: "Jean Paulhan, in October 1940, did not want to go back to work in an *NRF* purged of its Jews and its anti-Nazis. He found this contemptible." My translation.

15. The relationship between Drieu and Paulhan is discussed in greater detail in Herbert Lottman, "Capturing the *NRF,*" in *The Left Bank.* Lottman refers to Paulhan's office at rue Sebastian-Bottin as a "resistance cell" (p. 147).

16. See Gerhard Heller's memoirs of the Occupation, *Un Allemand à Paris* (Paris: Editions du Seuil, 1981), especially the chapter entitled "Mon maître Paulhan" (pp. 97–113).

17. For Paulhan's account of this week, see "Une semaine au secret," in *Oeuvres complètes,* vol. 1, pp. 291–97.

18. See Heller, *Un Allemand à Paris,* pp. 105–8.

19. For a more general history of the *épuration,* see Raymond Aron, *Histoire de l'épuration* (Paris: Fayard, 1975), 3 vols., especially vol. 3, no. 2, "Le monde de la presse, des arts et des lettres"; Jean-Pierre Rioux, "Epurer," in *La France de la quatrième République* (Paris: Seuils Points, 1980), pp. 49–67; and by the same author, "L'épuration en France (1944–1945)," in *L'Histoire,* no. 5, October 1978.

20. See Peter Novick, *The Resistance versus Vichy* (New York: Columbia University Press, 1968), p. 126.

21. The list, which was circulated privately among the members of the C.N.E., is reproduced in Pierre Assouline's *L'Epuration des intellectuels* (Paris: Editions Complexes, 1985), pp. 161–62.

22. The exchange of letters between Paulhan and Morgan was particularly acrimonious, and Morgan went as far as removing Paulhan's name as co-founder of *Les Lettres françaises*. (It had originally read: "Founded by Jacques Decour and Jean Paulhan.")

23. In *Les Lettres françaises*, 14 February 1947, quoted by Paulhan in an Appendix to *De la Paille et du grain*, p. 355.

24. *The Resistance versus Vichy*, p. 202.

25. *L'Epuration des intellectuels*, p. 108.

26. Ibid., p. 90.

27. "Le seul grief que vous reteniez contre les écrivains portés sur votre liste noire, ce n'est ni l'erreur ou la cupidité, ni la bassesse ou le goût de l'avilissement, c'est 'le crime irréparable, le tort irréversible, fait à la nation'" (*De la Paille et du grain*, Oeuvres Complètes, vol. 5, p. 344). Henceforth abbreviated as *Paille*, with the French original including the reference given in the footnotes. English translations are my own.

28. "Le goût des valeurs morales, la foi dans la justice ou la liberté, l'amour des peuples sont des sentiments louables; mais ils ne sont pas *le* sentiment qu'on appelle patriotisme. Non, pas plus que l'exotisme ou les plaisirs de l'anthropophagie. Et qu'est-ce donc que le patriotisme?" (The appreciation of moral values, the faith in justice or freedom, the love of other peoples, are all praiseworthy sentiments; but they are not *the* sentiment we call patriotism. No, not any more than exoticism or the pleasures of cannibalism. So, what is patriotism?) (*Paille*, p. 349).

29. "Que reprochez-vous donc, Benda, à ces collaborateurs, dont vous exigez le massacre? Est-ce d'avoir trahi leur patrie? Non, si vous étiez prêt vous-même à la trahir. C'est d'admirer un régime que vous vomissez. C'est d'appartenir à un parti qui n'est pas le vôtre. Vous n'êtes pas un patriote et s'il vous arrive, en telle ou telle circonstance, de trouver la patrie de votre côté, vous pouvez loyalement dire que ce n'est pas votre faute. Vous êtes un partisan, c'est tout différent" (*Paille*, p. 349).

30. In his *Lettre aux directeurs de la Résistance*, Paulhan quotes the number of 60,000 executions, which historians have agreed to be a grossly exaggerated figure, but one which was in public circulation for a long time. The officially accepted estimate is around 10,000. Cf. Novick, *The Resistance versus Vichy*, p. 202, and Rioux, "L'épuration en France (1944–1945)," *Histoire*, no. 5 (October 1978).

31. "Or le patriotisme consiste à ne pas plus séparer cette France charnelle de la France spirituelle, que la face dans un homme ne se sépare du profil" (*Paille*, p. 349).

32. For a more extensive discussion of the question of the legitimacy and legality of the Vichy government, see Peter Novick, *The Resistance versus Vichy*, pp. 191–97.

33. "Tant qu'il s'agit d'actes un peu extraordinaires, comme de fabriquer une montre, de rédiger un contrat de mariage ou de bâtir un Palais de Justice, un seul homme peut y arriver: l'architecte, le notaire, l'horloger. Oui, mais sitôt qu'il s'agit de simplement lire l'heure, d'être amoureux, ou de rendre la Justice qui est (ou qui devrait être) dans le Palais, eh bien, nous en sommes tous capables. Et même il arrive—en amour, par exemple—que le plus ignorant s'en tire mieux que le professionnel" (*Lettre*, p. 441).

34. "Jean Paulhan et le discours politique," in *Jean Paulhan le souterrain*, p. 225. Ferenczi is one of the few commentators to acknowledge the consistent and active interdependence between the linguistic and the ideological in Paulhan. Cf. also on this question his "Politique des littérateurs" *Cahiers Jean Paulhan* 3, pp. 33–40.

35. "Voici où je voulais en venir: tant qu'ils n'auront pas décrété qu'il existe des opinions coupables, et dignes de mort, les pacifistes de 1914 n'ont pas le droit de se montrer si agressifs pour les pacifistes de 1940. Ni les fusillés de 1915 (si je peux dire) de regarder de si haut les fusillés de 1945. Du simple point de vue de la patrie, ils se valent: c'est blanc bonnet et bonnet blanc" (*Paille*, p. 350).

36. Paulhan himself lists hyperbaton in his *Traité des figures (Treatise on Figures)* as a figure of language, in a sub-section on figures of construction (*Oeuvres complètes*, vol. 2, p. 216).

37. "Ces Blancs ont trahi la Patrie!—Vous conveniez vous-mêmes de la trahir, le cas échéant. Avouez donc la vérité. Vous les exterminez parce qu'ils sont blancs" (*Paille*, p. 348).

38. "Il est trop vrai qu'il existe du Droit à la Justice le même écart, peu s'en faut, qui sépare la lettre et l'esprit: la lettre, toujours près d'empiéter sur l'esprit, de le restreindre et l'amoindrir—toujours prête à passer lettre morte. Mais l'esprit vivace est libre, échappant aux pièges de l'automatisme, renaissant à tout instant" (*Lettre*, p. 436).

39. "Il joue ici une sorte de grammaire des idées qui n'est ni moins prompte ni moins décisive que notre grammaire des mots (cette grammaire spontanée qui nous rebrousse, ou nous fait éclater de rire devant une phrase mal bâtie, un mot prononcé de travers)" (*Lettre*, pp. 440–41).

40. The more usual French term for separating the wheat from the chaff is "séparer le bon grain de l'ivraie." I have chosen to use the appropriate Eng-

lish proverb to retain the proverbial flavor of the French, which is undoubtedly present in the original.

41. "Quel plaisir de lire, dans les dernières pages d'Eugène Marsan: Ce cheval a deux joquets. . . . *Joquet,* comme *croquet,* comme *jacquet,* cela fait un gentil mot français" (*Paille,* p. 315).

42. ". . . de savoir si la langue française est encore capable de se défendre, et d'habiller à sa guise les mots exotiques qu'elle accueille" (*Paille,* p. 316).

43. "Il tient, si l'on aime mieux, dans un conseil: (A quoi j'ajouterais volontiers: traite les mots étrangers comme s'ils ne voulaient rien dire.) Et je ne dis pas que ce soit là une maxime claire. Non. A la bien examiner, elle est même absurde. Reste à savoir si pour prendre une vue juste des choses—et de la littérature en particulier—il ne faut pas commencer par tolérer certaine absurdité, l'accueillir, lui faire place" (*Paille,* pp. 318–19).

44. "Et je sais bien que plus d'un homme s'imagine, au fond de lui, que les mots par quelque mystère nous révèlent la nature des choses: le malheur est que c'est une opinion qui risque de s'évanouir assez vite—précisément quand on apprend une autre langue que la sienne" (*Paille,* p. 318).

45. "Nous avons toujours été fiers, non pas sans raison, des Français qui malmenaient quelque peu la France" (*Paille,* p. 330).

46. "Les antipatriotes, c'est le luxe des patries" (*Paille,* p. 329).

47. "Et pour peu que l'on soit resté naïf, on n'arrête pas de faire jouer ce mystère, et de s'en étonner: de lancer en l'air des mots, pour les voir se transformer en idées. Et même des quarts de mots, un accent, une simple lettre" (*Paille,* p. 32).

5. AESTHETIC SPACES, DOMESTIC TRACES

1. "(Les critiques) se taisent . . . pour nous donner à entendre que le peintre lui aussi—lui d'abord—renonce à commenter, à détailler, à situer, nous jette dans l'espace plutôt qu'il ne le démontre, participe au lieu de décrire, et donc à sa façon se tait. . . . Bref , il y aurait eu, de peintre à critique, une contagion un peu gauche de ce silence.

"Mais les voies de l'écriture ne sont pas celles des arts, et je ne regrette pas tout à fait d'avoir tenté de le rompre." *La Peinture cubiste,* in *Oeuvres complètes,* vol. 5, p. 146. Quotations from this essay will be in my English translation. The French original including the reference to the text, abbreviated as *Peinture,* will be given in the footnote.

2. In "Writing and Deference" (art. cit.), Jeffrey Mehlman sees the relationship between Paulhan and Heller as prefigurative of a generalized "adulation" of French intellectuals by outsiders. According to Mehlman, Heller is able to appreciate the works of Braque and Picasso, thanks to Paulhan's ability to "domesticate" the violent energies of Cubist painting. I would again see Mehlman's summary of Paulhan's "aesthetics" as distorted, and based upon an inadequate reading of the relevant texts themselves. The relationship between aesthetics and "domestication" (the aesthetics of the domestic, the domestication of aesthetics, and aesthetics as a domesticating force), are key problems of Paulhan's writings on art, and will be explored later on in the present chapter. For a more detailed discussion of Mehlman's comments on Paulhan's aesthetics, see my "Domesticated Reading: Paulhan, Derrida and the Logic of Ancestry," in J. Wolfreys, ed. *French Connections* (Albany: State University of New York Press, 1998).

3. The texts concerned are, for rhetoric: *Les Fleurs de Tarbes,* 1941; "La Rhétorique renaît de ses cendres" (Rhetoric is Reborn from its Ashes), 1938; "La Rhétorique était une société secrète" (Rhetoric Was a Secret Society), 1946; "Traité des Figures, ou la Rhétorique décryptée" (Treatise on Figures, or Rhetoric Decoded), 1949; and "L'illusion de l'étymologie" (The Illusion of Etymology), 1950; and for art: "Lettre à Jean Dubuffet" (Letter to Jean Dubuffet) and "Braque ou le sens du caché" (Braque or the Sense of the Hidden), 1944; "Fautrier l'enragé" (Fautrier the Furious One), 1945; *Braque le patron (Braque the Boss),* 1946; and *La Peinture cubiste (Cubist Painting),* 1953.

4. Christine Poggi, *In Defiance of Painting* (New Haven, Conn.: Yale University Press, 1992), p. 28.

5. "On symbolise volontiers les révolutions par l'assaut donné à quelque palais. Et la peinture moderne, elle aussi, brise avec le décor de théâtre, l'architecture et la perspective, et prend sa Bastille avec un bon siècle de retard" (*Peinture,* p. 57).

6. ". . . les brouillons et les études qu'ils présentent aux jeunes peintres ressemblent aux cages d'une ménagerie où l'on aurait enfermé, au lieu de tigres et de panthères, des cubes vus de près ou de loin, de face ou de travers, des cubes et encore des cubes" (*Peinture,* p. 72).

7. "De quel nom cependant appeler un souci—une révélation—qui a trait non plus à la beauté (ou à la laideur, ou au caractère) de la maison, de la caisse ou de la fleur, ni même au détail des pétales, des planches, des pierres dont elles sont faites et autres éléments et traits naturels—non, mais qui les dépasse (ou, si l'on aime mieux, les transcende)" (*Peinture,* p. 75).

8. "Au feu les gracieusetés et les belles nuances, les fleurs et les di-aprures!" (*Peinture*, p. 62).

9. "On dirait une initiation. On dirait une conversion. Il lui semble toucher, ne fût-ce qu'un instant, au tuf même des choses, par-delà les ap-parences, les idées, les faux-semblants" (*Peinture*, p. 74).

10. "Il semblerait donc qu'avec les tableaux modernes le toucher prend le pas sur la vue, l'espace tactile sur l'espace visuel" (*Peinture*, p. 57).

11. "De Bergson à Husserl, d'Alexander à Heidegger, un nouveau réal-isme se propose de nous conduire aux choses elles-mêmes, vierges d'inter-prétation, et refuse de considérer la moindre réflexion, la perception la plus fugitive sans y inclure notre présence au monde. Tantôt elle insiste sur l'in-tention ou le projet, essentiels (prétend-elle) à tout état de conscience, qui nous mêlent étroitement aux choses—et les cubistes, eux aussi, refusaient le 'point de vue', extérieur et fixe, de la vieille perspective—, tantôt sur l'iden-tité profonde qui nous unit au monde, de toute façon mettant l'accent sur le pré-donné, le non-réfléchi, bref sur *ce* qui existe avant que nous en prenions conscience—et de l'espace cubiste aussi, il faudrait dire qu'il précède toute pensée que nous en formions" (*Peinture*, pp. 134–35).

12. "L'univers entier se disloque" (*Peinture*, p. 50).

13. "Le peintre parle espace, comme un Anglais parle anglais; ou un Chinois, chinois. C'est un langage qui a ses mots et ses locutions familières, ses lignes et ses combinaisons de lignes, ses couleurs et ses rencontres de couleurs; qui a même ses clichés: le cercle, la sphère, la section d'or; ses ono-matopées, les trompe-l'oeil; qui a sa grammaire, qui a même, on l'a vu, sa rhétorique, ses règles et ses unités—et il arrive, comme pour l'autre rhétorique, que ces règles paraissent soudain artificielles et de pure convention" (*Pein-ture*, p. 102).

14. "Ainsi les mots, à force de servir, deviennent inertes et perdent la pointe de leur sens. L'usage avilit, et le recommencement" (*Peinture*, p. 137).

15. Jean-Claude Zylberstein refers to this recycling process as "réécrit-ure" (rewriting) or "montage" [. . .] "Paulhan réutilisait sans cesse ses pro-pres textes" (Paulhan endlessly reused his own texts), in *Jean Paulhan le souterrain*, p. 390.

16. ". . . la réunion d'éléments hétérogènes" (*Peinture*, p. 114).

17. "C'est qu'une pyramide, à qui se place au-dessus d'elle et la regarde de haut, peut donner également l'impression de s'avancer vers notre oeil la pointe en avant, et tout aussi bien de s'enfuir et creuser devant notre regard un vide, au fond duquel se trouve la pointe. En sorte qu'il est facile, au prix d'un léger exercice, et passant rapidement de l'un à l'autre aspect, de voir la pyramide animée d'un mouvement de va-et-vient et tantôt se rapprochant

jusqu'à toucher l'oeil, tantôt s'enfuyant au contraire. Ainsi de l'espace obtenu par le jeu du papier collé" (*Peinture,* p. 133).

18. "... le trait s'est émoussé, la vivacité s'est amortie [...] dont la force est redoublée" (*Traité des figures,* pp. 210, 211).

19. "La métaphore n'arrête pas d'apparaître et de disparaître: elle est à n'en plus finir" (*Les Fleurs de Tarbes,* p. 226).

20. "... faire vaciller le langage à nos yeux" (*Peinture,* p. 237).

21. As Jean-Claude Zylberstein points out, it resurfaces in many different guises: "This nocturnal exploration of his studio/bedroom is an exceptional model of transhumance, and Paulhan will offer it up to us in many different contexts. It appears in 1948 in "L'espace sensible au coeur" (The space which the heart can feel), disappears in "L'espace d'avant les raisons" (Space prior to reason), 1953, makes a strong comeback in "Les peintres de la tache noire" (The painters of the black mark), 1959. In between, this little adventure makes an appearance in *Le Clair et l'obscur (The Clear and the Obscure),* where it is used as part of an argument which is not pictural this time, but rather metaphysical. Finally in 1962, Paulhan will place this text, "La Petite aventure" (The Little Adventure) on its own in the collection *Paroles peintes (Painted Words).* And this text returned once again in a short text entitled "Introduction à l'on ne sait quoi" (Introduction to Who Knows What), unpublished and originally intended to close the first volume of the *Oeuvres complètes (Jean Paulhan le souterrain,* p. 396).

22. "Eh bien, il n'avait rien de commun avec l'espace que l'on découvre d'une fenêtre, avec cet espace vaguement étoilé, par exemple. . . . Non, c'était même tout le contraire. Point de ces places lointaines et de ces places voisines! Ici, tout m'était voisin" (*Peinture,* pp. 76–77).

23. "C'est que j'avais traversé l'espace d'un tableau moderne. J'étais très précisément entré dans une toile de Braque ou de Picasso (et je venais d'en sortir)" (*Peinture,* p. 78).

24. "J'avais parfaitement vu tous mes obstacles, je ne les avais jamais tant vus, je les avais presque trop vus, à cette lumière aveuglante—comme s'ils n'avaient jamais encore été là; comme s'ils venaient d'être créés; comme s'ils venaient de se créer eux-mêmes!" (*Peinture,* p. 78).

25. "Dans cette aimable chambre que je connais bien—que je connais trop, un peu fatiguée vraiment [...] Avec sa vieille armoire paysanne, fabriquée pour les noces de ma grand-mère—mais elle a très bien tenu le coup jusqu'à moi [...] Ah! c'est pourtant une belle pendule transparente . . ." (*Peinture,* p. 79).

26. "Mais ne nous laissons pas distraire" (*Peinture,* p. 79).

27. "C'était le contraire d'un rêve, c'était à l'opposé d'une pensée: non pas l'un de ces espaces fluides et qui s'approfondissent à mesure; non, par-

faitement opaque et volumineux; et moi, non moins volumineux que lui ni moins opaque. Exactement de même race. Pris dans la même gelée" (*Peinture*, p. 79).

28. ". . . comme s'il m'était poussé dans la nuque des yeux, dans le dos des antennes" (*Peinture*, p. 80).

29. "Chaque personnage de mon aventure se trouvait avoir sa vertu propre, irréductible à tout autre. . . . La commode était fidèle, mais distante; la cheminée pointue, mais loyale; la machine à écrire, pleine de hargne; le paravent, compatissant (quoique peu sûr)" (*Peinture*, p. 81).

30. "Bref l'espace où j'avançais m'était énigmatique, et me le fût demeuré, si je ne m'étais par chance, je l'ai dit, juste sur le point de m'endormir, rappelé la peinture moderne" (*Peinture*, p. 81).

31. ". . . se déroulait dans le temps, il m'arrivait par vagues successive. . . . Il était fait, si je peux dire, d'une suite d'ébauches" (*Peinture*, p. 80).

32. ". . . le temps du moins restait fidèle [. . .] même le temps se déréglait" (*Peinture*, p. 77).

33. "Quelle joie de disposer à la fois de l'expérience de la vieillesse, mais de l'invention de l'enfance" (*Peinture*, p. 84).

34. "vieille armoire paysanne . . . qui a bien tenu le coup jusqu'à moi. . . . Que de morts sur nos murs, à nos vitres! Que de momies, qui ont été jadis des personnages actifs, agités, inquiétants et puis se sont fanés comme des feuilles" (*Peinture*, p. 79).

35. "L'une a trait à *l'usure des sens*. Elle porte que le mot s'épuise avant l'idée et laisse aisément altérer, s'il ne la perd—plus l'idée est de soi vive et frappante—sa vertu expressive. . . . Loin que le mot survive à l'idée, c'est l'idée qui survit au mot" (*Les Fleurs de Tarbes*, p. 44).

36. "Comment le rendre *sensible*, sinon par métaphore? ici le mot *usure*. On ne peut en effet accéder à l'usure d'un phénomène linguistique sans lui donner quelque représentation figurée. Que pourrait être l'usure *proprement dite* d'un mot, d'un énoncé, d'une signification, d'un texte?" "White Mythology," trans. Alan Bass, in *Margins of Philosophy* (Brighton: Harvester Press, 1982), p. 209. The original French is "La Mythologie blanche" in *Marges de la philosophie*, p. 249. Derrida touches on the question of *usure* somewhat elliptically in his discussion of the fate of metaphorical language in the Western philosophical tradition. The main focus of his text is on the visual analogues of metaphor (the sun as the source of all figures, the heliotrope, etc.).

37. Dominique Fisher, in her article "Jean Paulhan: Towards a Poetic/Pictural Space" (*The French Review* 61, no. 6 [May 1988], pp. 878–83) translates "enseigne," literally a "shop-sign," as "image-sign," a term she borrows from Meyer Schapiro. It is, according to Fisher, "a visual sign which negates the representational function of an iconic sign" (p. 882).

38. "Et que veut dire une enseigne? Elle ne prétend pas qu'il soit bon pour la santé de fumer ni qu'un veau à deux têtes soit un spectacle instructif. Non. Elle n'insinue même pas que le tabac dont il s'agit a bon goût, ni que le veau est particulièrement gracieux. *Il ne s'agit avec elle ni de morale, ni d'esthétique.* Elle dit simplement: on trouve ici du tabac, on voit un veau à deux têtes. Tout ce qu'on dit, c'est: 'il y a' (et même IL Y A!). Elle le dit brutalement, sans d'ailleurs le moins du monde chercher à rendre l'aspect véritable de la civette ou du veau. Elle n'a rien d'un trompe-l'oeil. Personne ne la prendrait pour l'animal lui-même . . ." (*Peinture,* p. 81).

39. "Mais quoi! elle suffit bien, comme la bribe d'armoire, à nous convaincre" (*Peinture,* p. 82).

40. "Un papier collé, le plus souvent, n'est pas signé. Mais ce serait peu: il semble fortement qu'il ne prête pas à signature . . ." (*Peinture,* p. 114).

41. "Signature event context," in *Margins of Philosophy,* trans. Alan Bass (Brighton: Harvester Press, 1982), p. 220.

42. The text was first published with Editions de l'Echoppe (Caen, 1989), and then as an appendix to the Folio edition of *La Peinture cubiste* (1990, ed. Jean-Claude Zylberstein). It is this latter edition I shall be referring to.

43. "Bref il y avait dans le tableau une faille, un défaut, un élément anti-pictural. Il s'y trouvait aussi, plus ou moins clairement présenté, un objet précis. Seulement par l'effet de l'opération du peintre, c'est l'élément anti-pictural qui devenait l'occasion de la peinture, la faille qui permettait l'objet—l'élément caché qui justifiait l'apparence" (*La Peinture Cubiste,* Folio edition, 1990, pp. 214–15).

44. Jean Fautrier, *Sur la virtuosité (Lettre à Jean Paulhan)* (Paris: Editions Envois, 1987).

45. ". . . il paraît obéir à présent aux volontés de l'huile et de l'enduit, à quelque besoin de sa pâte.

"C'est une étrange pâte, et fort gênante à détailler. Ce qui forme tant de vapeurs et de poudroiements, les plus subtils peut-être mais les plus violents qu'on ait jamais vus dans un tableau, ce sont d'épais grumeaux aplatis, un badigeon de fard, un écrasis d'huile et de pastel, tout un sabrage de craie grasse. On découvre alors que Fautrier s'est fabriqué une matière à lui, qui tient de l'aquarelle et de la fresque, de la détrempe et de la gouache; où le pastel broyé se mêle à l'huile, et l'encre à l'essence. Le tout mastiqué, pilé, bouchonné à la main et qui s'applique à la hâte, sans repentirs (à la façon des fresquistes), sur un papier gras, qu'un enduit colle à la toile" (*Fautrier l'enragé, Oeuvres complètes,* vol. 5, p. 200).

46. "Car cette maîtrise n'aurait rien de plus pressé que d'effacer sa trace, et se rendre invisible" (*Fautrier,* p.205).

47. "Car *beau*, de nos jours, fait curieusement penser à des arbres de soie, et des fleuves en verre filé" (*Fautrier,* p. 199).

48. For a more detailed account of the relationship of Fautrier to Paulhan, see Jean-Yves Pouilloux, "Ecrire avec . . . ," *Critique,* no. 490 March 1988), pp. 187–95.

49. "C'est comme quand on se réveille en pleine nuit, ou même le matin au moment de se lever. Qu'est-ce qu'on voit, au sortir d'un rêve (en général un peu convenu, et même académique, où les maisons ont toits et fenêtres; et les personnages, bras et jambes), qu'est-ce qu'on voit, sinon un zigzag, un éclair, un éclat; quelque chose comme une haie de brindilles, des morceaux de carrés et de losanges (qui tiennent aux plinthes du mur), un nuage où courent des rais lumineux. Quoi! des débris, des déchets. Il arrive qu'on referme les yeux, de la déception qu'on a. (Sans compter l'envie de dormir encore.) Et pourtant, c'est ça qui est vrai. Ce sont ces déchets qui portent tout le reste du monde. Ce sont ces débris qui sont présents" (*Fautrier,* p. 215).

50. "Et pour peu que l'on soit resté naïf, on n'arrête pas de faire jouer ce mystère, et de s'en étonner: de lancer en l'air des mots, pour les voir se transformer en idées. Et même des quarts de mots, un accent, une simple lettre" (*De la Paille et du grain,* p. 321).

51. The reference is of course to Derrida's essay "White mythology," in *Margins of Philosophy.*

CONCLUSION

1. "DissemiNation: Time, narrative and the margins of the modern nation," in *The Location of Culture* (London: Routledge, 1994), pp. 139–70.

2. "DissemiNation," p. 147.

3. "DissemiNation," p. 164.

4. "DissemiNation," p. 163.

5. L'un des hommes se plaignit: il souffrait de la tête. Son voisin se leva et s'allongeant à son côté lui pressa le front de ses mains: «Plus fort», dit l'autre. Ces mots rappelèrent ma surprise.

Presque aussitôt j'en appris la raison. A la droite du malade étaient des joueurs de cartes. L'un eux reprenait son partenaire: «Je ne t'avais pas dit de mettre la plus faible, eh tête! Ce sont des mots *nifis* simples.» Ils parlaient une langue étrangère.

Les mots sans doute m'auraient arrêté; j'avais dû saisir plus avant leurs sens, dans l'instant juste où ils allaient se traduire en phrases—et comme en détournant une part pour moi. (*Oeuvres complètes,* vol. 1, p. 98. English translation: *The Crossed Bridge,* in *Progress in Love on the Slow Side,* trans. Christine Laennec and Michael Syrotinski [Lincoln: University of Nebraska Press, 1994], p. 74)

6. Clifford Geertz, "Native's point of view: anthropological understanding," in his *Local Knowledge* (New York: Basic Books, 1983), p. 70. Quoted by Bhabha in *The Location of Culture,* p. 59.

BIBLIOGRAPHY

Anceschi, Luciano. "Paulhan, o dell'ambiguità delle lettere." *Il Verri*, no. 32 (March 1970).

Aron, Raymond. *Histoire de l'épuration*, 3 vols. Paris: Fayard, 1975.

Assouline, Pierre. *Gaston Gallimard* (Paris: Balland, 1984).

———. *L'Epuration des intellectuels*. Paris: Editions Complexes, 1985.

Austin, John Lloyd. *How to Do Things With Words*, ed. J. O. Urmson and Marina Sbisà. Cambridge, Mass.: Harvard University Press, 1975.

———. *Philosophical Papers*, ed. J. O. Urmson and G. L. Warnock. Oxford: Oxford University Paperbacks, 1961.

Bachelard, Gaston. "Une Psychologie du langage littéraire." In *Le Droit de rêver*. Paris: PUF, 1970.

Badré, Frédéric (ed.). *L'Infini 55* (Autumn). Issue devoted to Jean Paulhan. Paris: Gallimard, 1996.

Baetens, Jan. "Je m'appelle Jacques Maast." In *Poétique,* no. 78 (April 1987): 173–84.

Barthes, Roland. *La Chambre claire.* Paris: Editions de l'Etoile, Gallimard, Seuil, 1980.

———. *Le Plaisir du texte.* Paris: Seuil Points, 1973.

———. *Le Système de la mode.* Paris: Editions du Seuil, 1967.

———. *Mythologies,* trans. Annette Lavers. London: Paladin, 1973.

Belaval, Yvon (ed.). *Cahiers Jean Paulhan 3.* Paris: Gallimard, 1984.

Bennington, Geoffrey. *Sententiousness and the Novel.* Cambridge: Cambridge University Press, 1985.

Benveniste, Emile. *Problèmes de linguistique générale,* vol. 1. Paris: Tel Gallimard, 1966.

Berne Joffroy, André (ed.). *Jean Paulhan à travers ses peintres.* Paris: Editions des musées nationaux, 1974.

Bersani, Jacques (ed.). *Jean Paulhan le souterrain* (Colloque de Cérisy). Paris: 10/18, 1976.

Bhabha, Homi K. *The Location of Culture.* London: Routledge, 1994.

Blanchot, Maurice. "La Terreur dans les lettres." *Journal des Débats* (21 October 1941): 3.

———. "Comment la littérature est-elle possible?" *Journal des Débats* (25 November 1941): 3.

———. "Comment la littérature est-elle possible?" *Journal des Débats* (2 December 1941): 3.

———. *Comment la littérature est-elle possible?* Paris: José Corti, 1942.

———. "How is Literature Possible?" trans. Michael Syrotinski. In Michael Holland (ed.), *A Blanchot Reader.* Oxford: Blackwell, 1995.

———. *Faux Pas.* Paris: Gallimard, 1943.

———. "La Facilité de mourir." In *L'Amitié.* Paris: Gallimard, 1972, pp. 172–91.

———. "La Littérature et le droit à la mort." In *La Part du feu.* Paris: Gallimard, 1949, pp. 291–331.

———. "Literature and the Right to Death," trans. Lydia Davis. In *The Gaze of Orpheus and Other Literary Essays.* Tarrytown, N.Y.: Station Hill Press, 1981.

———. "Le Paradoxe d'Aytré." In *La Part du feu.* Paris: Gallimard, 1949, pp. 66–78.

———. "Le Mystère dans les lettres." In *La Part du feu*. Paris: Gallimard, 1949, pp. 49–65.

Boulestreau, Nicole. ". . . Comme une langue commune: Eluard à l'école de Paulhan." *Littérature*, no. 27 (October 1977): 44–45.

Bousquet, Joë. "A Propos des *Fleurs de Tarbes*." In *Cahiers du Sud* [Anthologie Joë Bousquet]. Marseille: Rivages, 1981. Text dates from 1939, pp. 138–61.

Brooks, Peter. "Aesthetics and Ideology: What Happened to Poetics?" *Critical Inquiry* 20, no. 3 (Spring 1994): 509–23.

Caillois, Roger. "Illusion à rebours." *Nouvelle Revue Française* (new series), no. 24 (December 1954): 1010–24; and no. 25 (January 1955): 58–70.

———. *L'Homme et le sacré*. Paris: Gallimard, 1963.

———. *The Necessity of the Mind*, trans. Michael Syrotinski. Venice, Calif.: Lapis Press, 1990.

Chemama, Roland. "L'Expérience du proverbe et le discours psychanalytique." *Ornicar?*, nos. 17–18 (1979): 43–55.

Clifford, James. *The Predicament of Culture: Twentieth Century Ethnography, Literature and Art*. (Cambridge, Mass.: Harvard University Press, 1988.

Cornick, Martyn. *The Nouvelle Revue Française under Jean Paulhan, 1925–1940*. Amsterdam: Rodopi, 1995.

de Man, Paul. *Allegories of Reading*. New Haven, Conn.: Yale University Press, 1979.

———. *Blindness and Insight*. Revised edition. Minneapolis: University of Minnesota Press, 1983.

———. *Critical Writings 1953–1978*. Minneapolis: University of Minnesota Press, 1988.

———. "Le Néant poétique: Commentaire d'un sonnet hermétique de Mallarmé." *Le Monde nouveau*, no. 88 (April 1955): 63–75.

———. "Roland Barthes and the Limits of Structuralism" (1972). *Yale French Studies* 77 (1990): 177–90.

———. *The Resistance to Theory*. Minneapolis, University of Minnesota Press, 1986.

———. *Wartime Journalism 1939–1943*, ed. Hamacher, Hertz, and Keenan. Lincoln: University of Nebraska Press, 1988.

Derrida, Jacques. *De la grammatologie*. Paris: Editions de Minuit, 1967.

———. "La Loi du genre." In *Parages*. Paris: Editions Galilée, 1986, pp. 249–87.

——. "La Pharmacie de Platon." In *La Dissémination.* Paris: Editions du Seuil, 1972, pp. 69–196.

——. "Like the Sound of the Sea Deep Within a Shell: Paul de Man's War." In *Responses. On Paul de Man's Wartime Journalism.* Lincoln: University of Nebraska Press, 1989.

——. *Marges de la philosophie.* Paris: Editions du Seuil, 1972. *Margins of Philosophy,* trans. Alan Bass. Brighton: Harvester Press, 1983.

Descombes, Vincent. *Modern French Philosophy.* Cambridge: Cambridge University Press, 1980.

Dhôtel, André. *Jean Paulhan.* Lyon: La Manufacture, Collection "Qui Suis-Je?" 1986.

Du Marsais, César Chesneau. *Traité des tropes.* Paris: Le Nouveau commerce, 1977.

Ducrot, Oswald, and Tzvetan Todorov. *Dictionnaire encyclopédique des sciences du langage.* Paris: Seuil Points, 1972.

Fautrier, Jean. *Sur la virtuosité (Lettre à Jean Paulhan).* Paris: Editions Envois, 1987.

Felman, Shoshana. *Le Scandale du corps parlant.* Paris: Editions du Seuil, 1980.

Fernandez, Ramon. "Les Fleurs de Tarbes." *Nouvelle Revue Française,* no. 333 (1 November 1941): 595–602.

Fisher, Dominique. "Jean Paulhan: Towards a Poetic/Pictural Space." *The French Review* 61, no. 6 (May 1988): 878–83.

Geertz, Clifford. *Local Knowledge.* New York: Basic Books, 1983.

Genette, Gérard. *Figures III.* Paris: Editions du Seuil, 1972.

Golding, John. *Cubism: A History and Analysis 1907–1914.* London: Faber and Faber, 1988.

Grover, Frederic J. "Les Années 30 dans la correspondance Gide-Paulhan." *Modern Language Notes 95,* no. 4 (May 1980): 830–49.

Hamacher, W., N. Hertz, and T. Keenan (eds.). *Responses. On Paul de Man's Wartime Journalism.* Lincoln: University of Nebraska Press, 1989.

Hegel, G. W. F. *Phänomenologie des Geistes Werke in zwanzig Bänden,* vol. 3. Frankfurt: Suhrkamp Verlag, 1970.

Hiedegger, Martin. *Sein und Zeit.* Tübingen: M. Niemeyer, 1963.

——. *Was ist Metaphysik?* Frankfurt: Klostermann, 1969.

Heller, Gerhard. *Un Allemand à Paris.* Paris: Editions du Seuil, 1981.

Hollier, Denis (ed.). *The College of Sociology.* Minneapolis: University of Minnesota Press, 1988.

———. "Afterword." In Roger Caillois, *The Necessity of the Mind*, trans. Michael Syrotinski. Venice, Calif.: Lapis Press, 1990.

Hountondji, Paulin. *African Philosophy, Myth, and Reality*. Bloomington, Ind.: Indiana University Press, 1983.

Hughes, Peter. "The Usual Terror, The Usual Suspects." In *Colloquium Helveticum: Cahiers Suisses de littérature comparée* 11–12 (1990): 21–38.

Jakobson, Roman. *Essais de linguistique générale*. Paris: Editions de Minuit, 1963.

Jenny, Laurent. "Un Bonheur sans emploi." *Critique,* no. 511 (December 1989): 410–22.

———. *La Terreur et les signes: Poétiques de rupture*. Paris: Gallimard, 1982.

———. Preface to *Cahiers Jean Paulhan 6: Correspondance Jean Paulhan-Roger Caillois*. Paris: Gallimard, 1991, pp. 7–22.

Kant, Immanuel. *Kritik der Urteilskraft Werke in zwölf Bänden* 10. Frankfurt: Suhrkamp Verlag, 1968.

Kohn-Etiemble, Jeannine (ed.). *226 Lettres inédites de Jean Paulhan. Contribution à l'étude du mouvement littéraire en France 1933–1967*. Paris: Klincksieck, 1975.

Lacan, Jacques. *Ecrits*. Paris: Editions du Seuil, 1966.

Laserra, Annamaria. "Paroxysmes." In Jenny Laurent (ed.), *Roger Caillois, la pensée aventurée*. Paris: Editions Belin, 1992, pp. 249–70.

Lefèbve, Maurice-Jean. *Jean Paulhan: Une Philosophie et une pratique de l'expression et de la réflexion*. Paris: Gallimard, 1949.

Lévi-Strauss, Claude. "Diogène couché." *Les Temps modernes,* no. 110 (1955): 1187–1220.

Levy, Karen. "From Duality to Triplicity: The Multidimensional Undertaking of Jean Paulhan." *Symposium* 44, no. 3 (1990): 180–90.

Lévy, Yves. "Jean Paulhan. Du Jardin fleuri aux catacombes." *Preuves,* no. 153 (November 1963): 3–21.

Lottmann, Herbert. *The Left Bank*. (Boston: Houghton Miffin, 1982.

Mallarmé, Stéphane. *Oeuvres Complètes*. Paris: Bibliothèque de la Pléiade, 1945.

Mehlman, Jeffrey. "Blanchot at Combat." In *Legacies of Anti-Semitism*. Minneapolis: University of Minnesota Press, 1983.

———. Interview with Christian Delacampagne. *Le Monde* (23 September 1994), p. 8.

———. "Perspectives: On Paul de Man and *Le Soir*." In *Responses. On Paul de Man's Wartime Journalism*. Lincoln: University of Nebraska Press, 1989, pp. 324–33.

————. "Response" to "More on Writing and Deference" (cf. Smock, Ann). *Representations* no. 18 (Spring 1987): 162–64.

————. "Writing and Deference: The Politics of Literary Adulation." *Representations,* no. 15 (Summer 1986): 1–14.

Mercier, Pascal. "Les écrits de Jean Paulhan dans la presse clandestine: Une Résistance appliquée." In *Actes du colloque "La Littérature française sous l'Occupation.* Reims: October 1981, pp. 93–99.

Meschonnic, Henri. "Jean Paulhan." In *Le Signe et le poème.* Paris: Gallimard, 1975, pp. 195–207.

————. "Paulhan et la terreur." In *La Rime et la vie.* Paris: Verdier, 1989.

Miller, Christopher. *Theories of Africans: Francophone Literature and Anthropology in Africa.* Chicago: University of Chicago Press, 1990.

Miller, Nancy K. *Getting Personal: Feminist Occasions and Other Autobiographical Acts.* New York and London: Routledge, 1991.

Mudimbe, V. Y. *The Invention of Africa: Gnosis, Philosophy and the Order of Knowledge.* Bloomington, Ind.: Indiana University Press, 1988.

Nash, Suzanne. "Paulhan lecteur de Valéry." *Nouvelle Revue Française* 452 (September 1990): 54–72.

Norris, Christopher. *Paul de Man: Deconstruction and the Critique of Aesthetic Ideology.* London: Routledge, 1988.

Novick, Peter. *The Resistance versus Vichy.* New York: Columbia University Press, 1968.

Paulhan, Jacqueline (ed.). *Bulletin de la Société des Lecteurs de Jean Paulhan,* no. 9 (October 1986).

Paulhan, Jacqueline, and Roger Judrin (eds.). *Cahiers Jean Paulhan 2.* Paris: Gallimard, 1982.

Paulhan, Jean. *Choix de lettres I. 1917–1936: La Littérature est une fête.* Paris: Gallimard, 1986.

————. *Chroniques de Jean Guérin 1927–1940, and 1953–1964,* ed. Jean-Philippe Segonds. Paris: Editions des Cendres, 1991.

————. *Essai d'introduction au projet d'une métrique universelle.* Paris: Le Nouveau Commerce, 1984.

————. *Jean Paulhan-Francis Ponge. Correspondance 1923–1968.* Edition critique annotée par Claire Boaretto. 2 vols. Paris: Gallimard, 1986.

————. *La Vie est pleine de choses redoutables,* ed. Claire Paulhan. Paris: Seghers, 1989.

————. *Le Pont traversé.* Le Revest-les-Eaux: Spectres Familiers, 1986.

————. *Progress in Love on the Slow Side,* trans. Christine Moneera Laennec and Michael Syrotinski. Lincoln: University of Nebraska Press, 1994.

———. *Le Repas et l'amour chez les Merinas.* Paris: Fata Morgana, 1970.

———. *Les Incertitudes du langage.* Paris: Gallimard Collections Idées, 1970.

———. *Oeuvres Complètes.* 5 vols. Paris: Cercle du livre précieux, 1966–1970.

———. *Traité du Ravissement.* Paris: Périple, 1983.

———. "Une lettre de Jean Paulhan." In *Preuves,* no. 155 (January 1964): 91–94.

Poggi, Christine. *In Defiance of Painting.* New Haven, Conn.: Yale University Press, 1992.

Pouilloux, Jean-Yves. "Ecrire avec . . ." *Critique,* no. 490 (March 1988): 187–95.

Rioux, Jean-Pierre. "Epurer." In *La France de la quatrième République.* Paris: Seuil Points, 1980.

———. "L'Epuration en France (1944–1945)." *L'Histoire,* no. 5 (October 1978).

Sakakibara, Naobumi. "La Fonction de 'la littérature' dans Aytré qui perd l'habitude." Unpublished article, n.d.

———. "Passivité de l'"être dans les récits de Jean Paulhan." Unpublished article, n.d.

Sartre, Jean-Paul. *Qu'est-ce que la littérature?* Paris: Gallimard, 1948.

Smock, Ann. "More on Writing and Deference." *Representations,* no. 18 (Spring 1987): 158–62.

———. "On Jean Paulhan's Récits." *Qui Parle* 8, no. 1 (Fall/Winter 1994): 130–51.

Stoekl, Allan. "Paulhan and Blanchot: On Rhetoric, Terror, and the Gaze of Orpheus." In *Agonies of the Intellectual.* Lincoln: University of Nebraska Press, 1992, pp. 145–73.

Syrotinski, Michael. "1941: Maurice Blanchot reviews Jean Paulhan's enigmatic *Les Fleurs de Tarbes.*" In Denis Hollier (ed.), *A New History of French Literature.* Cambridge, Mass.: Harvard University Press, 1989.

———. "Domesticated Reading: Paulhan, Derrida and the Logic of Ancestry." In *French Connections,* ed. J. Wolfreys. Albany: State University of New York Press, 1998.

———. "Jean Paulhan's Allegories of Translation." In *Translation and Literature, vol 3.* Edinburgh: Edinburgh University Press, 1994.

———. "Some Wheat and Some Chaff: Jean Paulhan and the Post-War Literary Purge in France." *Studies in Twentieth Century Literature* 16, no. 2 (Summer 1992): 247–63.

———. Introduction to *Progress in Love on the Slow Side: Récits by Jean Paulhan with an Essay by Maurice Blanchot,* trans. Christine Moneera

Laennec and Michael Syrotinski. Lincoln: University of Nebraska Press, 1994.

Trémolières, François. "L'art de Jean Paulhan." *Nouvelle Revue Française,* no. 356 (September 1982): 101–6.

Ungar, Steven. "Paulhan before Blanchot: From Terror to Letters between the Wars." *Studies in Twentieth Century Literature* 10, no. 1 (Fall 1985): 69–80.

Waters, Lindsay, and Wlad Godzich (eds.). *Reading De Man Reading.* Minneapolis: University of Minnesota Press, 1989.

Yeshua, Silvio. *Le Texte, le secret et l'exégèse.* Préface de Jean Starobinski. Paris: Champion, 1992.

INDEX

Abel, Karl, 15
Abetz, Otto, 108, 127, 181n.13
Adorno, Theodor, 158n.7
allegory: 14, 15, 39; *La Peinture cubiste* as, 134, 135, 139, 141, 163n.39; of public gardens of Tarbes, 87–89, 91, 120, 122, 123, 135
anarchism, 6
Apollinaire, Guillaume, 84, 108, 130–31
aporia, 12
Aragon, Louis, 2, 111, 114
Arland, Marcel, 2, 9

Artaud, Antonin, 2
Assouline, Pierre, 112
Audiberti, Jacques, 2
Augé, Marc, 28, 44, 165n.51
Aury, Dominique, 74, 75
Austin, J. L., 16, 170n.35
autobiography: and fiction, 5, 6, 50, 54, 69, 71; and linguistic enigma, 51, 55, 62; and personal writing, 48, 54–55, 63–64, 73, 168n.20

Barthes, Roland, 10, 11, 13, 22–23
Bataille, George, 2, 40, 41

Baudelaire, Charles, 143
Beaujour, Michel, 85
Benda, Julien, 109, 112, 115
Benjamin, Walter, 153, 155
Bennington, Geoffrey, 161n.19
Benvéniste, Emile, 10, 13
Bergson, Henri, 82, 133
betrayal, 96, 114, 148, 152
Bhabha, Homi K., 152–54
Blanchot, Maurice, 2, 9, 56, 63,
  116, 155, 166n.4; Blanchot-
  Sartre debate, 5, 79, 113–14;
  as reader of Clef de la Poésie,
  92, 93, 98–100; as reader of
  Les Fleurs de Tarbes, 15,
  19–21, 77, 84, 88, 90, 91;
  relationship to Paulhan, 15,
  16, 17, 19–21, 77, 78, 101–4
  WORKS: L'Arrêt de mort (Death
  Sentence), 15; "Comment la
  littérature est-elle possible?"
  (How is Literature Possible?),
  20, 77–80, 91; L'Espace
  littéraire (Literary Space), 20,
  103; "La Facilité de mourir"
  (The Ease of Dying), 17, 19,
  62–63, 72–73, 78; La Folie du
  jour (The Madness of Day), 18;
  "La littérature et le droit à la
  mort" (Literature and the
  Right to Death), 19–21, 79,
  102, 103; "Le Mystère dans les
  lettres" (Mystery in Literature),
  78, 92, 93, 98–100
Blum, Léon, 108
Bousquet, Joë, 2, 9
Brasillach, Robert, 108, 111
Breton, André, 1, 2, 6, 54
Brooks, Peter, 180n.2
Bruller, Jean, 110, 111

Caillois, Roger, 2, 3, 9, 40–44, 54,
  164nn.49,50. See also College

of Sociology; the sacred
Camus, Albert, 111, 113
Church, Barbara and Henry, 2
citationality, 16, 34, 86, 98, 148
Classicism, 83, 86, 97; in painting,
  131, 134, 137, 138
Claudel, Paul, 140
clichés, 5, 16, 33, 82, 86, 88–89,
  117–18, 154
Clifford, James, 27, 160n.7
collaboration. See Paulhan, Jean,
  and Second World War
College of Sociology, 40–44,
  164n.50
colonialism, 5, 25, 26, 28, 45–46,
  153
Comité National des Ecrivains
  (C.N.E., National Committee
  of Writers), 7, 115–16,
  118–20, 125; blacklist of, 108,
  111–13, 123, 182n.21
commonplaces, 5, 11, 81, 82, 86,
  87, 89, 134
Communism, 108, 111, 117, 118
Comte, Auguste, 40
Condillac, Etienne Bonnot de, 13
Crevel, René, 2
Cubism, 5, 10, 27, 28, 54, 160n.7;
  history of, 129–32; Paulhan's
  relationship to, 128, 131–33,
  139, 142, 149; and poetry,
  130–31

Dadaism, Paulhan's relationship to,
  1
Daumal, René, 2
Davis, Gary, 123
de Beauvoir, Simone, 111
deconstruction, 4, 106, 107, 125,
  147, 180n.2, 188n.36; Paulhan
  as precursor of, 15–18, 21. See
  also Derrida; de Man
Decour, Jacques, 7

Decourdemanche, Daniel, 110, 111
de Gaulle, Charles, 111, 115
de Man, Paul, 12–15, 21, 80, 106,
    107, 158nn.6,7,9, 180n.2
Derrida, Jacques, 1, 12, 15–19, 21,
    78, 107, 116, 142, 147,
    188n.36
Descombes, Vincent, 71
Dhôtel, André, 4, 5
Diderot, Denis, 13
domestication, 66, 136, 148,
    159n.15, 185n.2
Drieu la Rochelle, Pierre, 2, 7, 110,
    111
Dubuffet, Jean, 2, 128
du Gard, Roger Martin, 2
Duhamel, George, 111
duplicity, 3, 5, 8, 21, 42–44, 96,
    98, 129, 149; as ethical
    question, 17, 18, 114, 124,
    152; as narrative self-
    reflexivity, 63, 92; as rhetorical
    structure, 95, 116, 117, 124,
    152

Editions de Minuit, 7
Eluard, Paul, 2, 6, 84
epistemology, 10, 15, 28
épuration (postwar purge), 5, 7, 16,
    17, 21, 105–7, 111–13, 116,
    119, 123, 181n.19, 182n.30
Ernst, Max, 1
ethnography, 5, 27–30, 33, 39, 46,
    164n.50
Etiemble, René, 2
etymologism, 10, 15, 148

Fargue, Léon-Paul, 84
fascism, 77, 108, 117, 118, 123
Fautrier, Jean, 128, 143–46,
    190n.48
Felman, Shoshana, 170n.35
Flaubert, Gustave, 9, 82

Follain, Jean, 3
Freud, Sigmund, 73, 74

Gautier, Théophile, 84
Genet, Jean, 9
Genette, Gérard, 54
Gide, André, 2, 54, 108
Golding, John, 160n.7
Gourmont, René de, 83
Gracq, Julien, 2
grammar, 14, 33, 60–62, 118, 119,
    134. *See also* linguistic theory
grammatology, 15, 16
Grenier, Jean, 2
Griaule, Marcel, 27
Gris, Juan, 128, 140
Groethuysen, Bernard, 2
Guéhenno, Jean, 111
Guérin, Jean (pseudonym, Jean
    Paulhan), 22, 49

hain-teny, 6, 25, 26, 29–31, 154,
    163n.35
Hegel, Georg Wilhelm Friedrich,
    20, 79, 80
Heidegger, Martin, 19, 21, 133
Heller, Gerhard, 15, 110, 127,
    185n.2
Hess, Rudolf, 22
Hollier, Denis, 54, 168n.18
Hountondji, Paulin, 27
Hugo, Victor, 11, 85
Husserl, Edmund, 133
Hyppolite, Jean, 79, 80

indifference, 61, 69, 98–101,
    108–9, 118, 125; to death, 53;
    as a linguistic problem, 16, 96,
    117, 120, 124, 151
irony, 5, 14, 16, 17, 38, 88, 155,
    163n.38
Jacob, Max, 130
Jakobson, Roman, 10,

Jouhandeau, Marcel, 2, 108, 181n.9
Judrin, Roger, 3, 4

Kant, Emmanuel, 20
Kierkegaard, Søren, 20
Kojève, Alexandre, 79

Lacan, Jacques, 170n.35
La Fontaine, 11
Larbaud, Valéry, 2
Lautréamont, le comte de, 20
Leiris, Michel, 2, 27, 54
Lescure, Pierre, 110
Lévi-Strauss, Claude, 16, 164n.50
Levitsky, Anatole, 110
Lévy-Bruhl, Lucien, 6, 28
linguistic theory, 5, 8, 10, 11, 13, 115, 117, 119–21, 135, 140; Saussurean, 10. *See also* grammar
literary theory, 4, 8, 10, 11–23 *passim,* 48, 82, 107, 125, 158n.7, 166
Loti, Pierre, 26

Malagasy: language, 5, 10, 15, 25–39 *passim,* 42, 82, 124, 154; people and culture, 25–39 *passim,* 154, 160n.4, 161n.18
Mallarmé, Stéphane, 20, 82, 92, 99, 179n.58
Malraux, André, 108
Marinetti, Filippo, 131, 132, 140
Marxism, 22
Maulnier, Thierry, 108
Mauriac, François, 2, 111, 112
Maurras, Charles, 111
Mehlman, Jeffrey, 4, 15–17, 77, 78, 107, 159, 179n.61, 185n.2
Merleau-Ponty, Maurice, 79
Meschonnic, Henri, 21
metaphor, 21, 34, 36, 66, 69–70,

119, 135, 142, 147, 188n. 36. *See also* rhetoric, as tropology
metonymy, 21, 34, 46, 67. *See also* rhetoric, as tropology
Michaux, Henri, 2
Miller, Christopher L., 29
Miller, Nancy K., 168n.20
Modernism, 48, 54
modesty, 3, 48, 57, 63, 89, 93, 105; as linguistic tension, 64–68
Montherlant, Henri de, 158n.7
Morgan, Claude, 101, 112, 182n.22
Mudimbe, V. Y., 27
mystery, 3, 4, 121–24, 146–48. *See also* poetic mystery

Nadeau, Maurice, 81
Nazism, 44, 109, 110, 128
negrophilia, 27
Nizan, Paul, 108
Nouvelle Revue Française, 5, 7, 8, 22, 74, 80, 87, 101; and collaboration, 108–13; and the College of Sociology, 40; and the 1936 version of *Les Fleurs de Tarbes,* 42, 80, 87, 88; Paulhan as secretary and editor of, 1, 2, 7, 8, 9, 54, 108, 110
Novick, Peter, 113

onomatopoeia, 141, 144
ontology, 12, 18, 133

papiers collés, 131, 133–34, 141, 142, 148
parabasis, 59–60
paralepsis, 59–60
paralipsis, 59–60
patriotism, 107, 114–17, 121, 123, 154
Paulhan, Claire, 165n.1, 172n.49
Paulhan, Frédéric (father), 6

Paulhan, Germaine (née Pascal), 6, 7, 49, 50, 65, 66, 136

Paulhan, Jean: and Chinese thought, 6; as correspondant, 3, 42, 63; and First World War, 6, 48, 102, 114, 127–28; and Jacques Maast, 49, 64, 167n.8; and literary history, 3, 5, 80, 151; and Madagascar, 5, 6, 10, 25–46 *passim*, 48, 82, 155; and politics, 15, 21, 77–79, 82, 87, 88, 96, 104, 106–25 *passim*, 147, 152; and Second World War, 7, 15, 43, 49, 102, 104, 106–25 *passim*, 127–28

WORKS: *Alain, ou la preuve par l'étymologie*, 10, 12, 15; *Aytré qui perd l'habitude*, 45–46, 48; *Le Bonheur dans l'esclavage*, 74–75; *Braque le patron*, 8, 128, 143; *Les Causes célèbres*, 8, 64–68, 136, 145, 147; *Le Clair et l'obscur*, 68; *Clef de la Poésie*, 7, 14, 16, 18, 19, 20, 54, 92, 93–101, 114, 146, 148, 152; *La Démocratie fait appel au premier venu*, 109, 116; *Le Don des langues*, 5, 11, 81; *Enigmes de Perse*, 12; *Entretien sur des faits divers*, 81, 85; *Essai d'introduction au projet d'une métrique universelle*, 93; *L'Expérience du proverbe*, 30–39 *passim*, 42, 45, 48, 55, 63; *Fautrier l'enragé*, 128, 131; *Les Fleurs de Tarbes*: Blanchot as reader of, 9, 17, 78, 80, 86; ending of, 54, 89–92, 101; historical context of, 5, 77, 79–81, 108, 174n.10, 175n.18; in relation of Paulhan's other texts, 7–9, 12, 81, 119, 129, 135, 139; *La Guérison sévère*, 7, 49–54, 63, 69; *Le Guerrier appliqué*, 6, 49; *Jacob Cow le pirate, ou si les mots sont des signes*, 10, 81; *Lalie*, 71–73; *D'un langage sacré*, 40–44; *Lettre aux directeurs de la Résistance*, 14, 88, 116, 119; "Manie," 64–68, 136, 145, 147; *La Mentalité primitive*, 28; *Modestie de l'Occident*, 105; *De la Paille et du grain*, 106, 107, 114–25, 147, 154; *La Peinture Cubiste*, 8, 54, 127, 129, 131–43, 147; *Petite préface à toute critique*, 11, 93; *Le Pont traversé*, 63, 69–71, 73, 154; *Progrès en amour assez lents*, 49–51, 56–62, 72, 74; *Le Repas et l'amour chez les Merinas*, 28, 30, 45, 161n.18; *La Rhétorique renaît de ses cendres*, 81; *Un rhétoriqueur à l'état sauvage, ou la littérature considérée comme un faux*, 9; *La Sémantique du proverbe*, 6; *Traité des figures*, 13, 81, 135; *La Vie est pleine de choses redoutables*, 4

Paulhan, Pierre and Frédéric (sons), 7

Paulhan, Suzanne (mother), 6

performativity, of language, 16, 57, 58, 170n.35; of text, 29, 38, 56, 59, 60, 89, 90, 97, 104, 131, 152, 155

Pétain, Maréchal Philippe, 115

philosophy, 6, 15, 16, 18, 19, 55, 121, 133

Picasso, Pablo, 2, 27, 128–30, 136, 140

poetic mystery, 11, 14, 18, 19, 92, 93–101, 152, 160–65

Ponge, Francis, 1, 9, 20, 80, 157n.1
Popular Front, 108, 181n.9
pornography, 74, 75
post-colonialism, 152
post-modernism, 48, 152
Pouilloux, Jean-Yves, 190n.48
Poulet, George, 13
Proust, Marcel, 2, 48, 54
proverbs, 6, 9, 25–39 *passim*, 40,
    117, 124, 151, 154
psychoanalysis, 48, 73–75, 161n.18

Queneau, Raymond, 79

Racine, Jean, 87
Réage, Pauline (pseudonym,
    Dominique Aury), 74, 75
Rebatet, Lucien, 111
récit, 6, 18, 45, 114, 142, 151;
    Blanchot's concept of, 15,
    55–56, 62–63, 68, 93, 102–3,
    166n.4; *La Guérison sévère*,
    49–54; *Lalie*, 71–73; and
    narrative uncertainty, 29, 39,
    46, 59, 68, 92, 100; *Le Pont
    traversé*, 69–71; *Progrès en
    amour assez lents*, 56–62;
    readings of, *Aytré qui perd
    l'habitude*, 45–46. *See also*
    allegory
Renan, Ernest, 82
Resistance. *See* Paulhan, Jean, and
    Second World War
Reverdy, Pierre, 2, 130
reversibility, 16, 61, 63, 70, 73, 88,
    94, 119, 137–38
rhetoric: and aesthetics, 119, 129,
    135, 137, 145, 146, 148,
    185n.2; anamorphosis, 135;
    catachresis, 139; opposed to
    terror, 12, 14, 22, 43, 81, 82,
    84, 85, 88, 92, 114, 128; and
    politics, 88, 119, 128, 146,

183n.34; "reinvented," 16, 86,
    87; as tropology, 65, 67–68,
    81, 83, 87, 95, 120, 129, 134,
    135
rhetorician, 12, 13, 84, 88, 97
Rimbaud, Arthur, 9, 84, 114
Rivière, Jacques, 7, 108
Rolland, Romain, 114
romanticism, 83, 103, 131, 151

sacred, the, 40–44, 88, 146,
    164n.50. *See also* Caillois,
    Roger
Sade, Marquis de, 20
Salomon, André, 130
Sartre, Jean-Paul, 3, 5, 9, 11, 12,
    79, 111, 113, 132. *See also*
    Blanchot, Maurice
Saussure, Ferdinand de, 10
Schapiro, Meyer, 188n.37
secret of language, the, 5, 8, 11, 63
Segalen, Victor, 27
semiology, 22–23
Smock, Ann, 16
Stendhal, 11, 12, 83
Stoekl, Alan, 72, 78, 87–89, 101
Suarès, André, 2
Supervielle, Jules, 2
Surrealism, 1, 27, 28, 48, 54, 68
Syrotinski, Michael, 159n.15,
    185n.2

Taine, Hyppolite, 82
Tempel, Placide, 28, 29
temporality, 61–62, 78, 104,
    138–39
terror, 14, 15, 22, 44, 77–92
    passim, 123, 132–34, 142,
    145, 158n.7; as bypassing
    language, 14, 84, 85; opposed
    to rhetoric, 22, 44, 81, 82, 84,
    85, 88, 92, 114, 128; as
    political ideology, 79, 80, 82,

83, 119; as purification of language, 15, 84, 85, 90, 135; "reinvented," 12, 91
terrorist writers, 82, 84, 97
Thibaudet, Albert, 2
Thomas, Edith, 111
translation, 8, 33, 34, 122, 124, 152–55

Triolet, Elsa, 111, 127
triplicity, 5

Ungaretti, Giuseppe, 2

Valéry, Paul, 2, 9, 11–12, 20, 84, 94